Family Of God

A Study Of The New Testament Church

Batsell Barrett Baxter
Chairman, Department of Bible
David Lipscomb College
Nashville, Tennessee
1980

TABLE OF CONTENTS

INTRODUCTION

Recently, I asked a college Bible class to take a simple first-reaction test. Each student provided himself with a piece of paper upon which he wrote numbers one through ten. Then, each student was asked to listen to the reading of ten words, after each of which he was to write down the first word that came to his mind. It was made clear that no names would be signed to the papers, in order to get an honest and frank reaction to each of the words read. Reading somewhat deliberately, I then read the following words to the class of approximately 100 students: God . . . Christ . . . Bible . . . Worship . . . Preacher . . . Elder . . . Prayer . . . Modesty . . . Myself . . . Church. I was pleased to discover that, on the whole, their answers were positive and favorable, implying faith, respect and love.

Although it is not possible to give a complete summary of the reactions which the students registered to all of the words, I would like to give some typical reactions to the word "church." Selected at random from the lists of the 100 students were these responses: Worship . . . Building . . . Fellowship . . . Body . . . Love . . . People . . . God . . . Fantastic . . . Friends . . . Praise . . . Strength . . . Family . . . Joyful . . . Home . . . Brethren . . . Unity . . . Work . . . Sunday . . . Prayer . . . House of God . . . Christians . . . Salvation . . . Quiet . . . Go . . . and of course many others. On the whole these were positive, encouraging responses.

GETTING OUR PRIORITIES RIGHT

In a study of the church, it is imperative that we recognize at the outset that the church is important because of its relationship to God, Christ and the Holy Spirit, and only because of its relationship to the Godhead. Because of his special God-given role Christ is the center of the Christian religion and everything about Christianity is important because of its relationship to Christ. Apart from Christ the Lord's Supper would mean nothing. Baptism would have no significance whatever. The important work of evangelism would be an empty exercise. In short, the church would be unimportant.

It is because of our deep conviction that Jesus is the Christ, the divine Son of God, that all aspects of his church become significant. It is Christ's church, not ours. It was he who came to the earth and sacrificed his life that we might have salvation in his church. Christ's life and death made the church possible. It is God's will that is reflected in the New Testament teachings about Christ and the church. While we will not mention Christ over and over again in succeeding pages as we study the various aspects of his church, let it be clearly understood that all that we shall study is based upon the foundation of Jesus Christ as the Son of God and our Redeemer and Savior.

As we begin our study of the Lord's church another point needs emphasis. Christianity is not primarily a negative religion. It has certain negative aspects, as it must in view of the fact that much of the world is evil, but its primary emphasis is upon a positive note. There are two aspects of Christianity. There must be a turning away from evil, but there must also be a turning toward good. One is reminded of the epitaph which a biographer gave to Cato the Censor of ancient Rome: "He loved not right, half so much as he hated wrong." This is no compliment. The love of right ought to come first, for it is to furnish the motivation for the hating of wrong.

At this point I should like to mention a few typical passages of scripture which emphasize that Christianity has a positive side as well as a negative side. For example, Romans 12:9 says, "Abhor that which is evil; cleave to that which is good." Notice that the emphasis on "cleaving to good" is at least equal to the abhorrence of evil. Later in that same chapter, Romans 12:21, we read further, "Be not overcome of evil, but overcome evil with good." In this case the emphasis is upon overcoming evil with good. Still another passage which suggests this same balance is I Thessalonians 5:21-22: "Prove all things; hold fast that which is good; abstain from every form of evil."

When our Lord was on the earth he opposed many things because they were evil, but the primary, overwhelming emphasis of his life was a positive one. I like to make a comparison with our own pioneers who first moved across the eastern mountains and braved the frontiers in the early days of our nation. They felled many a tree, cut and burned underbrush and cleared much land. All of this is negative, destructive, tearing down. However, their motivation was not negative but positive. They cleared the fields in order that they might plant crops and sustain life. They cut clearings in the forest that they might build log cabins and houses in which to live and to work. So it was with Christ. He condemned and destroyed the evil in order that he might establish good. In a similar vein, we today turn from many elements of modern twentieth century life, not because we want to be negative, but because we want, in the deepest sense, to choose the good, the beautiful and the true. Our goal is to follow in the steps of Christ and to seek to live the highest type of Christian life possible.

THE CHURCH

In our effort to learn of the life that the Lord would have his disciples to live, we are setting out upon a careful study of the church as originally established in apostolic times. Our intention is to go back to the original documents which describe the church in its early purity and strength. Those earliest documents are, of course, the inspired New Testament scriptures. They not only reveal what the early church was, but even more importantly, what God intended it to be.

In the course of our study there are a number of key scriptures which we shall carefully examine. It is hoped that each student will want to become very familiar with these scriptures, remembering not only their content, but also where they are to be found in the New Testament. We live in a time when the study of the Bible is often crowded out by the busy routine of daily living. As a consequence, there is often a minimum of serious Bible study. Many people are comparatively ignorant of the teachings of the scriptures. Many people, likewise, have little or no knowledge about where to locate important teachings in the scriptures. Our goal in the study of the church is twofold: First, to learn the message of each scripture to be studied as it relates to the church, and, second, to learn scripture locations, so that we may have a familiar access to these important scriptures throughout the remainder of our lives.

Accordingly, a carefully chosen list of one hundred key passages of scripture is here printed at the very beginning of our study. Notice that in each case the location (book, chapter, and verses) is listed first, with a very brief summary of the content of each passage. It is suggested that in the course of our study each of us memorize the list of passages, along with the summary of the message of each scripture. Throughout the book the American Standard Version of the Bible is used for all quotations, unless otherwise noted.

100 KEY SCRIPTURES

1. Matthew 16:13-18 . . . . Peter's confession of Christ
2. Ephesians 5:22-32 . . . . Analogy of marriage and the church
3. John 3:16. . . . . God's love for the world
4. Acts 10:34-35 . . . . No respecter of persons
5. Matthew 28:18-20 . . . . The great commission
6. John 14:1-3. . . . . Preparing a home in heaven
7. I Peter 2:5, 9 . . . . Christians are living stones, a royal priesthood
8. Matthew 13:3-53 . . . . Christ's parables
9. I Corinthians 12:12-31 . . . . The church is like a body
10. Daniel 2:44 . . . . God's kingdom to be established
11. I Corinthians 3:11 . . . . Christ, the foundation
12. Mark 9:1 . . . . The kingdom to begin soon
13. John 17:20-21. . . . . Christ's prayer for unity
14. Acts 4:8-12 . . . . Salvation in no other name
15. I Peter 4:14-16 . . . . Suffer as a Christian
16. Matthew 21:23 . . . . Christ's authority questioned
17. Matthew 10:19-20 . . . . The Holy Spirit to guide the apostles
18. Galatians 1:8-9 . . . . Danger of falling away
19. Romans 3:10, 23. . . . . All are sinners
20. I John 1:8, 10 . . . . Those who claim no sin are deceived

We are now ready to embark upon what we hope will be both an enjoyable and valuable study of the scriptures, as they relate to the Lord's church. May we begin this study with an earnest prayer that God will bless our efforts and that our lives, because of this study, may be spiritually enriched and of greater service to him and to our fellowmen.

CHAPTER ONE
The Glory Of The Church

There is a very significant movement in modern Japan called the "No-church Movement." This means simply that many thousands of people who were formerly Buddhists and Shintoists have come in more recent years to realize the tremendous appeal of the person of Jesus Christ. Many of them have accepted him in a personal way and would call themselves Christians. While they have a great interest in Christ and are impressed by his teachings, his life, and his influence, they are not, however, impressed by his church. They want Christ, but do not wish to be involved in his church.

I had an occasion to see an actual demonstration of this when I visited Japan a few years ago. In speaking to the several hundred young people of Ibaraki Christian College I found that they were eager, as I spoke at two chapel periods, to hear about Christ. The things which I said about him and about his influence on the world seemed to challenge them, but on the third morning when I talked to them about the necessity of being in his church their eyes dropped to their books. I later talked to those who were in charge of the school, and they explained, "That is what we had expected. We find that they are very eager to know more about Christ, but somehow they do not want to be members of his church."

TARNISHED REPUTATION

Japan is not the only place where there are a great many people who are intensely interested in Christ, but not particularly interested in the church. In America there are many thousands of people who would classify themselves as Christians and yet they are not members of any religious body. To them, Christianity is something that you believe, something that you try to live by at home and in business, but it does not entail being a member of a church. Somehow the glorious reputation of the church has become tarnished.

Why has the church, this sacred institution of which we read so often in the New Testament, come into this position? Why has it become unimpressive and unappealing to so many people? It is largely because of two things: *First, it is because of the DIVISIONS which have fractioned the religious world.* Men have been confused by the more-than-250 different religious bodies here in the United States, most of whom call themselves Christians. Some have been alienated because these religious bodies, in their antagonisms and differences with each other, have behaved not at

1

all like Christ. All thoughtful people have decried the divisions which exist among people who believe in Christ. These divisions have been very costly and there are many today who are not active in the church because of these divisions.

The second reason is suggested by the word DISPARITY. There has been too great a disparity between the way Christians have lived and the way Christ lived (the practice gap). There has also been a disparity between the things which Christ taught and the doctrines and the theories which have been taught by the various religious bodies down through the ages. To say it more directly: When people have looked at Christ, he has been winsome and appealing; when they have looked at the church, it has often appeared unappealing.

Because of this negative attitude toward the church we need to think about the *glory of the church.* It is easy to speak of the glory of Christ, but our need is to talk about the glory of the church, because the church is an integral part of Christ and of Christianity. Sometimes we miss the glory of the church in the same way we miss the glory of the family. God has provided three, and only three, divinely approved institutions on earth— the home, civil government and the church. All are approved by God, but sometimes their glory escapes us. The home does not seem particularly glorious, for example, when you are washing dishes, or when you are mopping the kitchen floor, or when you are cleaning up the mess that a child has made.

Likewise, when we are enlarging a building, or when we are putting out a bulletin, or when we are writing letters, or when we are counting the collection after Sunday worship, the church does not seem particulary glorious. When we are passing out announcements of a meeting, or when we are counting the number who came to Vacation Bible School, or when we are doing any number of other things, the glory of the church seems rather remote. But the church is glorious and, lest we forget it, we need to review some of the reasons why we know it is the grandest and most glorious institution on earth.

ONE: ITS ORIGIN

It is glorious because of its origin. The church began in the mind of God rather than in the minds of men. No one on earth dreamed of the establishment of the church; it was God's idea and it was God's idea from the very beginning. It was no afterthought, as some have theologically contended in later centuries. Back in the beginning of time, God planned for the church. Hence, it is a divine, eternal institution. The apostle Paul wrote to the Ephesians, "Unto me, who am less than the least of all saints, was this grace given, to preach unto the Gentiles the unsearchable riches of Christ; and to make all men see what is the dispensation of the mystery which for ages hath been hid in God who created all things; to the intent

2

that now unto the principalities and the powers in the heavenly places might be made known *through the church* the manifold wisdom of God, *according to the eternal purpose* which he purposed in Christ Jesus our Lord" (Ephesians 3:8-11). The message of this scripture is that according to the eternal purpose of God, which he purposed in Christ Jesus our Lord, the will of God is made known through the church.

In the beginning of history man sinned against God. Man was lost. Then, God set about the redemption of man. God selected the Hebrew race through whom he would eventually be able to lift man up. He gave the law to be a schoolmaster to bring us to Christ. In the fullness of time he gave his only begotten Son to come and live among us, to show us how to live, and then to die on the cross, redeeming us from our sins. Then it was that the church was born. The church is no mere institution; the church is involved in God's salvation of all mankind. The beginning of its glory is in its origin.

TWO: ITS FOUNDATION

In the second place, the church is glorious because of its foundation. "For other foundation can no man lay than that which is laid, which is Jesus Christ" (I Corinthians 3:11). The foundation of the church is not a human being or a set of doctrines, but rather the person of Jesus Christ, the divine Son of God. Look for a moment at the conversation recorded in Matthew 16, in which Jesus began by asking his disciples:

> Who do men say that the Son of man is? And they said, Some say John the Baptist; some, Elijah; and others, Jeremiah, or one of the prophets. He saith unto them, But who say ye that I am? And Simon Peter answered and said, Thou art the Christ, the Son of the living God. And Jesus answered and said unto him, Blessed art thou, Simon Bar-Jonah: for flesh and blood hath not revealed it unto thee, but my Father who is in heaven. [The fact that Jesus was the Christ, the Son of God, was Peter's confession. It was not revealed unto him by men, but by God.] And I also say unto thee, that thou art Peter, and upon this rock [the grammar of this passage conclusively proves that the thing referred to is *the fact that he is the divine Son of God*] I will build my church; and the gates of Hades shall not prevail against it.—Matthew 16:13-18

Death shall not destroy it.

THREE: ITS BEGINNING

The glory of the church is further seen in its wonderful beginning. How recently have you read the second chapter of Acts and gloried in the beginning of the church? There were prophecies which told that it would begin in Jerusalem and that certain other events would happen, so it was a great fulfillment of prophecy. It was also a great day, Pentecost. It occurred in a great city, Jerusalem. There was a great sermon by the apostle Peter. A great crowd of several thousand people heard him. Then there

3

was a great response of 3,000 people who became Christians. Never has there been so glorious a beginning of any other institution on earth.

Four: Its Relationship

Again, the church is glorious because of its relationship to God and to Christ. The church is the people. It is not a building; it is not essentially an organization. It is the people. Part of its glory lies in the relationship which Christians sustain to God and to Christ. It is wonderful to be God's family, God's household. In I Timothy 3:15, Paul used the expression "the house of God, which is the church." In Ephesians 2:19, we find a similar phrase, "No more strangers and sojourners, but . . . the household of God." It is a wonderful thing to be a part of a family. We are part of God's family when we become Christians. In Galatians 3:26, there is this additional sentence, "For ye are all sons of God, through faith, in Christ Jesus."

There is also a wonderful new relationship to Christ. The scriptures describe him as the bridegroom and Christians as his bride. A wedding is a wonderful thing, and to see two people who love each other promise their love for life is a beautiful picture. That is the picture which the apostle Paul chose to present in the Ephesian letter concerning Christ and the church. While he is talking to wives and husbands about their relationship to each other, he is also talking about the church's relationship to Christ:

Wives, be in subjection unto your own husbands, as unto the Lord. For the husband is the head of the wife, as Christ also is the head of the church, being himself the savior of the body. But as the church is subject to Christ, so let the wives also be to their husbands in everything. Husbands, love your wives, even as Christ also loved the church, and gave himself up for it; that he might sanctify it, having cleansed it by the washing of water with the word, that he might present the church to himself a glorious church, not having spot or wrinkle or any such thing; but that it should be holy and without blemish. Even so ought husbands also to love their own wives as their own bodies. He that loveth his own wife loveth himself: for no man ever hated his own flesh; but nourisheth and cherisheth it, even as Christ also the church; because we are members of his body. For this cause shall a man leave his father and mother, and shall cleave to his wife; and the two shall become one flesh. This mystery is great: but I speak in regard of Christ and of the church.—Ephesians 5:22-32

Christ is the bridegroom and Christians are the bride. Part of the glory of the church is in this wonderful new relationship with Christ.

Five: Its Universality

The glory of the church is further evidenced by its universality. There is no one on earth excluded from the church. "God so loved the world, that he gave his only begotten Son, that whosoever believeth on him should not perish, but have eternal life" (John 3:16). In Acts 10:34-35 Peter says, "Of

4

a truth I perceive that God is no respecter of persons: but in every nation he that feareth him, and worketh righteousness, is acceptable to him." Also, think of Galatians 3:28, a passage which says, "There can be neither Jew nor Greek, there can be neither bond nor free, there can be no male and female; for ye all are one man in Christ Jesus."

Six: Its Work

The glory of the church is further made known by its work. While there is not time in this chapter to detail all the work of the church, it falls under three headings: Evangelism, Edification, and Benevolence. *Evangelism* is the carrying of the gospel to the lost world. The great commission is the charge: "Go ye therefore, and make disciples of all the nations, baptizing them into the name of the Father and of the Son and of the Holy Spirit . . ." (Matthew 28:19-20). Taking new-born babes in Christ and building them up through worship, through study, through Christian service, and through other means, is *edification.* Ephesians 4:11-13 states the purpose of edification—"Till we all attain . . . unto a fullgrown man, unto the measure of the stature of the fulness of Christ." *Benevolence* is an active concern for orphans, for the hungry, for the poor, and for everyone else who is in need. These constitute the work of the church. It is glorious work indeed!

· Seven: Its Simplicity

The glory of the church is further seen in its simplicity. In Matthew 18:20, Christians are promised by the Lord that where two or three are gathered together in his name there he will be in their midst. This means that a congregation can begin wherever there are two or three people who want to be Christians. A young Christian serviceman wrote to say, "Now there are five of us." He and four more had started a congregation in which to worship. It is wonderful to know that the organization of the church and the plan of worship are so simple that people can become Christians and serve God anywhere on earth—on shipboard and at far-off military posts, as well as at home in small towns and large cities.

Eight: Its Destiny

Finally, the glory of the church is evidenced by its destiny. We Christians are on a journey. We are going somewhere. Earth is not our home, for we will be here only for a little while and then "over there" forever. Remember the words of Jesus:

> Let not your heart be troubled: believe in God, believe also in me. In my Father's house are many mansions; if it were not so, I would have told you; for I go to prepare a place for you. And if I go and prepare a place for you, I come again, and will receive you unto myself, that where I am there ye may be also.—John 14:1-3

The glory of the church is partially in its destiny.

5

Sometimes it is a bit frightening to read in those last chapters of Revelation of the books which will be opened at the judgment. Our destiny will depend on whether we have been "written in the Lamb's book of life," as the last sentence in Revelation 21 phrases it. No one will enter into heaven except those who are written in the Lamb's book of life. It need not be frightening, however, for it is within our power to accept God's grace and to be certain that our names are written there. As Christians, it is wonderful to contemplate eternity.

The church is the grandest institution on earth. It is more important than any government, any business, any home, any fraternal order, or anything else on earth. May we never lose sight of its glory! When you give yourself to Christ in obedient faith, you become a part of his church. There is no separation of Christ and his church. As we give ourselves to Christ to live for him and work for him in his church, we are making sure that some day we shall live with him eternally. We enter his church in this life and beyond the river of death we continue in the church or family of God forever.

CHAPTER TWO

What Is The Church?

Because words mean different things to different people, it is important that we define the word "church." The Greek word *ekklesia* appears in the New Testament more than one hundred times. It is generally translated into English by the word "church." Literally, it means "the called out" or "assembly."

In ancient Greece, the word *ekklesia* had special reference to the calling of certain citizens out of the total population to serve as juries in court cases. In order to prevent bribery and corruption the ancient juries were very large, often consisting of five hundred and one citizens. From the total population of qualified men, this large number would be called for jury duty. Later on, when Christianity was established this familiar Greek word was used to convey the idea that the gospel of Christ would be preached to the whole world and that those who responded to the Lord would become his church, his assembly, his *called out body of people.*

It is important to notice that the church is composed of people. The church is the people. The church cannot exist apart from people. At the very beginning of the church we read, "And the Lord added to them day by day those that were saved" (Acts 2:47). Another scripture emphasizing that the church is made up of people is a statement found in Acts 5:11, "And great fear came upon the whole church, and upon all that heard these things." Obviously fear cannot come upon a building, or an organization, but only upon people. Another clearcut indication that the church refers to people is Luke's statement, "But Saul laid waste the church, entering into every house, and dragging men and women committed them to prison" (Acts 8:3). The church was made up of people and they were the church even when they were in their own homes, not just when they were together in the general assembly. Christians constitute the church wherever they are and whatever thay may be doing.

Used in Two Senses

The word "church" is used in the New Testament in two distinct senses. It may refer to the *Church Universal.* When such is the meaning it includes all of the saved in all the world. It was in that sense that Christ spoke when he said, "And I also say unto thee, that thou art Peter, and upon this rock I will build my church; and the gates of Hades shall not prevail against it" (Matthew 16:18). The same was Paul's meaning when he wrote to the Ephesians, "For the husband is the head of the wife, as Christ also is the head of the church. . . . Husbands, love your wives, even

7

as Christ also loved the church . . ." (Ephesians 5:23, 25).

The word "church" is also capable, however, of being used to refer to the *Local Church.* It then refers to all of the saved in one community or congregation. Such was Paul's usage when he addressed his letter to the Corinthians, "Paul . . . unto the church of God which is at Corinth . . ." (I Corinthians 1:1-2). Similarly, this was his meaning in I Thessalonians 1:1, where he wrote, "Paul . . . unto the church of the Thessalonians. . . ." Used in this sense the word "church" refers to a voluntary association of Christians who band themselves together to carry out God's plans. It has no specific geographic boundaries, except that the people must live close enough together to meet regularly for worship and to cooperate with each other in doing the Lord's work.

At this point it might be well to raise the question: How does one determine the congregation of which he should be a part? In many places this is not a problem, for there is only one congregation near enough to one's home to make active participation possible. In other localities, however, there are many congregations from which to choose one's church home. What criteria should guide one in the choosing of his home congregation in such cases?

There appear to be at least five important elements to be considered:

1. The choice may well be made upon the basis of *where one can do the most good*—where one is needed most. This would be an appropriate choice for mature Christians who are already well-trained and are capable of rendering valuable service in the Lord's work.

2. In other situations, *where one can get the most help* and can, therefore, prepare himself best for future service may be a major concern. This would be a concern especially for younger, less mature Christians, who need further training and growth.

3. In every case the congregation must be *within regular reach*, close enough geographically to make regular attendance possible.

4. Still another factor is *compatibility.* While the Lord's church is a great equalizer or melting pot where people of divergent backgrounds, talents, training and interests meet on a common level, there are also times when a person may feel more at home in one congregation than in another. When a choice among many congregations is possible, one may well choose the group where one can best worship and can best participate in the work of the Lord. This must not be, however, a defense of racial, social, educational or economic discrimination among God's people.

5. Very significant in the choice of one's home congregation is *the requirement of scriptural soundness.* To become a part of a doctrinally impure church simply because it is convenient, or because one's friends are attending, is not a defensible choice. Only those congregations which are loyal to Christ and his word should be given

8

consideration.

Perhaps a word of caution should be given. While for convenience and effectiveness of work it is quite defensible for several congregations to exist in relatively close proximity, there must not develop a destructive rivalry or competitiveness among them. While we may worship and work primarily in one congregation, we must be concerned about the whole church, the entire body of Christ, rather than for our home congregation alone. As mature Christians we rejoice with the successes of neighboring congregations and encourage them and cooperate with them in every good work.

MISCONCEPTIONS CONCERNING THE CHURCH

There are some who think of the church as an organization like other organizations. It is true that the church is an organization, but it is not primarily an organization. Rather, it is a new way of life. Those who have the view that being a part of the church is like being a member of a lodge, a luncheon club, a political party, or even a business are seriously mistaken. Such people feel that they should give to the church the same kind of support and loyalty which they give to these other organizations. It becomes "my church," as it is "my club, or lodge, or party, or team." The Christian's loyalty to the church, however, should be unique, for in reality it is a loyalty to Christ and his way of life. The church is like no other institution on earth and a person's membership in the church is like no other membership which he may sustain. The church is more like a vibrant, living *organism*, than it is like a cold, structured *organization.*

Some make the mistake of thinking that the church is like a social club, which exists for the entertainment and enjoyment of its members. On the contrary, the church exists in order that its members may have an intimate relationship with Christ and God, as well as a close relationship with each other. It does not exist for itself, but rather in order to honor and worship God and to accomplish God's will on the earth through service to mankind. While there is a fellowship among the members, which provides love and encouragement and enjoyment, the church serves many other purposes as well. It is not self-centered, but looks upward to God and outward to all mankind.

Some think of the church merely as a building. It may be that the church meets in a building, though this was not historically true for several centuries after its beginning. The church is made up of people. The apostle Peter wrote:

> Ye also, as living stones, are built up a spiritual house, to be a holy priesthood, to offer up spiritual sacrifices, acceptable to God through Jesus Christ. . . .But ye are an elect race, a royal priesthood, a holy nation, a people for God's own possession, that ye may show forth the excellencies of him who called you out of darkness into his marvelous light. —I Peter 2:5, 9

Paul wrote, "For we are God's fellow-workers: ye are God's husbandry;

God's building" (I Corinthians 3:9). The building in which the church meets is merely a meeting house. While it may be permissible in a kind of short-cut epigrammatic way to refer to a meeting house as the church, in the deep sense it must be understood that the church is made up of people. Buildings are of only incidental importance, as tools useful in the carrying on of the work and worship of the church.

Some may consider the church as perfect. While it is true that the *divine* side of the church is perfect in its plan, the church is far from perfect on its *human* side. To measure the members of the church by Christ's perfect standard is inevitably to be disillusioned. Sadly, it is sometimes true that there are hypocrites in the church. While this is certainly no defense of hypocrisy, it must be recognized that the members of the church are in the process of becoming the men and women that Christ wants them to be. The church is not a showcase in which to display perfect people; it is more like a hospital in which spiritually sick people are becoming well. The goal is for every member of every congregation to be like Christ, but this does not happen immediately upon conversion. It takes a lifetime of spiritual growth to reflect the likeness of the Lord. Those who observe the church from outside need to recognize the process that is underway in the lives of the Christians, a process not yet complete.

Some have the idea that any group which calls itself a church is acceptable to God. This is far from true, for the acceptability of a church depends upon the degree to which it is following the teachings of Christ. Many churches are far from the New Testament pattern. As an individual decides upon the church of which he will become a part, he needs to study the scriptures carefully and then to measure the doctrines and practices of the church by them. In our day some churches are far from what God would have them be. Witness, for example, the newly established "Church of Satan" and the equally reprehensible "Church of Witches," both of which are legal entities in our nation today. It is not true that the various churches are of approximately equal value. The value of the church is to be determined by the degree to which it believes and practices the Lord's teachings as found in the New Testament.

Some have considered the church as an activist organization. While it is true that the church, through the active work of its members in their commitment to follow the teachings of Christ, will influence and change the world about it, it is not true that the church is primarily an activist group. The church is not a revolutionary organization in the sense of using radical physical means to foment and encourage change. It is not primarily concerned with social or economic issues, but rather is a spiritual organization which follows the teachings of Christ. As yeast leavens dough, it influences and changes society, always for the better. Christ's teachings change every immoral and unwholesome condition in a permanent, lasting way, which violent revolutionary tactics are unable to do.

10

CHAPTER THREE
Analogies—The Church Is Like . . .

As an important part of his plan for the redemption of man, Christ came to the earth to lay the foundation for the establishment of· his church. In doing so he faced a difficult problem. There had never been an institution on the earth quite like his spiritual kingdom. Men would find it difficult to understand exactly what Jesus was doing. In facing the difficult task of communicating to earth-bound, materialistically-minded men the idea of a spiritual realm, Jesus resorted to the use of parables.

By definition a parable is a story suggesting a parallel between familiar facts and spiritual truths. It has been called an earthly story with a heavenly meaning. The term "parable" occurs some fifty times in the New Testament, for it was a favorite means employed by Christ to teach new concepts concerning his church.

A number of Christ's parables concerning his kingdom are to be found in the thirteenth chapter of the gospel of Matthew. Let us look at some of these parables:

1. *The sower* (Matthew 13:3-9, 18-23). This is the story of a farmer who went out to sow seed in his field, only to discover that some seed fell upon the hard pathway beside the field, while other seed fell on rocky ground, thorny ground, and good ground. Only the seed planted in the good ground matured and brought forth a crop, and even the good ground varied in productivity. The meaning of this simple story is that the gospel was like the seed which the farmer planted. It fell, as it was preached, into hearts comparable to the different kinds of soil. Some of the seed was lost, but some of it produced a valuable harvest.

2. *The tares* (Matthew 13:24-30, 36-43). Again seed was planted in a field, and grew side by side with tares or weeds. The owner of the field did not make any effort to separate the good grain from the tares during the growing season, but at the harvest there was a separation, with the grain being saved and the tares burned in the fire. Similarly, in the world today, righteous people live side by side with wicked people, all of whom enjoy God's natural blessings. Only at the judgment will there be a separation between the righteous and the unrighteous.

3. *The mustard seed* (Matthew 13:31-32). The mustard seed is very tiny when planted, but it grows to be a sizeable tree. Similarly, the Lord's church would begin small, but ultimately grow in size until

11

it reached great proportions.

4. *The leaven* (Matthew 13:33). As yeast causes an entire batch of dough to rise, so Christians have a leavening influence upon the world about them.

5. *The hidden treasure* (Matthew 13:44). Just as a man who finds a treasure in a field would sell all that he has in order to buy the field, so those who discover Christ's church should be willing to sacrifice everything in order to have this spiritual treasure.

6. *The merchant seeking goodly pearls* (Matthew 13:45). Just as a merchant who discovers a great and valuable pearl might wish to sell all that he has in order to own the pearl, so Christians should be willing to sacrifice everything in order to have Christ's kingdom.

7. *The fishnet* (Matthew 13:47-50). The story is of a net cast into a sea, bringing forth all kinds of fish. The good edible fish were kept and the bad were cast away. In like manner, Christ's gospel will draw all kinds of people, with the righteous being kept for salvation and the insincere and hypocritical being separated from God through eternity.

These parables, while simple, served to convey the idea of a spiritual kingdom and how it would operate among men. Each parable emphasized a different facet of God's plan, so that together they created a complete picture of what his kingdom would be like.

ANALOGIES

As Jesus made use of parables to convey his ideas of the church, so he and the New Testament writers used analogies to convey various concepts concerning the church. One of the most effective ways to teach is by laying the known alongside the unknown. Comparisons and analogies are prominent in the teaching methods of all effective teachers. An analogy is a special kind of comparison. It does not necessarily compare two objects that are outwardly and obviously alike, but rather draws a parallel between certain functions or relationships of two objects.

For example, the United States of America is sometimes called "the ship of state." Obviously, our nation is not outwardly and visibly like a ship in a sea, yet it has certain properties in which the two are alike. As a ship may be buffeted and tossed by the waves, so a nation has troublesome times. As a ship may be in danger of sinking, so a nation may be in danger of perishing. Another example is the comparison of the slow movement of traffic at a busy rush hour in a major city to "a snail's pace." There is little in common between automobiles on busy streets and the lowly snail, except that the movement of each is very slow. Similarly, a shiny new automobile may sometimes be called "a lemon," though it has no outward physical characteristics like a lemon. Rather, because of poor workmanship or faulty parts, the automobile leaves an unpleasant memory, in its

12

owner's mind, as a lemon leaves a sour taste in a person's mouth. Now, notice some New Testament analogies.

First, the church is like a physical body. Christ is the head of the body, with Christians being like the various members of a physical body—all under the direction of the head. To the church at Colossae Paul wrote, "And he is the head of the body, the church: who is the beginning, the firstborn from the dead; that in all things he might have the preëminence" (Colossians 1:18). To the Corinthians Paul wrote, "Now ye are the body of Christ, and severally members thereof" (I Corinthians 12:27). The same message was also conveyed in Romans 12:3-8.

Among the several meanings of this particular analogy, there is the idea that the body and the members are under the headship of Christ. There is also the idea of diversity among Christians, yet a unity provided by their being members of the same body. Other concepts conveyed by this particular analogy are: the importance of coordination among the members of the church, a mutual concern for each other, and an equality among the various members.

Second, the church is like a kingdom. In the Old Testament book of Daniel, there are the lines:

> And in the days of those kings shall the God of heaven set up a kingdom which shall never be destroyed, nor shall the sovereignty thereof be left to another people; but it shall break in pieces and consume all these kingdoms, and it shall stand for ever.—Daniel 2:44

Christ also referred to the disciples as a kingdom when he said, "I will give unto thee the keys of the kingdom" (Matthew 16:19).

Among the meanings intended by this analogy there is the obvious indication that Christ is to be considered as king. Christians, then, are subjects of the king and are obligated to be obedient to his commands. This parable indicates that the church is not a democracy. Christians do not legislate, or vote, or change God's plans for the church. There is a clear-cut relationship between king and subjects, with respect for and obedience to authority being an important part of the message of this analogy.

Third, the church is like a building. The apostle Paul wrote to the Ephesians: *but isnt its people*

> So then ye are no more strangers and sojourners, but ye are fellow-citizens with the saints, and of the household of God, being built upon the foundation of the apostles and prophets, Christ Jesus himself being the chief corner stone; in whom each several building, fitly framed together, groweth into a holy temple in the Lord; in whom ye also are builded together for a habitation of God in the Spirit.—Ephesians 2:19-22

In this passage Christ is referred to as the chief corner stone of the

13

building which is the temple of God, with the teachings of God as presented by the apostles and prophets being the foundation.

In a parallel passage Jesus himself, including his teachings, is referred to as the foundation: "For other foundation can no man lay than that which is laid, which is Jesus Christ" (I Corinthians 3:11). In either case it is the message of the gospel of Christ that is the foundation—either embodied in the life and teachings of Jesus, or in the message presented by the apostles and prophets. In this analogy Christ and his teachings serve as the foundation for the church, and individual Christians are living stones built upon that foundation. The apostle Peter wrote, "Ye also, as living stones, are built up a spiritual house . . ."(I Peter 2:5).

The figure of a building built upon a solid foundation is also indicated in a conversation between Jesus and Peter: "And Simon Peter answered and said, Thou art the Christ, the Son of the living God . . ." To which Jesus replied, "And I also say unto thee, that thou art Peter, and upon this rock [the basic bedrock fact that Peter had just confessed—that Jesus was the Christ the Son of God] I will build my church; and the gates of Hades shall not prevail against it" (Matthew 16:16, 18).

Practical applications of this idea of the church being a building or temple, with each Christian being a stone in that building, are numerous. Among them is the very important realization that as a building is brought into existence and can later go out of existence, so each local congregation has the possibility of both coming into existence and going out of existence. The church universal, however, is declared in other scriptures to be eternal (Daniel 2:44; Matthew 16:18). Extensive planning and diligent effort are required in the building of a house. Similarly, careful planning and diligent effort are required in the building of the church in any local community.

Fourth, the church is like a family. In Ephesians 3:14-15, Paul wrote, "For this cause I bow my knees unto the Father, from whom every family in heaven and on earth is named." God is the Father and Christ is the Son in this spiritual family. While on the earth Jesus had said, "And call no man your father on the earth: for one is your Father, even he who is in heaven" (Matthew 23:9). Paul later wrote of ". . . one God and Father of all, who is over all, and through all, and in all" (Ephesians 4:6). In this analogy individual Christians are the children in the household. In Romans 8:16 Paul recognized this when he said, "The Spirit himself beareth witness with our spirit, that we are children of God." In his Galatian letter he added, "For ye are all sons of God, through faith, in Christ Jesus" (Galatians 3:26).

Practical applications of this particular analogy concerning the church include the fact that in the Christian family, as well as in every well-regulated human family, children must be submissive to their father.

14

This analogy comparing the church to the home is less meaningful than it ought to be for many people because of the faulty character of the human father. Such is not the case in the spiritual family of God, the church, for God is perfect. To others whose fathers are devout Christians, this figure of the church is one of the richest and most meaningful of all. This obviously has important implications for those who serve as human fathers. A child's first concept of God is in terms of his own father. This is implied in the model prayer which Christ taught his disciples and which we teach our children very early in life: "Our Father who art in heaven, Hallowed be thy name" (Matthew 6:9).

Just as one may turn the facets of a diamond so as to reflect light from many angles and achieve a comprehensive view of the stone, so the parables of Jesus and the analogies of the inspired writers of the scriptures reveal the various facets of God's church. As Christ and the apostles undertook the task of explaining the new, different kind of spiritual organization through which men must be saved, parables and analogies were imperative. The richness and the permanence of the comparisons which they made are evidence of the remarkable way in which God inspired the writers of the scriptures.

Jesus foretold coming of his
Kingdom.

CHAPTER FOUR
When Did The Church Begin?

Different people have held different ideas about when the church
began. There are those who speak of it as beginning in the Old Testament
period, though such a view is a misunderstanding of what the church is.
Others believe that it began with the ministry of John the Baptist. Still
others believe that the Lord's kingdom has not yet been established. In the
midst of these divergent ideas, what is the correct idea about when the
church began?

The correct answer is rather easily determined, if one notices the
tense of the verbs that is used in reference to the church. Throughout the
Old Testament all references to Christ's kingdom are future. For the most
part the statements are prophecies concerning an event somewhat remote
in the future. Some of these prophecies we will notice later in this chapter.

To the surprise of many, every reference to the church found in the
four gospels is also stated in terms of the future. The fact is that Christ
lived his entire life under the Law of Moses, keeping the Ten Commandments, making regular pilgrimages to Jerusalem, and keeping the
other vestiges of the law. The Mosaic Dispensation continued in full sway
until Christ died upon the cross, thus taking the old Mosaic Law out of the
way. In his Ephesian letter Paul wrote, ". . . having abolished in his flesh
the enmity, even the law of commandments contained in ordinances . . ."
(Ephesians 2:15). In his Colossian letter Paul was even more specific: ". . .
having blotted out the bond written in ordinances that was against us,
which was contrary to us: and he hath taken it out of the way, nailing it to
the cross . . ." (Colossians 2:14). It is quite true that during his ministry
Jesus did teach many things which would be a part of his kingdom, but the
kingdom, or church, had not been established until after he died on the
cross, taking the old dispensation out of the way.

This is also apparent in the discussion which Jesus had with his
disciples near the climax of his ministry, as found in Matthew 16:13-19.
After asking the question, "Who do men say that the Son of man is ?" he
received Peter's answer, which came to its climax with the words, "Thou
art the Christ, the Son of the living God." To this Jesus responded, "I also
say unto thee, that thou art Peter, and upon this rock [the fact which Peter
had just confessed] I will build my church; and the gates of Hades shall
not prevail against it." Notice that the future tense was used—"I will build
my church." During Christ's entire lifetime on earth the church was still in

16

Kingdom – Christ reigns as king in my life

church assembly of believers

after Penecost

prospect and not yet actually established.

It was on Pentecost, likely in the year A.D. 30, that the church actually was established. We read of this great new beginning in Acts 2. After the momentous event described in this chapter three thousand people believed in Christ, repented of their sins and were baptized, after which God added them to his church. The chapter closes with the words, "And the Lord added to them day by day those that were saved" (Acts 2:47). From Pentecost on, the church is no longer spoken of as something in the future, but as an actuality. References throughout the remainder of the book of Acts and throughout the remainder of the New Testament speak of the church as being in existence.

DANIEL'S PROPHECY OF THE KINGDOM

In line with what has just been said, there is a very significant prophecy in the Old Testament book of Daniel, a prophecy written some six centuries before Christ lived upon the earth. The second chapter of the book of Daniel, verses 31-45, tells the story of King Nebuchadnezzar's momentous dream, which later was interpreted by Daniel. The king had dreamed of a great image which had a head of gold, a breast and arms of silver, belly and thighs of brass, legs of iron, and feet of iron mixed with clay. In the God-inspired interpretation which Daniel gave, the head of gold represented the Babylonian Kingdom, over which Nebuchadnezzar was presiding, a kingdom which lasted from 612 B.C. to 536 B.C. The breast and arms of silver represented the Medo-Persian Empire ruled by kings Cyrus and Darius among others, an empire which fell in 330 B.C. The belly and thighs of brass represented the Macedonian Empire, ruled by Alexander the Great, which was divided at his death in 323 B.C. The legs and feet of iron and clay represented the Roman Empire, headed by the various Caesars. This empire began about 30 B.C. and fell in 476 A.D.

There is one other very important element in Nebuchadnezzar's dream. In addition to the great image which he envisioned, there was a stone cut out of the mountain without human hands which came rolling down the mountainside until it struck the image and broke it into pieces. The interpretation of this great stone is that a different kind of kingdom—a spiritual kingdom established by God—would be established in the days of the final empire represented by the image and that it would triumph over that empire. This interpretation fits perfectly with the fact that the Lord's church, or kingdom, was established during the Roman Empire, on Pentecost, A.D. 30, during the reign of Tiberius Caesar.

Thus, 600 years before the event, long before the establishment of some of the kingdoms mentioned in the prophecy, God revealed through his prophet Daniel that he would establish his spiritual kingdom which would ultimately outlive and triumph over the physical kingdoms which would be dominant in the world. The Roman Empire was divided into ten

17

provinces, represented by the ten toes of the image, and was a weakened empire, as signified by iron being mixed with clay. It was at that point in history—Pentecost, A.D. 30—that God chose to establish his kingdom.

OTHER PROPHECIES

There is further corroboration of the correctness of this date for the beginning of God's kingdom found in such passages as Mark 9:1, where Christ is quoted as saying during his active ministry on earth, "Verily I say unto you, There are some here of them that stand by, who shall in no wise taste of death, till they see the kingdom of God come with power." Some of those living during Christ's active ministry did live on through Pentecost and did see his kingdom come with power.

The Old Testament prophet Isaiah, who lived some seven hundred fifty years before Christ, also foretold the establishment of God's kingdom. In Isaiah 2:2-3, he wrote:

> And it shall come to pass in the latter days, that the mountain of Jehovah's house shall be established on the top of the mountains, and shall be exalted above the hills; and all nations shall flow unto it . . . and he will teach us of his ways, and we will walk in his paths: for out of Zion shall go forth the law, and the word of Jehovah from Jerusalem.

At the very end of the gospel according to Luke, reference is made to this prophecy of Daniel as Luke quotes the words, "Thus it is written, that the Christ should suffer, and rise again from the dead the third day; and that repentance and remission of sins should be preached in his name unto all the nations, beginning from Jerusalem" (Luke 24:46-47). Christ told his apostles, "tarry ye in the city, until ye be clothed with power from on high" (Luke 24:49). They did just that, waiting in Jerusalem during the forty days of Christ's appearances and further teaching, and an additional ten days beyond his ascension into heaven, until Pentecost (which means fifty) on which day they did receive the Holy Spirit's power from on high. On that day Peter and the other apostles spoke in tongues and announced the new regime or kingdom of Christ. Those who accepted it were added together and constituted the church.

One final evidence that Pentecost was the beginning date of the church is found in a reference from the apostle Peter sometime later when he was explaining that the Holy Spirit had guided him to preach the gospel to Cornelius and other Gentiles. In this explanation he said, "And as I began to speak, the Holy Spirit fell on them [the household of Cornelius], even as on us at the beginning" (Acts 11:15). Pentecost was the beginning. Any church or organization which began prior to Pentecost is not God's church; any church or organization which began later than Pentecost is likewise not God's church. The New Testament discusses the Lord's kingdom, or church, in promise, in preparation and, after Pentecost, in actuality.

18

THE USE OF SPECIAL TERMS

There are various ways in which the writers of the New Testament refer to the church. Sometimes it is called the "kingdom of heaven" and at other times the "kingdom of God." "Kingdom of heaven" and "kingdom of God" are used interchangeably in the scriptures, as indicated in Matthew 21:43: "Therefore I say unto you, the kingdom of God shall be taken away from you, and shall be given to a nation bringing forth the fruits thereof," and Matthew 22:2, "The kingdom of heaven is likened unto a certain king, who made a marriage feast for his son." Matthew alone, of all the gospel writers, uses "kingdom of heaven." All four gospels use "kingdom of God."

Whenever either of these terms refers to an institution the church is meant. Notice Matthew 16:18-19, for example: "And I also say unto thee, that thou art Peter, and upon this rock I will build my church; and the gates of Hades shall not prevail against it. I will give unto thee the keys of the kingdom of heaven: and whatsoever thou shalt bind on earth shall be bound in heaven; and whatsoever thou shalt loose on earth shall be loosed in heaven."

Somewhat strangely the word church occurs only three times in the gospel narratives, in Matthew 16:18 and Matthew 18:17, which read, ". . . upon this rock I will build my church. . . . And if he refuse to hear them, tell it unto the church: and if he refuse to hear the church also, let him be unto thee as the Gentile and the publican." While it occurs only three times in the gospel narratives, the word church appears scores of times in the rest of the New Testament.

The Lord uses "kingdom of heaven" and "kingdom of God" thirty-six times in Matthew alone, and also throughout the New Testament, to mean the regime he came to establish. However, the term church cannot always be substituted for "kingdom of God." In Luke 17:21, for example, the statement, "The kingdom of God is within you, . . ." means rather a power or atmosphere of godliness. Similarly, in Matthew 8:11, we read that "many shall come from the east and west, and shall sit down with Abraham, and Isaac, and Jacob, in the kingdom of heaven." Here it refers to the kingdom of glory, or heaven itself.

14 times mark 38 times in Luke 3 times in John

Still other terms are used later in the New Testament to refer to the church, but these will be given attention in a later chapter. Suffice it to say at this point that "in the fullness of time" the Lord established his church at the end of his ministry on earth, through his inspired apostles, and that it has spread and grown until it has reached into all parts of the world and all corners of the earth. Like the mustard seed, referred to in one of his parables, the church has grown up to be a great tree and after nineteen centuries is still thriving throughout the world.

19

CHAPTER FIVE

What's In A Name?

Serious Bible students are inevitably impressed by the powerful emphasis which the New Testament gives to the theme of Christian unity. From one end of the New Testament to the other there is a continuing emphasis on the essentiality of unity among all believers in Christ. Perhaps the strongest single passage is found in the prayer which Jesus prayed on the night in which he was betrayed, just a few hours before he was to be nailed to the cross: "Neither for these only do I pray, but for them also that believe on me through their word; that they may all be one; even as thou, Father, art in me, and I in thee, that they also may be in us: that the world may believe that thou didst send me" (John 17:20-21). In this intimate glimpse into the innermost yearnings of our Lord we see his urgent desire for unity. The degree of unity is impressive, for he prays that all his disciples may achieve the same unity which exists between himself and God. The purpose of this plea was that the world might believe. *Truly, the price that has been paid for a divided Christendom is an unbelieving world.*

One of the greatest barriers to unity is found in the distinctive religious names which men wear. Names, like fences, separate one group from another, helping to destroy the unity for which Christ prayed. When a person is identified as a Republican, he is automatically separated from Democrats or those of other political persuasions. When one is identified as a Texan, he is automatically separated from those who live in the other forty-nine states. Names fence us in; names fence others out. To be marked as a Pharisee or a Sadducee, in apostolic times, destroyed all practical possibility of fellowship between them. In this connection it is intensely interesting to study the emphasis of the scriptures.

EMPHASIS ON CHRIST

On one occasion Christ was discussing with his disciples the question, "Who do men say that the Son of man is?" At one point in the discussion Jesus further said, "Upon this rock I will build my church" (Matthew 16:13-18). When Jesus talked with his disciples during the last hour that he was on earth, he gave them his final marching orders in these words: "Go ye therefore, and make disciples of all the nations, baptizing them into the name of the Father and of the Son and of the Holy Spirit: teaching them to observe all things whatsoever I commanded you: and lo, I am with you always, even unto the end of the world" (Matthew 28:19-20).

20

Sometime later when Peter preached the first great sermon of the Christian era he concluded it by commanding the people, "Repent ye, and be baptized every one of you in the name of Jesus Christ unto the remission of your sins; and ye shall receive the gift of the Holy Spirit" (Acts 2:38). Still later the apostle Paul wrote to the Galatians, "For as many of you as were baptized into Christ did put on Christ" (Galatians 3:27). Notice the constant emphasis upon Christ. Notice that no other names were given.

In the remarkable history of the beginning of the church, the book of Acts, we find this passage:

> Then Peter, filled with the Holy Spirit, said unto them, Ye rulers of the people, and elders, if we this day are examined concerning a good deed done to an impotent man, by what means this man is made whole; be it known unto you all, and to all the people of Israel, that in the name of Jesus Christ of Nazareth, whom ye crucified, whom God raised from the dead, even in him doth this man stand here before you whole. He is the stone which was set at nought of you the builders, which was made the head of the corner. And in none other is there salvation: for neither is there any other name under heaven, that is given among men, wherein we must be saved.—Acts 4:8-12

Still later in the book of Acts we learn that "the disciples were called Christians first in Antioch" (Acts 11:26). Still later we learn that the apostle Paul preached to King Agrippa and at the end of the sermon Agrippa said, "With but little persuasion thou wouldest fain make me a Christian. And Paul said, I would to God, that whether with little or with much, not thou only, but also all that hear me this day, might become such as I am, except these bonds" (Acts 26:28-29).

In the first epistle that Peter wrote there are these words:

> If ye are reproached for the name of Christ, blessed are ye; because the Spirit of glory and the Spirit of God resteth upon you. For let none of you suffer as a murderer, or a thief, or an evil-doer, or as a meddler in other men's matters: but if a man suffer as a Christian, let him not be ashamed; but let him glorify God in this name.—I Peter 4:14-16

We are to glorify God in the name of Christ—as Christians.

All of this reminds us of a passage from the pen of the prophet Isaiah: "And the nations shall see thy righteousness, and all kings thy glory; and thou shalt be called by a new name, which the mouth of Jehovah shall name" (Isaiah 62:2). This prophecy, written some seven centuries before Christ came to the earth, foretold a new name. While we do not know exactly how the name was given, we cannot help but identify the name Christian with this prophecy of Isaiah. What other possibility is there?

As Bride and Bridegroom

In writing to the Ephesians the apostle Paul uses a marvelous illustration. He speaks of Christ as the bridegroom and the church as the bride, comparing the relationship to that between husband and wife:

> Wives, be in subjection unto your own husbands, as unto the Lord. For the husband is the head of the wife, as Christ also is the head of the church, being himself the saviour of the body. But as the church is subject to Christ, so let the wives also be to their husbands in everything. Husbands, love your wives, even as Christ also loved the church, and gave himself up for it; that he might sanctify it, having cleansed it by the washing of water with the word, that he might present the church to himself a glorious church, not having spot or wrinkle or any such thing; but that it should be holy and without blemish.—Ephesians 5:22-27

Just as the husband gives his name to his bride, so Christ gives his name to the church.

In all these passages, in fact throughout the entire New Testament, the emphasis is upon Christ. The church is built upon the foundation that Jesus is the Christ, the Son of God. Its doctrines take their importance from the fact that Christ commanded them. The lives of Christians are to be patterned after the life of Christ. The whole scheme of redemption stems from and depends upon Christ. How apparent it is, when one stops to think, that those who are redeemed should wear the name of their redeemer rather than the name of some man or some ordinance. How apparent it is that when the church came into being it should wear the name of the divine Son of God who made it possible and who serves as its head.

New Testament Usage

When one makes a careful check of the New Testament (American Standard Version) to discover the names which were used in referring to God's people, he finds the following usages:

95 times. . . . . "the church".
68 times. . . . . . . "kingdom of God"—Matthew 13 and elsewhere.
32 times. . . . . "kingdom of heaven"—Matthew 13 and elsewhere.
11 times. . . . . "the church of God"—I Corinthians 1:2.
1 time . . . . "body of Christ"—I Corinthians 12:27.
1 time . . . . "churches of Christ"—Romans 16:16.
1 time . . . . "my church"—Matthew 16:18.
1 time . . . . "church of the Lord"—Acts 20:28.
1 time . . . . . . "church of the first born [ones]"—Hebrews 12:23.
1 time . . . . "church of the saints"—I Corinthians 14:33.

All of these names were applied to the church in general.

Now, notice some names which were applied to individual members of God's family:

"Christians" . . . . Acts 11:26.
"Saints" . . . . Philippians 4:21-22.
"Disciples" . . . . Acts 19:1.

THE TRAGIC STORY

There was no recognition in the apostolic period of a multiplicity of churches, for this has been an invention of man rather than of God. Instead, the disciples were called Christians and were spoken of as "the church," which belonged to their Lord. In the beginning there were no names (fences) to divide the Lord's people into the various sects and denominations. All were one, united in the church which belonged to God and Christ. So ought it to be now! Ninety-five times the expression "the church" is used and in every other instance the church is identified with Christ or with God. This indicates clearly the Lord's desire concerning the names that his disciples should wear.

What has happened during the nineteen hundred years of church history? The tragic story began even in the first century, for we read of incipient division in the Corinthian church:

> For it hath been signified unto me concerning you, my brethren, by them that are of the household of Chloe, that there are contentions among you. Now this I mean, that each one of you saith, I am of Paul; and I of Apollos; and I of Cephas; and I of Christ. Is Christ divided? was Paul crucified for you? or were ye baptized into the name of Paul?—I Corinthians 1:11-13

In the third chapter of the same book the apostle Paul gives the same important emphasis:

> And I, brethren, could not speak unto you as unto spiritual, but as unto carnal, as unto babes in Christ. I fed you with milk, not with meat; for ye were not yet able to bear it: nay, not even now are ye able; for ye are yet carnal: for whereas there is among you jealousy and strife, are ye not carnal, and do ye not walk after the manner of men? For when one saith, I am of Paul; and another, I am of Apollos; are ye not men? What then is Apollos? and what is Paul? Ministers through whom ye believed; and each as the Lord gave to him. I planted, Apollos watered; but God gave the increase. So then neither is he that planteth anything, neither he that watereth; but God that giveth the increase. Now he that planteth and he that watereth are one: but each shall receive his own reward according to his own labor. For we are God's fellow-workers: ye are God's husbandry, God's building.
> According to the grace of God which was given unto me, as a wise masterbuilder I laid a foundation; and another buildeth thereon. But let each man take heed how he buildeth thereon. For other foundation can no man lay than that which is laid, which is Jesus Christ.—I Corinthians 3:1-11

VOICES OF RELIGIOUS LEADERS

Not only does inspiration command that all believers be one, but

23

many of the outstanding religious leaders of succeeding centuries join in that same emphasis. Note particularly the following quotations:

Martin Luther: I pray you to leave my name alone, and call not yourselves Lutherans, but Christians. Who is Luther? My doctrine is not mine. I have not been crucified for anyone. St. Paul (I Corinthians 1:13) would not that any should call themselves of Paul, nor of Peter, but of Christ. How, then, does it befit me, a miserable bag of dust and ashes, to give my name to the children of Christ. Cease, my dear friends, to cling to these party names and distinctions; away with them all; and let us call ourselves only Christians after him, from whom our doctrine comes (Stork, *Life of Luther*, p. 289).

John Wesley: Would to God that all party names and unscriptural phrases and forms which have divided the Christian world were forgot; that we might all agree to sit down together as humble, loving disciples at the feet of the common Master, to hear His word, to imbibe His spirit, and to transcribe His life into our own. (Quoted by C. C. Crawford, *Sermon Outlines*, Vol. I, 1927, p. 47).

Charles Spurgeon: (Baptist) I look forward with pleasure to the day when there will not be a Baptist living. I hope they will soon be gone. I hope the Baptist name will soon perish; but let Christ's name last forever (*Spurgeon Memorial Library*, Vol. 1, p. 168).

Alexander Campbell: But, alas, the enemies have blasphemed the blessed gospel by pasting our sinful names upon it to bring it into disrepute. (Crawford, p. 103.) (Campbell said this in reference to the practice of some being called "Campbellites" and others being called "Stoneites." See *Christian Baptist*, Vol. III, pp. 8-10.)

The substitution of the names of men for the name of our Lord in connection with the church is just another of the many steps which men have taken in getting away from the emphasis which the New Testament places upon Christ as the center of our religion. What we need in doctrine, in worship, and in every phase of our Christian activities is a return to the centrality of Christ. We need to forget the creeds and councils of men. We need to forget the subtractions and additions that men have made to the religion of Christ. We need to remember Christ and him alone. This also holds true in the matter of names. As Paul wrote, "And whatsoever ye do, in word or in deed, do all in the name of the Lord Jesus, giving thanks to God the Father through him" (Colossians 3:17).

Is it defensible that the name of some ordinance of the church should be exalted as the name of the church? Is it proper that the name of some reformer or some church leader should be exalted as the name of the church? Is it appropriate that some phase of the government of the church should become the church name? Is it logical that anything but the name of Christ should be the name that his disciples wear? Is it reasonable that anything but his name should be used as a designation of his church? May our practice come to conform to the very meaningful words of the great Christian hymn, "All Hail the Power of Jesus' Name."

24

CHAPTER SIX

Authority In Religion

Every thinking person realizes that authority plays a very significant role in the life of all of us. We must have adequate authorization for everything that we do. For example, in a large department store there are many employees. Some have been hired as buyers, and from time to time they go to the various markets and buy merchandise for their company. Others have been employed to work in the business office of the department store and certain ones have the authority to extend credit to approved customers. Still others are employed in the advertising phase of the business and their authority empowers them to speak through the mass media: newspaper, radio and television, on behalf of their company. Then, there are many who are authorized to serve as clerks, or salespeople, in the various departments where the merchandise is offered for sale. Notice that in every case an employee is given certain limited responsibilities and must operate within those specific areas.

Can you imagine what would happen if every employee of the store decided that he was a buyer and went forth with reckless abandon to purchase merchandise for the company? Can you imagine what would happen if every employee decided that he was a credit manager and extended credit right and left? Can you imagine what would happen if every employee decided that he was employed to announce the policies and prices of the company in the newspaper and over the radio? Can you imagine what would happen if every salesperson decided that he had the power to fix the prices at which each item should be sold? Just how long would a salesperson keep his employment if he decided to double the price of certain items and cut other prices in half? Obviously, each employee must do that which he is authorized to do and nothing else.

The vital place which authority plays in every phase of our lives is seen no matter in which direction we may look. Before we may drive a car we must have the authority of a license. Before we can write a check we must have the authority which comes from having made a previous deposit in a bank. Even to get married, we must have a license from the County Court Clerk. A doctor must have a diploma from a reputable medical school before he can practice. A policeman must have a badge which authorizes him to carry out his duties. Travel from nation to nation is possible only when we have the authority of a passport. We cannot even attend a football game until we are authorized to do so through the purchase of a ticket. Authority comes from many sources and is of many kinds, but there is little that we can do in life without proper authorization.

Is it not reasonable to believe that in the realm of religion man must also have proper authority for all he does? Religion is essentially a personal relationship with God, to whom the soul surrenders in loving obedience and from whom it receives blessing and salvation. It is the most important thing in our lives. Surely, in the worship and the service of God we must do that which we are authorized to do and nothing else.

Late in the earthly ministry of Jesus the chief priest and the elders came to him and asked, "By what authority doest thou these things? and who gave thee this authority?" (Matthew 21:23). Jesus demonstrated that his authority came from God in a number of ways. The fulfillment of the many prophecies concerning his life was ample evidence that he was God's Messiah. The miracles which he worked constantly throughout his active ministry were further evidence of his divine authority and power. The superior quality of his teaching was still another unanswerable evidence that he was no mere man. Further, the perfection of his life was unassailable evidence of his authority. Ultimately, his resurrection from the dead was the absolute proof that he was the Son of God and that he spoke with God's authority.

But the question asked of Jesus in the long ago is a good one to be asked in our time. "By what authority doest thou these things? and who gave thee this authority?" This is one of the most fundamental questions in the realm of religion and every religious person or group should welcome the question. Each of us should be willing and ready to demonstrate his authority for everything that he believes and practices in his religion. What is our authority?

POSSIBLE SOURCES OF AUTHORITY

The final or ultimate authority in religion must eventually rest in one of three possible sources. *First of all, it may conceivably rest in the church.* This is the Roman Catholic view of authority. Although the Bible is considered to be significant, it is to be officially interpreted by the hierarchy of the church. The traditions of the church also have significance for Catholics, but the final authority rests in the supreme official of the church, the Pope. When speaking *ex cathedra,* his pronouncements are binding upon Roman Catholics throughout the entire world. While there are other religious bodies who hold a similar position, the Catholic example is probably the clearest and most familiar to people generally.

Through the centuries since Christ was on earth this idea that authority rests in a group of men constituting some council or synod or church has become very widespread. Many councils, like the council of Nicea in 325 A.D., and succeeding councils, such as those of Chalcedon, Ephesus, Constantinople, and those of more recent times, have been held. Various

26

creedal statements have come from these meetings and have had tremendous influence on the various streams of doctrine which have developed. The Roman Catholic Church places great emphasis upon its tradition— the ever-changing doctrines which have come through the action of the various Popes and councils. It is from these human councils that such doctrines as that of purgatory, the adoration of Mary, the seven sacraments, papal infallibility, and a host of others have come, rather than from the inspired word of God, the Bible.

We cannot help but be appreciative of the forthright statement of Martin Luther, when he stood in defense of his life before the Diet of Worms and said:

> If his imperial Majesty desires a plain answer, I will give it to him, and it is this: It is impossible for me to recant unless I am proved to be in the wrong by the testimony of Scripture or by evident reasoning; I cannot trust either the decisions of Councils, or of Popes, for it is plain that they have not only erred but have contradicted each other . . . (Richard Friedenthal, *Luther: His Life and Times*, p. 278)

How right Luther was!

The councils of men do not change the teachings of God's word. A case in point is that which occurred a few years ago in a meeting of the legislative assembly of a large American church. A newspaper wire service announced that after much debate the delegates to this particular meeting had voted to relax the restrictions against divorce and remarriage which had long been binding in their church. As I read the news release, I could not help but think, "Christ's words in Matthew 19:3-9 still read just as they did before the council voted." The voting of men in San Francisco did not change the will of God.

The second possibility is that the final authority rests in the reasoning power of men. This view holds that authority is internal, resting within the person himself. It is the authority of one's own conscience, one's inner feelings, one's own reason. There was a time when Saul of Tarsus believed in this internal kind of authority, at least in part. When standing before the Sanhedrin in Jerusalem he said, "Brethren, I have lived before God in all good conscience until this day" (Acts 23:1). Later, he further said, "I verily thought with myself that I ought to do many things contrary to the name of Jesus of Nazareth. And this I also did . . ." (Acts 26:9-10). He was referring to the very earnest, sincere feelings which led him to be the foremost persecutor of Christians. In spite of his honesty of purpose and intensity of zeal, he was wrong, and he spent the remainder of his life trying to undo the wrongs which he had honestly but mistakenly done.

Conscience is a creature of education, and, hence, it may be defiled by the wrong kind of training. Many a person, guided by his own inner feelings, believes and practices that which is contrary to the will of God.

27

This is especially true of those who accept the philosophy of existentialism. For them, truth is discovered in subjective, personal experience. These are not evil persons, but like Saul of Tarsus, they are mistaken.

In past years there have been many occasions on which someone would say, "I just know that I am all right with the Lord. I just feel it in here." Then, he would place his hand on his chest, covering the heart. He was wrong two ways: first, he was wrong when he pointed to the physical muscle that pumps blood throughout his body, for this marvelous muscle neither thinks nor feels. He should have been pointing to the brain, for it is here that man's feelings exist. Secondly, he was wrong because even the brain has no assurance that its thinking or feeling is always correct.

The diversity of religious doctrines in our twentieth century has largely grown out of different opinions and feelings of men. We do not question the integrity or sincerity of the people who have led to the establishment of the various churches with their different creeds and doctrines, but we do point out that God did not intend for his church to be so divided (I Corinthians 1:10-13). And his truth is still a single, united body of truth, just as it was in the first century. It is man's opinions and personal preferences which have taken the religious world into the deeply disturbing abyss of division. In following their own feelings, men such as Joseph Smith and women such as Ellen G. White and Mary Baker Eddy have claimed special revelations from God. To see the error of such dependence upon inner feelings one needs simply to ask, "Does God say one thing to Joseph Smith, and something entirely different to Ellen G. White and Mary Baker Eddy?" God is not the author of confusion; rather, confusion comes from the fallible feelings of men. ". . . it is not in man that walketh to direct his steps" (Jeremiah 10:23).

Liberalism, or modernism, in the realm of theology, makes the mistake of thinking that man's reason is the infallible authority in religion. Rudolf Bultmann, for example, speaks of "demythologyzing the Bible," by which he means that he or other theologians would go through the Bible and would decide what is truth and what is myth. Nels Ferré speaks of the Bible containing "meat and milk, but also sand and gravel." It then devolves upon man, through the use of his reason, to make the decisions as to which is which. Need we point out that man's reason is not so infallible? No two modern theologians agree on just how to demythologize the Bible. No two systems of theology are in even comparative agreement. When man turns to his own reason, there is nothing solid or sure or permanent.

The third possibility, as the absolute source of authority, is the Bible, the inspired word of God. The only dependable authority in religion is the authority of God. Neither the internal authority which man imagines within himself nor the authority which a group of men claim in concerted

28

efforts is real authority. The only authority in religion is the authority of God who created the universe. Is it not obvious that God, the object of our worship, should be the one to determine what he wants done by his creatures in their service and in their worship to him? How wrong it is for man to arrogate to himself the right to decide how God is to be worshiped or in what way he is to be served! It is our responsibility to read the scriptures, understand them and obey them. Let us say, as Samuel did, "Speak; [Lord] for thy servant heareth" (I Samuel 3:10).

The Line of Authority

God the Father has the final or ultimate authority, in religion as well as in everything else. In Genesis 1:1, we read, "In the beginning God created the heavens and the earth." The fact that our entire universe, including everything within it, originated in the mind of God and came into being by his creative power seems to establish God's priority in every aspect of authority.

There was a time, however, when God delegated this authority to Christ, during the period when he lived among men on the earth. At the end of Christ's ministry in his final recorded message, he said, "All authority hath been given unto me in heaven and on earth. Go ye therefore, and make disciples of all the nations, baptizing them . . . teaching them . . . and lo, I am with you always, even unto the end of the world" (Matthew 28:18-20). This is further borne out by his statements in the Sermon on the Mount, when he said, "Ye have heard that it was said . . . but I say unto you . . ." (Matthew 5). In each of these cases he stated part of the Mosaic Law, then modified and deepened the command as he defined the requirements of the Christian era. At the end of that sermon there is the significant statement, "And it came to pass, when Jesus had finished these words, the multitudes were astonished at his teaching: for he taught them as one having authority, and not as their scribes" (Matthew 7:28-29). So, the line of authority begins with God, the Father, but moves on to Christ, the Son, to whom God gave all authority in heaven and on earth.

The next step occurred when Christ left the earth, announcing that in his place he would send the Holy Spirit or Comforter. In John 16:13, we find, "Howbeit when he, the Spirit of truth, is come, he shall guide you into all the truth: for he shall not speak from himself; but what things soever he shall hear, these shall he speak: and he shall declare unto you the things that are to come." Christ plainly indicated that he would not leave his disciples alone, but would send them the Holy Spirit who would guide them into all truth.

A careful study of the scriptures indicates that authority has always rested with divinity—God the Father, Christ the Son, and the Holy Spirit. Never did it rest with men. Men, on the other hand, were merely the messengers or instruments through which the authoritative statements of

God came to mankind. This is borne out in many passages such as the following: "Ye shall recieve power, when the Holy Spirit is come upon you: and ye shall be my witnesses both in Jerusalem, and in all Judaea and Samaria, and unto the uttermost part of the earth" (Acts 1:8).

WITNESSES AND SPOKESMEN

Earlier, during his active ministry, Jesus said, "But when they deliver you up, be not anxious how or what ye shall speak: for it shall be given you in that hour what ye shall speak. For it is not ye that speak, but the Spirit of your Father that speaketh in you" (Matthew 10:19-20). Similarly, Christ told Peter, "I will give unto thee the keys of the kingdom of heaven: and whatsoever thou shalt bind on earth shall be bound [shall have been bound] in heaven; and whatsoever thou shalt loose on earth shall be loosed [shall have been loosed] in heaven" (Matthew 16:19). The same message was delivered to all of the apostles, as stated in Matthew 18:18, "Verily I say unto you, What things soever ye shall bind on earth shall be bound [shall have been bound] in heaven; and what things soever ye shall loose on earth shall be loosed [shall have been loosed] in heaven."

Just here it should be pointed out that men have sometimes mis-understood these two scriptures. Sometimes the view has been held that the Lord was giving Peter almost unlimited authority, saying that whatev-er Peter decided to bind upon men would be recognized as the basis of judgment in heaven. This is far from what the passage actually states. A careful study of the very tenses in the original Greek clearly indicates that the real meaning is, "whatsoever thou shalt bind on earth *shall have been bound in heaven.*" Similarly, "whatsoever thou shalt loose on earth *shall have been loosed in heaven.*" In other words, the things that Peter would be guided by the Holy Spirit to teach had already been established in heaven as the grounds upon which men would be judged. This is certainly reasonable. Peter, fickle as he was, could hardly have been given the authority to decide matters on his own whims. It is much more logical to believe that God was letting Peter be his spokesman. This interpretation runs parallel to all the other passages on the subject of authority.

There is yet another verse which deserves our attention. On Pentecost when the church began, it was obviously the Holy Spirit who guided the apostles. "And they were all filled with the Holy Spirit, and began to speak with other tongues, as the Spirit gave them utterance" (Acts 2:4). This is exactly what the Lord had told them to expect. This is exactly what happened. The apostles were God's messengers to declare his will and did not have authority resting within themselves. These men were also in-spired to write the Holy Scriptures, which are the authoritative statements of God's will for men. However, these men did not have the authority to originate the teachings nor to modify them. They were used simply as messengers to proclaim that which God had established.

OUR ONLY GUIDE

The Bible is our guide, our only guide. For this reason it is encouraging to hear people say. "Let us have a 'thus saith the Lord . . .' for all that we do in our religious faith and practice." It is also good to hear men say, "Let us call Bible things by Bible names." Still another way of saying it is, "Let us speak where the scriptures speak, and be silent where the scriptures are silent." Each of these is a statement indicating the acceptence of the authority of the scriptures.

At this point let us examine two opposite positions on the matter of the authority of the scriptures. *Martin Luther* championed the idea: *Whatever is not expressly prohibited in the scriptures is permissible.* His view can be summarized, "I favor bringing into the church of God and being a part and parcel thereof anything and everything not specifically forbidden and directly condemned." (*History of the Great Reformation of the Sixteenth Century*, by D'Aubigne, 1848 edition, Book II, p. 297). Luther's view would open the door to all kinds of innovations. Such things as the burning of incense, the lighting of candles, the use of images, and the like are nowhere expressly prohibited in the New Testament scriptures. Christening ceremonies for infants could be brought in under such an interpretation. The Lord's Supper might have other elements added to the unleavened bread and the fruit of the vine. If it is permissible to bring into Christian worship anything not expressly forbidden, then infinite variety is inevitable. This is much of the reason that the religious world is so divided today.

Huldrich Zwingli championed the second view: *Whatever is not expressly authorized in the scriptures is prohibited.* His view can be summarized: "My position is that in the matters of God and the service to the Lord we will accept nothing unless the Scriptures authorize it" (*A History of the Christian Church*, by Williston Walker, Charles Scribner's Sons, 1959, p. 322). The fact is that Zwingli's point of view is that which is stated in the scriptures themselves. Only what is authorized is permissible. In Galatians 1:8-9, Paul wrote:

> But though we, or an angel from heaven, should preach unto you any gospel other than that which we preached unto you, let him be anathema. As we have said before, so say I now again, If any man preacheth unto you any gospel other than that which ye received, let him be anathema.

This is a strong teaching and an unusual style of emphasis—the repetition of a sentence for double emphasis. The apostle John stated the same point in these words, "Whosoever goeth onward and abideth not in the teaching of Christ, hath not God: he that abideth in the teaching, the same hath both the Father and the Son" (II John 9).

In the final part of the final chapter of the final book of the Bible there is this emphasis:

31

I testify unto every man that heareth the words of the prophecy of this book, If any man shall add unto them, God shall add unto him the plagues which are written in this book: and if any man shall take away from the words of the book of this prophecy, God shall take away his part from the tree of life, and out of the holy city, which are written in this book.—Revelation 22:18-19

While this message primarily applied to the book of Revelation, the same general principle applies to the entire body of scripture. Anyone who adds to or takes from the inspired word of God has God's disapproval.

THREE AVENUES

In determining what the scriptures authorize there are three avenues through which we may receive guidance. First, there are *direct commands*. Such scriptures as Acts 2:38 exemplify what we mean by direct commands: "And Peter said unto them, Repent ye, and be baptized every one of you in the name of Jesus Christ unto the remission of your sins; and ye shall receive the gift of the Holy Spirit." There are many other commands which give us clear-cut, unequivocal evidence of what God expects us to do if we are to be his followers.

In the second place, there are *approved apostolic examples*. Here we might use as an illustration the missionary journeys which were made by the apostle Paul. Beginning in Acts 13, we discover that he was sent out by the church at Antioch, that he visited many places, preached and established congregations, and then returned to make a report to the church from which he had gone out. The same was true in his second missionary journey and in his third missionary journey. There was no establishment of a separate organization, such as a missionary society, to carry on the mission program of the early church. Congregations selected men, sent them out, supported them and received their reports upon their return. This is what we continue to do today.

The third avenue through which we can know the Lord's will is what we might call *necessary inference*. Each command of God authorizes whatever is necessary to carry it out. When the Lord commands Christians to meet for worship, he necessarily authorizes the providing of a place for the Christians to assemble for worship. The church cannot meet for worship without a location to meet in. It is that simple.

We might also suggest that when there are two positions under consideration, it is extremely wise to choose the safest and the surest of the two. We ought to make every religious act as sure as we possibly can. As an example, we might take the matter of eating the Lord's Supper each first day of the week. Another view is that it should be eaten each quarter, or even only semi-annually. Since the early Christians, according to church history, did eat the Lord's Supper each first day of the week, and since the scriptures themselves, in Acts 20:7, indicate exactly the same thing, the

32

safest, surest position is to have the Lord's Supper each Lord's Day.

Still another suggestion is that in interpreting any individual passage of scripture it is wise to interpret it in the light of all other passages of scripture on the same subject. Sometimes we may be puzzled about what a certain sentence means. What the Holy Spirit guided the same writer to say on another occasion, or guided other writers in other books to say on the same subject, will be helpful in our understanding of the puzzling sentence.

Our religion—our relationship to God—is our most important consideration. We ought to be absolutely certain about everything that we believe and practice. Let us return to the church of the New Testament in all things. Let us become Christians in the same manner that men became such during the time of the apostles. Let us worship as the early Christians worshipped. Let us see that the church is organized and governed as it was in the days when the Holy Spirit guided the apostles. Then, we are on solid ground. These suggestions form an approach to understanding the source of authority in religion. They will bring men closer together, and will eliminate divisions which plague the religious realm. They are taught in the scriptures themselves.

CHAPTER SEVEN
Salvation

One of the least recognized and yet one of the most serious problems of our day is an incorrect understanding of what is involved in man's salvation. This is critically important. Misinformation or partial information concerning a business investment may cost a man his money, but it will not cost him his soul. Misinformation or partial information concerning his physical health may cost a man his life, but it will not cost him his soul. On the other hand, misinformation or partial information concerning salvation will cost a man his eternal destiny in heaven.

A discussion of the subject of salvation presupposes that all men are sinners. Until man recognizes that he is a sinner and that he is lost, there is no real point in discussing salvation. The presupposition that all are sinners is supported solidly in the scriptures. For example, Paul, quoting from David, wrote in Romans 3:10, and 23, "There is none righteous, no, not one; . . . for all have sinned, and fall short of the glory of God."

These statements from the apostle Paul are strongly supported by sentences found in the writings of the apostle John: "If we say that we have no sin, we deceive ourselves, and the truth is not in us. If we say that we have not sinned, we make him a liar, and his word is not in us" (I John 1:8, 10). There is no uncertainty about it—all men who have lived long enough to reach the age of accountability (the age when they are old enough to choose meaningfully between right and wrong) have committed sin. When one realizes this, the subject of salvation becomes a live and vital subject.

God's Grace

Salvation is by God's grace. It is a gift from God, motivated by his love for us, and is provided through Jesus Christ. Grace means "unmerited favor." Salvation is an unearned, undeserved blessing, offered freely to all mankind, and made possible by the sacrificial death of Christ on the cross. In short, there was no way that man, the sinner, could earn or merit salvation, so God provided it for him as a gift. This is the Good News of the Gospel.

One of the clearest statements of this theme is from the pen of the apostle Paul in Ephesians 2:8-9, where he said, "For by grace have ye been saved through faith; and that not of yourselves, it is the gift of God; not of works, that no man should glory." A similar passage is found in Romans 5:8, where Paul wrote, "But God commendeth his own love toward us, in that, while we were yet sinners, Christ died for us." In the same chapter we read further:

> For if by the trespass of the one the many died, much more did the grace of God, and the gift by the grace of the one man, Jesus Christ, abound unto the many . . . even so through one act of righteousness the free gift came unto all men to justification of life . . . as sin reigned in death, even so might grace reign through righteousness unto eternal life through Jesus Christ our Lord.— Romans 5:15, 18, 21

All of these passages emphasize that salvation is God's gift—a matter of grace. The central point in salvation is the love of God manifested through Christ for the saving of men. It is a story of grace, pre-eminently, above everything else. It would be impossible to overemphasize the fact that salvation is a gift from God—a matter of grace.

As wonderful as grace is, there is something about it that man does not like. Instead of feeling that he is totally dependent upon God for the making of salvation possible, he would prefer to feel that he does it himself. Just as men glory in being "self-made" men in business, politics, or the professions, man would prefer to feel that he earns his own salvation and is in this regard self-sufficient. The fact is, however, that this is totally impossible. If man is to be saved at all, it must be because of God's love manifest in Christ.

When one comprehends this, his salvation becomes so much more precious. His love of God becomes so much greater. His gratitude to Christ for his sacrificial death on the cross becomes so much deeper. His religion becomes so much more satisfying. Instead of doing the right things and thereby earning salvation, much as one might pay the premium on an insurance policy, he worships God and serves his fellowmen out of sheer gratitude. His religion becomes a joy, rather than a duty. It becomes not a question of "How much is required for salvation?", but rather a question of "How much can I do to show my gratitude for the priceless gift of salvation?"

Although no human illustration is quite adeqate to express this spirit of gratitude to God for his grace, I can understand it more fully in my own life because of an incident a few years ago. My doctor, after giving me a physical examination, told me the sad news that I had cancer. It was serious and something needed to be done immediately. An operation was suggested. My doctor suggested a surgeon, one of his own professors in medical school, a man who was nearing retirement though he continued to teach surgery and to perform a limited number of operations.

When I first met him I thought that he looked more like a rancher or a fisherman than a surgeon. But in the days ahead, as I observed his skill and felt his kindly touch, I came to respect him and even to love him. His ability and training and concern combined to give me back my life.

Already there have been sixteen years to be with my family and to continue to do the work I love. My point is this: I feel a debt of gratitude to this man that I can never repay. If ever he should need anything that I could provide, I would be eager to provide it. Nothing that he could ask of me would be a duty. Rather, it would be a joy. He saved my life. To an infinitesimal degree this story suggests the gratitude which we Christians feel for the eternal salvation which God provides.

Three Aspects of Salvation

In order that we may feel the full significance of what God, through Christ, has done for us, let us look at three very special words—words which are too seldom used and appreciated. First is the word *redemption*, a word of the market place. This word implies an understanding of the "fall" of man. Man, created in God's image, did not remain pure and sinless, but sinned, thus becoming estranged from God. Then, man needed to be redeemed. He was in bondage to sin, and needed someone who would buy his freedom for him. In the days of American slavery, occasionally this very thing happened—some benevolent person would buy a slave's freedom. This is what God has done for us.

When Isaiah wrote concerning the Messiah, he described him as a redeemer. In Mark 10:45, there is this sentence, "For the Son of man also came not to be ministered unto, but to minister, and to give his life a ransom for many." A redeemer is one who pays the ransom for another. In Romans 3:24, Paul used this idea as he wrote, "Being justified freely by his grace through the redemption that is in Christ Jesus." In Ephesians 1:7, Paul further wrote, "In whom we have our redemption through his blood, the forgiveness of our trespasses, according to the riches of his grace."

A second word is *justification*, a word of the law courts. Visualize a man who stands before a judge, charged with a crime. The judge acquits the man, which means that he is justified and free to go his way. It may be that he was guilty of the crime but he is declared free from the penalty of the crime. Because of some special generosity he is given his freedom from paying the penalty for his sin. In Romans 4:25, Paul used the word *justification* when he wrote of Christ, "Who was delivered up for our trespasses, and was raised for our justification." Again in Romans 5:18, he used the word, "So then as through one trespass the judgment came unto all men to condemnation; even so through one act of righteousness the free gift came unto all men to justification of life."

A third word is *reconciliation*, a word often involved in family relationships. *Reconciliation* is the point of the story of the prodigal son—when the wayward boy comes home and is lovingly received by his father. In Romans 5:10, Paul used this word: "For if, while we were enemies, we were reconciled to God through the death of his Son. . . ." Again in II

36

Corinthians 5:19-20, Paul referred to this idea when he wrote: "God was in Christ reconciling the world unto himself, not reckoning unto them their trespasses, and having committed unto us the word of reconciliation ... We beseech you on behalf of Christ, be ye reconciled to God."

Redemption means that our freedom from sin has been bought. *Justification* means that we have been freed from the necessity of paying the price of our guilt. Then, sweetest of all, *reconciliation* means that we have been restored to the love of God.

If Grace, Why Anything Else?

It seems strange that something so wonderful as grace should be misunderstood or misinterpreted, but such has been the case. There have been some, for example, who have felt that grace was meted out only to certain ones and not to all. This doctrine is quite old, for the man who gave it its first really distinctive statement was Augustine, who lived in the fifth century. He said, in effect, "There is nothing man can do until God starts the process by his grace." Augustine believed that before a man could be saved God must do something specifically for that man. God must elect him to be saved. Augustine was one of the first to believe in predestination—that God before the foundation of the world determined those who were among the elect and those who were not among the elect. He believed that the number was so fixed that it could not be changed.

Later, John Calvin believed this same doctrine and taught it. Those millions who have followed in the theology of Calvin have believed it. They have believed that God predestined certain men to be saved and others to be lost and that man can do nothing about it. The scriptures have quite a different emphasis, for they indicate that man must play a crucial and determining part in his own salvation.

When T. B. Larimore, a Confederate scout in the war between the states, was a young man he earnestly desired salvation. He was misguided in that he was told that he must wait for some supernatural sign that he was among the elect. It never came. He was not of an emotional nature and he never dreamed a special dream nor heard a voice in the night or any other spectacular "call from God." He despaired of being saved, until someone taught him from the scriptures that in New Testament times they were never told to "pray through" or "wait for a call" but were simply told what they must do.

There have been others who mistakenly thought that God's love, providing grace for all men, meant that all men would be saved. The universal salvation of all men is not taught in the scriptures, however, for Jesus said, "Enter ye in by the narrow gate: for wide is the gate, and broad is the way, that leadeth to destruction, and many are they that enter in thereby" (Matthew 7:13). Many will be eternally lost.

If grace is for all men, and yet not all men will be saved, does this not mean that God is a respecter of persons, saving some by his grace and letting others be lost? The apostle Peter said not, for he wrote, "Of a truth I perceive that God is no respecter of persons: but in every nation he that feareth him, and worketh righteousness, is acceptable to him" (Acts 10:34-35). We must conclude from these scriptures that man is saved by God's grace, but not without an appropriate response from man himself.

SALVATION BY FAITH

At this point, let us go back to one of the key scriptures mentioned earlier. In Ephesians 2:8-9, Paul wrote, "By grace have ye been saved through faith; and that not of yourselves, it is the gift of God; not of works, that no man should glory." What does this mean? In the passage there are several key words, two of which stand out. The first is *grace*, the unmerited favor of God which provides salvation as a gift for all men. The second key word is *faith*, which is man's response to God's free gift. Salvation is by grace—on God's side; and by faith—on man's side.

Now it becomes very important for us to understand what faith means. Exactly what is meant by faith? Many people define faith as a mental acceptance of certain facts. That is historical faith and we have historical faith about many things. We believe, for example, that certain cities exist and that certain people have lived though we have neither seen the cities nor known the people. That kind of faith, however, is not sufficient to save a man. The devils believe and shudder (James 2:19), but they will not be saved. Saving faith is something beyond the mental acceptance of the existence of God and of Christ. It is that, but it is more.

The theme of the book of Romans is faith. When we study Romans we discover that faith meant, to the apostle Paul, a mental acceptance of the existence of God and Christ, plus an active commitment of his life. When a man has faith he not only believes, but also invests himself in Christ. The clearest way to convey Paul's meaning is to read a phrase from the opening sentence of Romans and another from the closing sentence. In the opening sentence we find the expression "unto obedience of faith" (Romans 1:5). Paul emphasized faith throughout the sixteen chapters which make up the book. It is obedient faith—faith which includes within itself obedience to God's will. When we come to the end of the book we find that Paul used the same expression, "unto obedience of faith" (Romans 16:26). We are saved by grace, to which we must respond in obedient faith (Romans 16:26). Grace is God's part and faith is our part. Faith, in order to be saving faith, includes within itself the obedience which God asks of us.

We are disturbed by those whose interpretation of faith leads them to preach, in many pulpits across the land and on many radio and television programs, that all one must do in order to be saved is to believe in one's heart. The emphasis often made is that whenever a person believes in the

38

Lord and mentally commits himself to the Lord, he is immediately saved. Sometimes this is called "being born again," and is described as having happened while riding on an airplane, or on one's knees in prayer, or while facing some special trial of life. This interpretation of faith, commonly held by many people, is not the interpretation of faith reflected in the pages of the inspired scriptures. Biblical faith is an obedient faith.

GRACE AND FAITH

Helpful here is the familiar passage, John 3:16, which reads, "For God so loved the world, that he gave his only begotten Son, that whosoever believeth on him should not perish, but have eternal life." Both elements are in this passage—God's gift and man's response. Later in that same chapter there is this additional sentence, "He that believeth on the Son hath eternal life; but he that obeyeth not the Son shall not see life, but the wrath of God abideth on him" (John 3:36). In this sentence, believing is the positive side, while its opposite is disobedience, the negative side.

Salvation is God's gift; there can be no question about that. But, the gift must be appropriated by man's response in obedient faith. *Grace makes salvation possible; obedient faith makes salvation actual.* When man responds in Biblical faith to God's offer of salvation, he is neither earning nor deserving the gift, but only accepting it on the conditions on which the Lord has promised to give it.

Each of us breathes God's fresh air every moment that he lives. It is God's free gift, but we must breathe it. We do not earn it by breathing it, but our breathing it is essential to life.

Imagine a brilliantly lighted room in the darkness of night. Inside the room are electrical fixtures through which light is provided in abundance. Behind these fixtures there are electric power lines which link them with the generating plant of some power company. Think, too, about all of the effort that has gone into the discovery of electricity, and the perfecting of the techniques of producing it, distributing it, and effectively translating it into light. Now, when someone opens the door and invites you to come into the lighted room, and you accept his invitation, you do not earn or deserve all of the effort that has gone into discovering electricity, inventing the means of using it, and developing the plants that produce it. You simply enjoy these unearned benefits as a result of being invited into the light. So it is with God's grace. We do not deserve it, but in order to have it we must accept it.

Somewhere in this study it is important also to mention the fact that God's grace is something that has already appeared. Paul wrote in Titus 2:11-14:

> For the grace of God hath appeared [past tense], bringing salvation to all men, instructing us, to the intent that, denying ungodliness and worldly lusts, we should live soberly and righteously and

godly in this present world; looking for the blessed hope and appearing of the glory of the great God and our Savior Jesus Christ; who gave himself for us, that he might redeem us from all iniquity, and purify unto himself a people for his own possession, zealous of good works.

Notice that God's grace has already come.

It is at this point that many people have a basic misunderstanding. Many expect the grace and mercy of God to be extended to man at the judgment, whereas we have no such promise in God's book. Rather, as stated in this passage, the grace of God has already come in the person of Jesus Christ. In other words, salvation and the freedom from sin which it provides are possible only in Christ. Man has the privilege of accepting God's gift of salvation by coming to Christ, or of rejecting it by staying away from Christ.

That salvation by grace involves obedience is clearly indicated in Christ's Sermon on the Mount, where he said:

> Not every one that saith unto me, Lord, Lord, shall enter into the kingdom of heaven; but he that doeth the will of my Father who is in heaven. . . . Every one therefore that heareth these words of mine, and doeth them, shall be likened unto a wise man, who built his house upon the rock: and the rain descended, and the floods came, and the winds blew, and beat upon that house; and it fell not: for it was founded upon the rock. And every one that heareth these words of mine, and doeth them not, shall be likened unto a foolish man, who built his house upon the sand: the rain descended, and the floods came, and the winds blew, and smote upon that house; and it fell: and great was the fall thereof.—Matthew 7:21, 24-27

Notice the emphasis upon doing the will of God in this passage.

In this connection let us also read II Thessalonians 1:7-9:

> . . . to you that are afflicted rest with us, at the revelation of the Lord Jesus from heaven with the angels of his power in flaming fire, rendering vengeance to them that know not God, and to them that obey not the gospel of our Lord Jesus: who shall suffer punishment, even eternal destruction from the face of the Lord and from the glory of his might.

Notice that the vengeance of the Lord at the time of judgment will be rendered against: (1) those that know not God, and (2) those that obey not the gospel. These passages obviously indicate that obedience to the commands of God is imperative if one expects to be saved eternally.

Do not misunderstand this emphasis upon obedience. We do not *earn* salvation, but we must comply with the *conditions* laid down by the Lord in order to receive the free gift of eternal salvation. Christ said, "Even so ye also when ye shall have done all the things that are commanded you, say, We are unprofitable servants; we have done that which it was our duty to do" (Luke 17:10). Man cannot earn salvation through works of merit, but

40

he must comply with the conditions that the Lord laid down in order to receive the gift of salvation.

New Testament Conversions

In the book of Acts there are eight major conversions, given as models for all people of all time. In every case the gospel of Christ was preached, the people believed in their hearts, made known their faith in some manner and then were baptized for the forgiveness of sins. It is strange that the only one of these elements in salvation which is mentioned in every example is baptism. Even faith is not mentioned each time, though, of course, we know that it must have been the foundation out of which obedience came in each case. Repentance is not mentioned every time; confession is not mentioned every time. Only baptism is mentioned in each of the eight cases.

Let us notice some of these God-given examples of how men became Christians:

PENTECOST: Peter preached a great sermon concerning Christ. Then we read, "Now when they heard this, they were pricked in their heart, and said unto Peter and the rest of the apostles, Brethren, what shall we do? And Peter said unto them, Repent ye, and be baptized every one of you in the name of Jesus Christ unto the remission of your sins; and ye shall receive the gift of the Holy Spirit. . . . And with many other words he testified, and exhorted them, saying, Save yourselves from this crooked generation. They then that received his word were baptized: and there were added unto them in that day about three thousand souls."—Acts 2:37-38, 40-41

ETHIOPIAN NOBLEMAN: God loved the man from Ethiopia enough that he called a preacher to come and sit beside him in his chariot. "And Philip opened his mouth, and beginning from this scripture, preached unto him Jesus. And as they went on the way, they came unto a certain water; and the eunuch saith, Behold, here is water; what doth hinder me to be baptized? And Philip said, If thou believest with all thy heart, thou mayest. And he answered and said, I believe that Jesus Christ is the Son of God. And he commanded the chariot to stand still: and they both went down into the water, both Philip and the eunuch; and he baptized him. And when they came up out of the water, the Spirit of the Lord caught away Philip; and the eunuch saw him no more, for he went on his way rejoicing."—Acts 8:35-39

SAUL OF TARSUS: When Saul came to believe that Christ was the divine Son of God, he traveled the Damascus road into the city and spent three days and three nights in fasting and prayer. At the end of this agonizing period, God sent Ananias to say, "And now why tarriest thou? arise, and be baptized, and wash away thy sins, calling on his name" (Acts 22:16). Even though he had believed in Christ, even though he had spent three days in fasting and prayer, Saul was not yet saved—his sins were not yet for-

41

given—until he was baptized. There is no property or power in the water to wash away sins, but there is a power in the obedience that one renders to the Lord which causes the grace of God to be applied in the salvation of his soul. We are saved by grace, through faith, which involves obedience to the conditions laid down by the Lord.

CORNELIUS: To those who think that all man must do in order to be saved is "just live a good life; be honest, sincere, and basically moral," the case of the conversion of Cornelius is especially significant. Here is the account: "Now there was a certain man in Caesarea, Cornelius by name, a centurion of the band called the Italian band, a devout man, and one that feared God with all his house, who gave much alms to the people, and prayed to God always" (Acts 10:1-2). Here is a good man, as good as any of us, yet the story tells how an angel was sent to tell him that his prayers had come up before God as a memorial and that God wanted him to be saved. Quoting the scriptures exactly: "Send to Joppa, and fetch Simon, whose surname is Peter; who shall speak unto thee words, whereby thou shalt be saved [future tense], thou and all thy house" (Acts 11:13-14). The rest of the story is that the apostle Peter did come and did preach Christ to Cornelius and his household. They believed the preaching, made known their faith and their desire to be Christians, and were baptized. From this detailed example we learn that there is no goodness within man himself that can cleanse from sin. Salvation is only in Christ. Apart from the redeeming blood of Christ there is no salvation (I John 1:7). It certainly is true that men must live good moral lives in order to reach heaven, but it is equally true that good moral lives by themselves will not save.

PHILIPPIAN JAILOR: The pagan Roman jailor, after the earthquake had jarred loose the doors of his prison, fell down before Paul and Silas and said: "Sirs, what must I do to be saved?" And they said, "Believe on the Lord Jesus, and thou shalt be saved, thou and thy house. And they spake the word of the Lord unto him, with all that were in his house. And he took them the same hour of the night, and washed their stripes; and was baptized, he and all his, immediately. And he brought them up into his house, and set food before them, and rejoiced greatly, with all his house, having believed in God" (Acts 16:30-34). Notice that this Roman jailor believed, but also notice that a part of "having believed in God" was obedience to God's command of baptism. Inseparably bound up with his hearing and accepting of the gospel was his doing what the gospel required.

Then Comes the Rejoicing

The realization that we are lost leads us to listen when the gospel is preached. As we hear the story of Jesus, faith takes hold of us, changes the direction of our lives, is then made known by word of mouth, and finally culminates in what the Bible calls the new birth. Jesus spoke of it in that fashion in the story of Nicodemus, who was a ruler of Israel:

42

> Verily, verily, I say unto thee, Except one be born anew, he cannot see the kingdom of God. Nicodemus saith unto him, How can a man be born when he is old? can he enter a second time into his mother's womb, and be born? Jesus answered, Verily, verily, I say unto thee, except one be born of water and the Spirit, he cannot enter into the kingdom of God.—John 3:3-5

This is the new birth. It begins when we believe and becomes actual and visible to others when we break forth from the water in baptism.

The apostle Paul in the letter to the Romans also compared baptism with a death:

> Are ye ignorant that all we who were baptized into Christ Jesus were baptized into his death? We were buried therefore with him through baptism into death: that like as Christ was raised from the dead through the glory of the Father, so we also might walk in newness of life.—Romans 6:3-4

Jesus was killed on the cross, buried in a tomb and then raised from the tomb. He who would become a Christian must be buried in water and raised to walk in newness of life. The old, sinful man dies and is buried. A new man is born—a Christian. Symbolically he does what Jesus did before him. Again we read:

> For if we have become united with him in the likeness of his death, we shall be also in the likeness of his resurrection; knowing this, that our old man was crucified with him, that the body of sin might be done away, that so we should no longer be in bondage to sin; for he that hath died is justified from sin.—Romans 6:5-7

After we have responded to God's grace through obedient faith, then comes the rejoicing:

> Being therefore justified by faith, we have peace with God through our Lord Jesus Christ; through whom also we have had our access by faith into this grace wherein we stand; and we rejoice in hope of the glory of God . . . and not only so, but we also rejoice in God through our Lord Jesus Christ, through whom we have now received the reconciliation.—Romans 5:1-2, 11

CHAPTER EIGHT
The Work Of The Church— Evangelism

As one reads the New Testament and analyzes all of the teachings concerning the work that the Lord wants Christians to do, he comes to the conclusion that there are three major areas of work: (1) *Evangelism*—the carrying of the good news of Christ to everyone in the whole world; (2) *Edification*—the nurturing and encouraging of all Christians to grow spiritually until their lives reflect the image of Christ; and (3) *Benevolence*—providing help to all those who are in need in any way. Obviously, each of these areas is vast in its implications. Together they cover the whole range of activities in which Christians ought to be engaged. Let us examine each one carefully to determine what is involved and even more especially how we may become active in doing each phase of the Lord's work.

EVANGELISM

The primary mission of the church is the same as the primary mission of Christ—the saving of lost souls. This is not to discount the importance of the other areas of work which the Lord outlined for his disciples, but it is to highlight the importance of bringing the message of Christ and salvation to the eternal souls who are not yet among the redeemed. In order that we may properly feel the importance of the work of evangelizing the world, let us notice a number of scriptures:

Romans 3:10, 23 —". . . There is none righteous, no, not one; . . . for all have sinned, and fall short of the glory of God; . . ."

I John 1:8, 10—"If we say that we have no sin, we deceive ourselves, and the truth is not in us . . . . If we say that we have not sinned, we make him a liar, and his word is not in us."

John 3:16—"For God so loved the world, that he gave his only begotten Son, that whosoever believeth on him should not perish, but have eternal life."

Matthew 1:21—"And she shall bring forth a son; and thou shalt call his name JESUS; for it is he that shall save his people from their sins."

Luke 19:10—"For the Son of man came to seek and to save that which was lost."

John 14:6—". . . I am the way , and the truth, and the life: no one cometh unto the Father, but by me."

44

Matthew 9:35-38—"And Jesus went about all the cities and the villages, teaching in their synagogues, and preaching the gospel of the kingdom, and healing all manner of disease and all manner of sickness. But when he saw the multitudes, he was moved with compassion for them, because they were distressed and scattered, as sheep not having a shepherd. Then saith he unto his disciples, The harvest indeed is plenteous, but the laborers are few. Pray ye therefore the Lord of the harvest, that he send forth laborers into his harvest."

Matthew 28:19-20—"Go ye therefore, and make disciples of all the nations, baptizing them into the name of the Father and of the Son and of the Holy Spirit: teaching them to observe all things whatsoever I commanded you: and lo, I am with you always, even unto the end of the world."

Romans 1:16-17—"For I am not ashamed of the gospel: for it is the power of God unto salvation to every one that believeth; to the Jew first, and also to the Greek. For therein is revealed a righteousness of God from faith unto faith: as it is written, But the righteous shall live by faith."

I Corinthians 15:1-2—"Now I make known unto you, brethren, the gospel which I preached unto you, which also ye received, wherein also ye stand, by which also ye are saved, if ye hold fast the word which I preached unto you, except ye believed in vain."

Romans 10:13-15—". . . Whosoever shall call upon the name of the Lord shall be saved. How then shall they call on him in whom they have not believed? and how shall they believe in him whom they have not heard? and how shall they hear without a preacher? and how shall they preach, except they be sent? even as it is written, How beautiful are the feet of them that bring glad tidings of good things!"

Each of these passages is typical of many other scriptures which emphasize, on almost every page of the New Testament, the supreme importance of the work of evangelism.

MASSES OF MANKIND

In Genesis 22:17, we read of God telling Abraham that his seed would be numberless "as the sands of the sea-shore" and "as countless as the stars of the heavens." While this has been fulfilled in Abraham's descendants, it is even more impressive in the whole of mankind. Imagine standing on a shore of one of the great oceans of the world and holding a single handful of sand in one's grasp. As the hundreds and thousands of grains of sand slip through the fingers, one is overwhelmed with the total number of grains of sand on the shores of all the oceans and all the seas of the world. Or, imagine standing on a summer's night and looking into the starry heavens above and contemplating the limitless expanse of stars. These God-given comparisons help us to realize the vastness of humanity. Truly mankind constitutes a great ocean of lost souls.

Several years ago the United Nations published a booklet on the

"Population Explosion." It was pointed out that all of the centuries from the beginning of time until 1830 A.D. were necessary for the population of the world to reach one billion people living simultaneously. From 1830 to 1935 was required for the population to reach two billion. It was then estimated that from 1935 to 1965 would be sufficient for the population to reach three billion. Actually, this mark was reached in 1964, even ahead of the estimated schedule. The estimates in that booklet also indicated that by 1980 there would be four billion people living simultaneously. That estimate too was reached ahead of time, for in 1976 the world population reached the four billion mark. It was further estimated that by 1990 there would be five billion, and before the turn of the century there would be more than six billion people living at the same time. These figures are impressive, yet it is almost impossible to comprehend a billion people—or rather, a billion souls.

In an effort to make a billion people more comprehendable, let us visualize this great unit of mankind in terms of something nearer our own experiences. Let us imagine an auditorium which will seat one thousand people. Then let us imagine that beginning at noon on a given day this auditorium is filled with a thousand different people, to whom the essence or heart of the gospel is preached. Let this process continue, with a different thousand people each hour of the day and night, until the entire population of the world should hear the barest essentials of Christianity. How long would it take to preach, at the rate of a thousand people an hour, to all of the four and one-quarter billion people who currently live on the earth? Obviously, if we should begin at noon on a certain day, we would have reached 24,000 people by the following day at noon. It would be possible to reach 168,000 people within the seven days of the first week. It would then take a total of forty-one days to reach one million people at the rate of a thousand people an hour.

It is when we reach above the million toward the ten million, the fifty million, the hundred million, and the billion mark that we find ourselves shocked by the enormity of the time that would be required. At the rate of a thousand people an hour, it would take 114 years to preach to a billion people. If we should begin today, it would require nearly 500 years to preach just a brief hour-long summary of Christianity to the people now living on the earth.

Yet, of course, at such a pace it would be utterly impossible to reach all mankind, for everyone now living will die within our own generation. The hope of bringing the good news of Christ to all mankind rests upon having more workers to enter the harvest fields. What at first seems a hopeless, impossible task, however, becomes a possibility if every Christian throughout the world will only share his faith with those about him.

The apostle Paul wrote to Timothy, "These things write I unto thee, hoping to come unto thee shortly; but if I tarry long, that thou mayest know how men ought to behave themselves in the house of God, which is the church of the living God, the pillar and ground of the truth" (I Timothy 3:14-15). The last expression in this sentence, "the pillar and ground of the truth," signifies that the church is to be *the foundation and support of the truth* as it is proclaimed throughout the world. The church, meaning the people who make up the church, has the responsibility of taking the message of salvation to all people everywhere.

This means that the church can do in its own organizational framework all that is necessary in the work of evangelism. It can SELECT workers, SEND them to a field, SUPERVISE them, and SUPPORT them. The church, through its elders, selects a field where the gospel needs to be preached, then selects workers to go into that field. After careful preparation the church sends them to the field, supervises the work while they are there, and provides the financial and spiritual support which the workers may need. There is no need for an extra-organization such as a missionary society, or any other organization to do the evangelistic work which the Lord has planned for his church to do.

As we examine the New Testament scriptures we notice that local churches were the media through which evangelism was carried on. In apostolic times the church was the only missionary organization that was used, or needed. As an example, the church at Antioch was guided by the Holy Spirit to select Barnabas and Saul and to send them out to preach (Acts 13:1-3). After they had gone through the island of Cyprus, and had preached extensively in Asia Minor they returned to Antioch and made a report of their missionary journey (Acts 14:27-28). At a later time the apostle Paul reminded the church at Corinth that when he first came preaching the gospel in their city he "robbed other churches, taking wages of them that I might minister unto you . . ." (II Corinthians 11:8-9). To the church at Thessalonica he wrote, speaking of their activity in preaching the gospel in many places, and included in his comments these words: "For from you hath sounded forth the word of the Lord, not only in Macedonia and Achaia, but in every place your faith to God-ward is gone forth; so that we need not to speak anything" (I Thessalonians 1:8). At still another time he thanked the church at Philippi because they had sent regularly to him while he preached in other locations (Philippians 4:14-20).

The plan outlined in the New Testament was for the gospel to be preached first at Jerusalem, where the church began, then in Samaria, and unto the uttermost part of the earth. These are the instructions Christ gave his apostles: "But ye shall receive power, when the Holy Spirit is come upon you: and ye shall be my witnesses both in Jerusalem, and in all Judaea and Samaria, and unto the uttermost part of the earth" (Acts 1:8). This was literally fulfilled, as we read in the early chapters of Acts. After persecution drove the Christians out of Jerusalem we find the statement, "They therefore that were scattered abroad went about preaching the word" (Acts 8:4). From Jerusalem, throughout the immediate surrounding area, the church spread to Antioch in Syria; then into Asia Minor, from which it moved on into Europe and throughout the rest of the populated earth. This has continued down through the centuries until today the gospel is known on every continent of the earth.

The spread of the gospel in that first generation of the church's existence was phenomenal. Beginning with 3,000 on Pentecost, the number of men soon came to be 5,000; then we note that the church multiplied and multitudes of men and women were added. By the time we reach Acts 19, we read of Paul's stay in Ephesus: "And this continued for the space of two years; so that all they that dwelt in Asia heard the word of the Lord, both Jews and Greeks" (Acts 19:10). Every Christian seemed to recognize his privilege and responsibility to help in carrying the message of salvation to all of those within reach. Today also each individual Christian needs to feel the challenge and to recognize the privilege of sharing his Christian faith with all those about him. Only in this way can the gospel be spread to the millions who are lost without Christ.

METHODS OF EVANGELISM

In order to be as practical as possible, let us notice some of the methods or techniques of evangelism that are currently being used to carry the message of Christ to people of our time. While this list may not be exhaustive, it does include a number of ideas that have been and are being used with great success in our generation.

1. *ADVERTISEMENTS IN NATIONAL MAGAZINES:* "Ads" of a religious nature are placed in national magazines in the same way that commercial advertisers use such space. The Granny White Church of Christ, Nashville, Tennessee, has been a leader among churches involved in this work.
2. *AMAZING GRACE BIBLE CLASS:* Sponsored by the Madison, Tennessee, church this class is televised weekly over approximately 240 television stations. Along with Biblical messages it presents a complete picture of a working congregation, concerned about its own young people and elderly people, as well as the needs of the community. Local churches pay for air time. Ira North is the "teacher" of the class.
3. *BIBLE CALL:* A series of approximately 200 five-minute recorded teaching messages are available by telephone to people living in 144 cities in 37 states. The range of subjects includes almost all areas about which people might be inquisitive, with special emphasis on those subjects having to do

48

with salvation. A local telephone number is advertised. An operator answers, allows the calling party to designate which category he or she wishes and then the tape is played. Many capable writers across the country have written the scripts.

4. *BUS MINISTRY:* In recent years many congregations have acquired buses, usually used school buses, and have sent them throughout areas within reach of the church building, inviting children and others to attend classes and worship. In some instances this work has been unusually successful, bringing in scores and even hundreds of young people for teaching. Some have matured to the point of becoming Christians. In some instances parents have also come and been converted.

5. *CAMPAIGNS:* A carefully planned evangelistic series of meetings in a foreign country, or in a section of this country where the church is either non-existent or very weak. A sizeable number of dedicated, trained Christian workers go for a relatively brief period of time (two weeks to one month usually), engage in intensive personal evangelism and conduct a series of public meetings. Example: The campaigns led by the Hillsboro church of Nashville in the London area of England, taking as many as 90 workers for a period of three weeks.

6. *CAMPUS MOVEMENTS:* This is an effort in connection with major universities and colleges to establish Christian centers for the students of the schools. It is an evangelistic effort to attract young people who otherwise would be engulfed in a secular university society. Lee Harrington, working with students of Michigan State University in East Lansing, Michigan, has led an effective work of this type.

7. *CITY-WIDE MEETINGS:* A series of evangelistic services in which the congregations of an entire city or area cooperate. Example: The Collins-Craig city-wide meeting held at the opening of the Municipal Auditorium in Nashville, Tennessee in the 1960's. The largest crowd was approximately 13,000 and the meeting continued for eight days.

8. *CORRESPONDENCE COURSES:* A number of correspondence courses, varying in length from four or six lessons to as high as thirty lessons, emphasizing various areas of Bible study are available. One such series is that of Monroe Hawley and another well-known series was written by John Hurt.

9. *EXODUS MOVEMENTS:* This is a movement of a number of families from an area where the church is strong and Christians are numerous, into an area of the country where the church is either non-existent or very weak. Families sell their homes, terminate their employment, and move to a new area with the primary motivation of helping the Lord's Cause to grow and spread.

10. *FILM STRIPS:* A series of five thirty-five minute film strips, accompanied by recorded narration, has been prepared by Jule Miller and distributed widely throughout this country and in some foreign lands. The series presents a clear view of

the entire Bible, dealing with the Patriarchal Period, the Mosaic Period, and the Christian Period. A new series of three filmstrips, featuring Christ, the Bible and the Church, was introduced in 1978, by the Religious Services Company, in which Batsell Barrett Baxter guides a young couple through a study of the Bible to the point of their conversion to Christ.

11. *GOSPEL MEETINGS:* A series of evangelistic services continuing daily for three, four, or eight days, or even longer. The cumulative effect of the series, together with the possibility of presenting a number of appropriate lessons in a relatively short time, helps people to make decisions to become Christians.

12. *HERALD OF TRUTH:* For more than twenty-five years hundreds of churches throughout the United States have cooperated, under the leadership of the Highland Church of Christ, in Abilene, Texas, in presenting international radio and television programs. While the number of stations fluctuates, the number of television stations has often been as high as 150 and the number of radio stations as high as 450, plus free time on the Armed Services Network. At times more than 2,000 congregations have contributed to this effort with many times that many individuals also doing so. Current speakers are: Harold Hazelip, Joe Barnett, Landon Saunders (Heartbeat), Juan Monroy, and Batsell Barrett Baxter. Heartbeat is a very successful, brief-message radio program designed for non-religious listeners.

13. *INNER-CITY WORK:* This is an effort in major cities, usually ghetto areas, to help underprivileged people in learning of Christ and salvation. Camp Shiloh, in addition to its summer camp periods, has conducted a year-long effort in Brooklyn, New York.

14. *MAGAZINES:* Many Christian magazines and papers have been published through the years. These are aimed at different groups of people, but are ultimately evangelistic in purpose. Among the best known are the *Gospel Advocate, Firm Foundation, Power for Today, 20th Century Christian, The Spiritual Sword,* and *Teenage Christian.*

15. *MISSIONARIES:* A family or families moves from an area where the church is strong into an area where the church is non-existent or very weak, either in our own country or in some foreign land. Usually the minimum period of stay is five years, with the possibility of returning for other similar periods. Recently, a program known as GOOD NEWS, at David Lipscomb College, has prepared college students to spend two years as "apprentices" in a foreign mission field. Local congregations send the individual students to the fields, after they are trained. *MISSION SEMINARS:* Many congregations are now conducting intensive, brief lectureships on mission work. These include the need for more evangelistic efforts, and the sharing of ideas of how best to conduct such efforts. A typical example is that held annually

50

in Tulsa, Oklahoma, with more than 20,000 in attendance at times.

16. *PERSONAL EVANGELISM BOOKS:* These are books to guide Christians in person-to-person evangelistic efforts. Among the better known of such books are: Otis Gatewood, *You Can Do Personal Work;* Fred Walker, *Following Through for Christ;* and Ivan Stewart, *From House to House.*

17. *PUPPETS:* The youth work in many congregations has included a "puppet ministry." This is an effort to present the stories and teachings of the Bible in such a way as to attract the attention, especially of young people, but also of adults. In parks and camp grounds, as well as in classes at the church building, this method has provided an interest and a motivation for the learning of the Bible message.

18. *STAR PUBLICATION:* A quarterly magazine of an evangelistic nature, distributed by mail to the residents in any city, town, or county in the country. A congregation or individual chooses the location, then Alvin Jennings, who conducts this service and edits the magazine, arranges for the mailing. Lists of residents are available for every part of the country.

19. *SUMMER CAMPS:* Many congregations take their own young people and the young people of their area to summer camps, where recreation and Bible teaching in a Christian environment help the young people make their life-long decisions about the church and related religious principles.

20. *TEACHING LETTERS:* A series of "teaching letters" has been prepared to teach in an incremental fashion those who have responded to radio or television messages, or other mass media appeals, but who need to be taught more extensively. In some instances the letters have been mailed on a monthly basis to all of the homes within the immediate area of a church building. The letters, twelve in number, begin in a general way to present the message contained in the Bible and gradually lead the person to understand God's will and to want to obey the gospel. The Hillsboro Church of Christ in Nashville, Tennessee, has been one of the pioneer churches using this method. They have also been used extensively with listeners to the Herald of Truth and Heartbeat programs.

21. *TRAINING SCHOOLS:* These consist of schools to train personal evangelistic workers, preachers, missionaries and the like. Example: "Great Commission School," conducted by Wingate Church of Christ, Nashville, Tennessee, and the "Sunset School of Preaching" conducted by the Sunset Church of Christ, Lubbock, Texas.

22. *TRACTS:* Many individuals and congregations produce small booklets, attractively printed, setting forth the New Testament teaching on a variety of subjects. The Hillsboro Church of Christ, Nashville, Tennessee has an extensive series of these tracts, available at printing cost.

23. *UP REACH:* A new attractive full-color, bi-monthly magazine, published by the Highland church in Abilene, Texas, exlusively for evangelistic purposes. Subscriptions are free

on request and now number 150,000.

24. *WORLD RADIO:* A national and international radio program sponsored by the West Monroe, Louisiana, church with Tom Holland and Thomas B. Warren as speakers. A similar program, THE INTERNATIONAL BIBLE HOUR, with V. E. Howard as speaker, is also widely heard.

25. *YOUTH SEMINARS:* From time to time congregations conduct youth meetings for the inspiration and guidance of young people. These appear throughout the brotherhood.

A Modern Parable

Our Lord often taught in parables and some of his most memorable teaching is couched in the language of parables. Here is a modern parable which is designed to encourage each of us to want to do more in soul-winning. It is not given facetiously or critically, but simply that we may be caused to think. The parable begins with a farmer who owns a large field of grain. It is harvest time, and the wheat is already golden brown and needs to be cut. It must not be left in the field very long because the wind or the rain may destroy the crop. Early in the morning he goes into the small town and calls for helpers to come and harvest his crop. The immediate response is favorable and many respond to his invitation.

When they arrive at the field they see the golden harvest and are deeply impressed. They talk about what a wonderful privilege it is to get to harvest so big and bountiful a crop. But someone points out that the fence around this field is not very attractive. It is an old rock fence and in many places the stones have tumbled down. So the people set to building a new fence. They spend all morning getting stones from a nearby stream which they use to build a beautiful wall around the field.

When the fence is finished, someone suggests, "Let's get to the work." Someone else responds, "Wait, if the sun gets any hotter, or if it should rain, we will need shelter." They all agree, so over in one corner of the field they build a shelter for themselves. It is so beautifully done that they decide to put a plaque on it, with names inscribed, so that everybody who passes by in generations to come will know just who was thoughtful enough to build such a wonderful shelter.

Then someone says, "Now let's get to the harvest." But others say, "It is noon and we ought first to eat." So they work diligently until quite a feast is prepared. It is in keeping with the beautiful wall and the fine shelter and is a wonderful feast indeed. After the dinner is finished, there is a period of rest, of course, and then someone says, "Now for the harvest." But someone else replies, "With such a great responsibility and with such a great challenge before us, do we not need to be better dressed than we are?" Immediately, each provides for himself better garments with which to do the harvesting. Then again they turn their thoughts to the golden grain and begin to sharpen the scythes with which to cut the grain. After a while they are razor sharp. But as they look at the grubby old handles they are not satisfied. They are unworthy instruments for so great a work. So they begin to carve those ugly handles into beautiful pieces, and some even add intricate filigree work of gold and silver. One man is even able to adorn his scythe with mother of pearl. It is truly a beautiful thing.

Now they are ready to go to the harvest. But suddenly someone says, "It is night, the sun is gone down." It is then that they realize that only a few have cut any grain. So these wonderful people (like us) turn back sorrowing with guilty feelings to meet the man who owns the field. He comes to meet them, expecting shoulders laden with heavy bags of grain, but instead he finds only beautiful tools and a story of wonderful fences and fine clothes and a good dinner and a shelter to take care of those who work. He asks sadly, "But where is the harvest?" The people are speechless and ashamed.

CHAPTER NINE

The Work of the Church—Edification

Growth is one of the most familiar processes in the world. The whole earth is alive and growing. Our children grow far faster than most of us parents would wish. Through the years I have been impressed with the suddenness with which tiny babies develop into toddlers, toddlers into pre-schoolers, and pre-schoolers into school children. Almost overnight they are in high school and then college. This growth is natural and beautiful to watch.

Many families also have pets. A wobbly-legged little puppy is a full-grown dog within a few short months. Trees grow. Flowers grow. Institutions grow. Nations grow. Growth is universal. But more important than any other growth is that which takes place in man. Man grows *physically* in body, *intellectually* in mind, *socially* among those about him, and *spiritually* in soul. The last of these, spiritual growth, is supremely important, and this is where the church becomes involved. Edification, one of the three major works of the church, stimulates, encourages and nurtures spiritual growth.

In some instances growth is almost automatic. In the physical realm, for example, we eat because we are hungry, we sleep because we are tired, and we exercise because we like to be active. Then, growth just happens. It is unsought and inevitable. Occasionally something goes wrong and growth is interrupted. This is tragic, as most of us have seen in some handicapped child. In some areas, however, growth is not automatic. In the spiritual realm, for example, growth does not take place without plan and effort. It can be achieved only by conscious desire and diligent work.

As Christians, our greatest desire should be to grow into the likeness of Christ. We often sing the much-loved hymn:

O, to be like Thee, blessed Redeemer,
This is my constant longing and prayer.
Gladly I'll forfeit all of earth's treasures,
Jesus, Thy perfect likeness to wear.

Much of the time this is our desire, but at other times it is crowded out by the trivia of the day. We find ourselves striving for the same goals in much the same manner as non-Christians. Our problem is that we live in an increasingly secular age and often the sheer mass of secular, non-spiritual activities crowds out the deepest longing of our hearts.

One of the responsibilities of the church, therefore, through its elders, and others whom they choose to assist them, is to see that newborn babes in Christ grow and mature into full-grown Christians. The arrangement of meaningful periods of worship, the scheduling of carefully-planned classes, and a variety of other activities are designed to bring about this program of edification.

The Bible often emphasizes the importance of soul growth. In the only chapter of III John there are these impressive opening sentences:

> The elder unto Gaius the beloved, whom I love in truth. Beloved, I pray that in all things thou mayest prosper and be in health, even as thy soul prospereth. For I rejoiced greatly, when brethren came and bare witness unto thy truth, even as thou walkest in truth. Greater joy have I none than this, to hear of my children walking in the truth.—III John 1-4

In this passage the aged apostle John is writing to a younger Christian who is growing and developing spiritually in the way which the apostle had hoped. He commends him and then expresses the wish that he may prosper and be in health to the same degree that he is prospering spiritually. What a wonderful wish! What a fine compliment!

Here is a negative warning in the Hebrew letter:

> For when by reason of the time ye ought to be teachers, ye have need again that some one teach you the rudiments of the first principles of the oracles of God; and are become such as have need of milk, and not of solid food. For every one that partaketh of milk is without experience of the word of righteousness; for he is a babe. But solid food is for fullgrown men, even those who by reason of use have their senses exercised to discern good and evil. Wherefore leaving the doctrine of the first principles of Christ, let us press on unto perfection . . . And this will we do, if God permit.—Hebrews 5:12—6:3

A positive emphasis on this same theme is found in Ephesians 4:11-15:

> And he gave some to be apostles; and some, prophets; and some, evangelists; and some, pastors and teachers; for the perfecting of the saints, unto the work of ministering, unto the building up of the body of Christ: till we all attain unto the unity of the faith, and of the knowledge of the Son of God, unto a fullgrown man, unto the measure of the stature of the fulness of Christ: that we may be no longer children, tossed to and fro and carried about with every wind of doctrine, by the sleight of men, in craftiness, after the wiles of error; but speaking truth in love, may grow up in all things into him, who is the head, even Christ.

Still another admonition to spiritual truth is found in II Peter 1:5-7:

> Yea, and for this very cause adding on your part all diligence, in your faith supply virtue; and in your virtue knowledge; and in your knowledge self-control; and in your self-control patience; and in your patience godliness; and in your godliness brotherly

kindness; and in your brotherly kindness love.

FIVE KEY WORDS

There are five key words which are extremely significant in the process of edification. Let us note each of these words in some detail.

ELDERS

If spiritual growth takes place within the members of a congregation, it will be largely as a result of the leadership which its elders provide. According to the qualifications laid down in the scriptures for the selection of elders, they are mature, spiritually-minded men and have demonstrated their ability to lead spiritually by nurturing their own children to the point that they have become Christians.

They are the kind of men to whom one would naturally go when he has some need for understanding of Biblical principles. They are the kind of men to whom one would naturally go when he faces some difficult problem and needs mature spiritual advice. They are the kind of men with whom one seeks to share his triumphs and joys, and from whom one seeks help and strength when there are disappointments and sorrows. Elders are deeply concerned about every phase of the welfare of each member of the church and often pray for and with those who are under their spiritual leadership. They have the same concerned, helpful, intimate relationship with the members of the congregation, over which the Lord has made them bishops, which a shepherd has with the sheep which make up his flock.

This closeness of relationship is reflected in Acts 20:28, in the account of Paul speaking to the elders of the church at Ephesus: "Take heed unto yourselves, and to all the flock, in which the Holy Spirit hath made you bishops, to feed the church of the Lord which he purchased with his own blood." In a related passage, Hebrews 13:7, 17, the inspired writer admonished Christians to respect and heed the advice of their elders:

> Remember them that had the rule over you, men that spake unto you the word of God; and considering the issue of their life, imitate their faith. . . . Obey them that have the rule over you, and submit to them: for they watch in behalf of your souls, as they that shall give account: that they may do this with joy, and not with grief: for this were unprofitable for you.

WORSHIP

A second source of spiritual growth is to be found in the periods of worship in a congregation. Periods of worship are carefully designed by the elders to accomplish certain important purposes, one of which is spiritual growth upon the part of the members of the church. The frequency of times of worship is also a matter of design, and each Christian should respect the elders' call to worship unless it is absolutely impossible to do so.

56

The New Testament has a great deal to say about worship. Among the passages is Acts 2:42, which describes the earliest Christian worship: "And they continued stedfastly in the apostles' teaching and fellowship, in the breaking of bread and the prayers." Colossians 3:16 also touches upon another important aspect of worship: "Let the word of Christ dwell in you richly; in all wisdom teaching and admonishing one another with psalms and hymns and spiritual songs, singing with grace in your hearts unto God." Still another is mentioned in I Corinthians 16:2: "Upon the first day of the week let each one of you lay by him in store, as he may prosper. . . ." In Hebrews 10:25 there is the admonition: ". . . not forsaking our own assembling together, as the custom of some is, but exhorting one another; and so much the more, as ye see the day drawing nigh."

There are three different means or plans of worship, all of which should have a place in the life of each Christian. First, there is the very important worship with the entire body of Christ making up a local congregation. This would include Sunday worship, when the Lord's Supper is eaten, as well as group worship at other times. Second, there is small, semi-private group worship. This occurs when a group of like-minded Christians feels a need for Bible study, prayer and discussion. The heart of such group worship is the study of the Bible, which should never be minimized or left out. It is ideal when one or more of the elders can be part of this group which is smaller than the total congregation. Third, there is individual or private worship. It is very profitable for each Christian to have quiet times when he reads the scriptures, prays and meditates alone with God. All three of these approaches to worship fit together with each other in the life of the growing Christian.

Toward the end of a lifetime spent in worship and service to the Lord, the mature Christian looks back and is surprised to see how tremendously significant those hours spent in worship have been in his spiritual development. As one becomes older and must give up one activity after another, the one that is given up last and with greatest reluctance is assembling for worship with one's fellow-Christians. Interest in travel, recreational activities, shopping trips and other activities, when compared with the desire to worship, declines as one reaches the sunset of life. Many of life's most meaningful experiences occur within the four walls of a church building while a person is engaged in worship.

TEACHING

Teaching rather obviously has a very close relationship with spiritual growth. The more one knows and understands God's will, the more likely he is to see the importance of letting God guide his life. Ideally, this program of instruction should begin very early in life, in the early pre-school years, and should continue as long as one lives. As Isaiah wrote, "For it is precept upon precept, precept upon precept; line upon line, line upon line; here a little, there a little" (Isaiah 28:10).

Christ gave emphasis to the importance of teaching, when he gave his great commission before leaving the earth:

> Go ye therefore, and make disciples of all the nations, baptizing them into the name of the Father and of the Son and of the Holy Spirit: teaching them to observe all things whatsoever I commanded you: and lo, I am with you always, even unto the end of the world.—Matthew 28:19-20

Notice that it is not enough simply to make disciples and baptize them, but the further step of teaching them to observe all things commanded is also important.

In writing to Timothy Paul said, "And the things which thou hast heard from me among many witnesses, the same commit thou to faithful men, who shall be able to teach others also" (II Timothy 2:2). To Titus he wrote, "But speak thou the things which befit the sound doctrine" (Titus 2:1). Christianity is a teaching religion, and where the scriptures are neglected and the people go untaught, Christians languish and die. To avoid this, thoughtful elders arrange a teaching program for the congregation for all ages and covering all phases of instructional needs. Teachers are trained and materials are prepared to carry out this major activity of edification.

ASSOCIATION

We are all aware of the spiritual giants of whom we read in the scriptures. By what means did the early Christians achieve their spiritual strength? The answer is a very simple one. *They grew by association.* Take the apostles for an example. They were very ordinary men, fishermen, tax collectors, and the like. Yet, after three years of close association with Jesus they were the great apostles who began the Lord's church. The book of Acts has this very revealing sentence concerning the reaction of some of the enemies of Christ: "Now when they beheld the boldness of Peter and John, and had perceived that they were unlearned and ignorant men, they marveled; and they took knowledge of them, that they had been with Jesus" (Acts 4:13).

This little band of men accompanied Jesus wherever he went, observing him under stress and strain. They watched him react to angry critics and answer their questions in love. They observed him in nights of prayer. They ate with him; they traveled with him. They grew spiritually through their association with Jesus.

Nor was this method of spiritual growth, by personal association, limited to Christ and his apostles. It is interesting to note in Acts 20:4, where the apostle Paul is returning from his third missionary journey, that he is accompanied by eight different men. The text reads, "And there accompanied him as far as Asia, Sopater of Beroea, the son of Pyrrhus; and of the Thessalonians, Aristarchus and Secundus; and Gaius of Derbe,

58

and Timothy; and of Asia, Tychicus and Trophimus." When the name of Luke, the writer of the passage, is added there were eight men who were traveling with Paul. All of these men were learning how to preach through observing him and his methods. They were growing into the great evangelists who helped to spread the kingdom during the first century.

In this twentieth century we also grow by association. *We grow by association with Christians of our own day.* By being with fellow-Christians in our homes and in our recreation and at other times, we develop spiritually. By worshipping and studying together we mature. It is a fine experience when young couples meet together for dinner or for an outing. The conversation often turns to spiritual matters—the church, the world's need of the gospel, and what they can do about it. They are growing through such association and such conversations.

We also grow spiritually through association with those in need—the sick, the disturbed, the bereaved, the poor, the young and the aged. By knowing of the problems and needs of others and by helping them with those problems we grow and develop. We grow as we share in the suffering of others.

We also grow spiritually by association with Christians of other generations. Through reading the writings of such men as T. B. Larimore we develop spiritually. One cannot read his writings, or those of David Lipscomb, without being drawn closer to the Lord. Through the means of reading we can associate with the great Christians of other generations.

We also grow through association with people of the long ago whose lives are described in the scriptures. Instead of reading chapters, or spending just so many minutes a day in reading the Bible, let us *associate* with the characters of the Bible of whom we read. Through the mind's eye let us actually be part of the crowd, feeling the tension of the crisis and participating in the events about which we are reading. In such a manner we can make the story of Joseph's life become real and its lessons meaningful in our own lives. By living with Moses, with David, and with the prophets, we can drink in their spiritual strength. As we read the New Testament we can travel with the apostles, feel the yearning of their hearts and be built up by their examples. Think of what it can mean to associate with Timothy, Titus, Mary, Dorcas, Lydia, and the many others!

We also grow spiritually through our association with Christ. As we live with him through the events of his ministry we, like the apostles, grow spiritually. II Corinthians 3:18 says it beautifully: "But we all, with unveiled face beholding as in a mirror the glory of the Lord, are transformed into the same image from glory to glory, even as from the Lord the Spirit." In the Roman letter Paul had this to say:

I beseech you therefore, brethren, by the mercies of God, to present your bodies a living sacrifice, holy, acceptable to God, which is your spiritual service. And be not fashioned according to this world: but be ye transformed by the renewing of your mind, that ye may prove what is the good and acceptable and perfect will of God.—Romans 12:1-2

We also grow spiritually through our association with God. Through periods of prayer and times of meditation on his word we develop spiritually. Likewise, we grow in inner strength as we contemplate the works which he has created in our world and our universe. "The heavens declare the glory of God; and the firmament showeth his handiwork" (Psalm 19:1).

The Greek traveler Ulysses returned home to say, "I am a part of all that I have met." How true! Our associations in school, at work, in marriage, in reading, in recreation and in worship will largely determine what we shall be. All of us are part of all we have met. Our lives are so full of the wrong kind of association—worldly people, the influences of radio and television, sensual music, and the like—that it is no wonder that we often do not grow spiritually. We need to remember the words of the apostle Paul in I Corinthians 15:33, when he said: "Be not deceived: Evil companionships corrupt good morals."

SUFFERING

Spiritual growth often comes out of times of suffering and sorrow. There is a maturing influence upon us that comes from struggle. Just as the young football player does not grow physically strong by a life of easy living and physical inactivity, so the Christian does not grow spiritually strong when everything in life is pleasant and easy. Struggle builds stamina, whether in the physical world or in the spiritual world.

The apostle Paul opened for us a window into his own life and in so doing gave us some understanding of his own great spiritual strength as he told us, ". . . we are pressed on every side, yet not straitened; perplexed, yet not unto despair; pursued, yet not forsaken; smitten down, yet not destroyed; always bearing about in the body the dying of Jesus, that the life also of Jesus may be manifested in our body" (II Corinthians 4:8-10). Later in the same chapter he added, "For our light affliction, which is for the moment, worketh for us more and more exceedingly an eternal weight of glory" (II Corinthians 4:17). See II Corinthians 11:24-27 for a list of Paul's afflictions.

The writer of the Hebrew letter indicated at least one of the major values of discipline when he wrote:

It is for discipline that you have to endure. God is treating you as sons; for what son is there whom his father does not discipline? If you are left without discipline, in which all have participated, then you are illegitimate children and not sons. Besides this, we have had earthly fathers to discipline us and we respected them. Shall we not much more be subject to the Father of spirits and live? For they disciplined us for a short time at their pleasure, but

60

he disciplines us for our good, that we may share his holiness. For the moment all discipline seems painful rather than pleasant; later it yields the peaceful fruit of righteousness to those who have been trained by it.—Hebrews 12:7-11 RSV

Fortunately, the whole matter of spiritual growth is ours to decide. We can grow spiritually, if we want to. The formula for such growth is relatively simple—suggested by the five key words in this chapter. Let us then desire this greatest of all personal virtues, and let us arrange our lives accordingly.

CHAPTER TEN

The Work of the Church—Benevolence

When Christ came to the earth he came for the purpose of saving the souls of men. "It is he that shall save his people from their sins" (Matthew 1:21). He also was concerned to help men in whatever difficulties they faced. He fed the multitudes because they were hungry and might faint before they could reach their homes. He healed the lepers; he cast out demons; he lifted up sinners. Over and over again the scriptures say of him, "He had compassion. . . ." He went about doing good for those in need. If we Christians are to follow in his steps, we must also be concerned to help those who are in need. Let us notice some of the scriptures which the Lord has provided to guide Christians in helping others.

Early in the ministry of Jesus he attended the synagogue in Nazareth, as his custom was, and was invited to read from the scriptures: He read from Isaiah, chapter 61, a prophecy concerning himself:

The Spirit of the Lord is upon me,
Because he anointed me to preach good tidings to the poor:
He hath sent me to proclaim release to the captives,
And recovering of sight to the blind,
To set at liberty them that are bruised,
To proclaim the acceptable year of the Lord.

Then he added: Today hath this scripture been fulfilled in your ears" (Luke 4:18-19, 21).

Matthew told the story of a conversation between Jesus and a rich young ruler, which began with the young man's question, "Teacher, what good thing shall I do, that I may have eternal life?" After Jesus had asked concerning the teaching of Moses' law and had received the right answer, he told the young man, "Go, sell that which thou hast, and give to the poor, and thou shalt have treasure in heaven: and come, follow me" (Matthew 19:21).

One of the most disturbing passages in all the New Testament in regard to this matter of using our material goods to help those who are in real need is found in the remarks of Jesus to a Pharisee who had invited him to dinner:

When thou makest a dinner or a supper, call not thy friends, nor thy brethren, nor thy kinsmen, nor rich neighbors; lest haply they also bid thee again, and a recompense be made thee. But when thou makest a feast, bid the poor, the maimed, the lame, the blind: and thou shalt be blessed; because they have not wherewith to recompense thee: for thou shalt be recompensed in the resurrection of the just.—Luke 14:12-14

"He Passed By"

Of all the teachings of Jesus few, if any, are more vivid and more widely remembered than this story:

> And behold, a certain lawyer stood up and made trial of him, saying, Teacher, what shall I do to inherit eternal life? And he said unto him, What is written in the law? how readest thou? And he answering said, Thou shalt love the Lord thy God with all thy heart, and with all thy soul, and with all thy strength, and with all thy mind; and thy neighbor as thyself. And he said unto him, Thou hast answered right: this do, and thou shalt live. But he, desiring to justify himself, said unto Jesus, And who is my neighbor? Jesus made answer and said, A certain man was going down from Jerusalem to Jericho; and he fell among robbers, who both stripped him and beat him, and departed, leaving him half dead. And by chance a certain priest was going down that way: and when he saw him, he passed by on the other side. And in like manner a Levite also, when he came to the place, and saw him, passed by on the other side. But a certain Samaritan, as he journeyed, came where he was: and when he saw him, he was moved with compassion, and came to him, and bound up his wounds, pouring on them oil and wine; and he set him on his own beast, and brought him to an inn, and took care of him. And on the morrow he took out two shillings, and gave them to the host, and said, Take care of him; and whatsoever thou spendest more, I, when I come back again, will repay thee. Which of these three, thinkest thou, proved neighbor unto him that fell among the robbers? And he said, He that showed mercy on him. And Jesus said unto him, Go, and do thou likewise.—Luke 10:25-35

As we let our minds range through the remainder of the New Testament, we recall many passages which emphasize the Christian's need to take care of the poor and others who need his help. For example, the apostle Paul told of his visit to Jerusalem with Barnabas to discuss the question of whether circumcision should be bound upon Gentiles. The verdict was followed by the statement, "Only they would that we should remember the poor; which very thing I was also zealous to do" (Galatians 2:10). Over and over again throughout the pages of the New Testament we are admonished to remember the poor and care for those in financial need.

Still another passage along this line with unmistakable emphasis is that found in the writings of James:

> My brethren, hold not the faith of our Lord Jesus Christ, the Lord of glory, with respect of persons. For if there come into your synagogue a man with a gold ring, in fine clothing, and there come in also a poor man in vile clothing; and ye have regard to him that weareth the fine clothing, and say, Sit thou here in a good place; and ye say to the poor man, Stand thou there, or sit under my footstool; do ye not make distinctions among

63

yourselves, and become judges with evil thoughts? Hearken, my beloved brethren; did not God choose them that are poor as to the world to be rich in faith, and heirs of the kingdom which he promised to them that love him? But ye have dishonored the poor man.—James 2:1-6

THE FINAL JUDGMENT

The most impressive passage of all, however, is the final judgment scene, as described by the Lord near the end of his life. If there were no other passage in all the New Testament teaching our responsibility to care for the needy, this would be enough. As we read this scripture, we need to remember that we will be in the great assemblage at the last day, here described by Jesus, and that his words, in one way or the other, will be spoken to us:

> But when the Son of man shall come in his glory, and all the angels with him, then shall he sit on the throne of his glory: and before him shall be gathered all the nations: and he shall separate them one from another, as the shepherd separateth the sheep from the goats; and he shall set the sheep on his right hand, but the goats on the left. Then shall the King say unto them on his right hand, Come, ye blessed of my Father, inherit the kingdom prepared for you from the foundation of the world: for I was hungry, and ye gave me to eat; I was thirsty, and ye gave me drink; I was a stranger, and ye took me in; naked, and ye clothed me; I was sick, and ye visited me; I was in prison, and ye came unto me. Then shall the righteous answer him, saying, Lord, when saw we thee hungry, and fed thee? or athirst, and gave thee drink? And when saw we thee a stranger, and took thee in? or naked, and clothed thee? And when saw we thee sick, or in prison, and came unto thee? And the King shall answer and say unto them, Verily I say unto you, Inasmuch as ye did it unto one of these my brethren, even these least, ye did it unto me. Then shall he say also unto them on the left hand, Depart from me, ye cursed, into the eternal fire which is prepared for the devil and his angels. . . .

At this point Jesus went through the same list of services to those in need and pointed out that none of these had been rendered. The passage closes with the words, "And these shall go away into eternal punishment: but the righteous into eternal life" (Matthew 25:31-41, 46).

THOSE IN NEED

There are many people in the world today who are in great need, and their needs are of many kinds. Let us notice some of the areas of man's greatest needs:

HUNGER. Many of the earth's population go to bed hungry each night. Not long ago our news media carried an appeal for the hungry of foreign lands, pointing out that the average yield of foodstuffs in the Middle East is only twenty bushels per acre, while here in the United

States our yield of foodstuffs is fifty bushels per acre. Then the statement was made, "We cannot eat all of our fifty and they cannot live on their twenty." We who have been blessed by being born in America, a land of vast natural resources, have a great responsibility in caring for those who are less fortunate. However, even in this land there are those who are hungry. To all of these, and especially to the children, we owe our concern.

SICKNESS. Throughout the land today there are hundreds of hospitals and multiplied thousands of people who are ill. Beyond the hospitals there are millions more who are in need of physical help which is not available. What must it be like to be seriously ill, or to have some member of one's family seriously ill, and yet live beyond the reach of medical care? I think of a guide who showed us some of the great temples in Luxor in Middle Egypt a number of years ago. At the age of forty-six he appeared to be an old man, and he told us that of the eleven children that had been born into his family only four still survived. His teeth were almost gone and he gave the impression of being more than a score of years older than his actual age.

MENTAL ILLNESS. One of the most difficult of all problems is the problem of mental illness. Perhaps it is because so many of us do not properly understand it. The problem is intensified because the mentally ill and their loved ones often feel some stigma attached to this particular kind of illness, and consequently are ashamed to ask for competent professional help. No problem is more difficult for a family to face than the problem of mental illness. These need our help.

DISTRESS. There are others who face problems in difficult situations which are almost beyond their ability to bear. What must it be like for a mother, who has brought several children into the world, to have a husband who comes home drunk night after night? This creates financial and emotional problems, and has a devastating effect upon the proper upbringing of the children. There are many other problems faced in the home and in daily work which place a burden upon those involved. These also need help.

JOBLESSNESS. What must it be like to have a family who are in need of food, clothing, shelter and other necessities of life, and to be able and willing to work, yet have no job? This situation, known to millions, would destroy a man's confidence in himself and make him feel that he was a failure in providing for his family. Those who are willing and able to work need our help to find employment.

ORPHANS. Still others in need are the children whose parents are gone. In our land no orphan will permanently go without some kind of home. Often it is provided by government agencies and has the limitations of professional, impersonal care; however, every child will ultimately be taken care of by some kind of home. This is not true in many other sections of the world. The orphans in Korea and in South Viet Nam, products of American soldier fathers and native prostitute mothers, often have to prowl the streets, sleeping where they can and finding food wherever they can steal or beg. While visiting in Palestine some years ago, I watched as a little orphan boy walked into an alley in Haifa, Israel, took the lid off a garbage can and then found some food and ate it. He was not the first, nor will he be the last such orphan to have to provide for himself. Surely these are in need of help.

PRISONERS. In the prisons throughout the land there are some men and women who see the error of past mistakes and who want to turn toward a higher and better way of life. These people need our encouragement and help. Think of a boy who in his late teens or early twenties commits a crime in an irresponsible and reckless moment. After he has spent years in prison, he realizes that his life is not what he wants it to be and genuinely desires to change its direction. Think of how much it would mean for some Christian friend to provide for him the reading that he needs in order to learn new principles and new goals in life, and then when he is released from prison to give him some help in finding a job where he can begin to earn his living. Many of those released from prison find it extremely difficult to locate work that will provide an honest living after they have come back into free society. Surely this is a place where Christians can render help that is needed.

AGED. As we grow older and our physical faculties fail, we inevitably face discouragement, so far as this world is concerned. Not to be able to do the things that we once did with ease is disturbing. Think how much more disturbing it must be for those who reach the end of their earning period of life, yet have inadequate funds to provide for themselves in old age, and no children to care for them. Surely these need our encouragement, our attention and our financial help.

UNGUIDED YOUTH. Some years ago The Saturday Evening Post printed an article entitled, "We Waste a Million Kids a Year." This article told of the many teen-agers across the land who become disinterested in school and drop out. Then they drift around, seeking employment, joining gangs, and failing generally to establish solid beginnings for productive lives. Many of them come from homes where they have been taught few of the basic principles which must undergird a successful life and where they may have been discouraged by family disintegration and other problems. These young people need the help of Christians. Think of what it would mean for a boy who has dropped out of high school, has been unable to find a job, and has come in desperation to consider a life of crime, if he could be transported into another area and be made a part of a Christian family. The adjustment at first would be difficult, but in the course of the months and the years think what a different life he would

66

live and how both God and our country would be blessed by this help to a boy in need.

GROSS SINNERS. There are still others who need our help. They are physically healthy and financially prosperous, but they are living in the grossest kind of sin. Think of the Las Vegas crowd who are addicted to gambling. Think of those who brazenly make their living by pornography, being involved in printing such material, or in displaying it in adult bookstores and movie houses. Think of the prostitutes who destroy their bodies and souls for hire. Think of the homosexuals who brazenly practice their special kind of immorality, as did the men of Sodom in the long ago. Although Christians have a tendency to turn away from such people, these also need help, for in each is an eternal soul and each is made in the image of God.

How Shall It Be Done?

In the area of benevolence the scriptures often do not give detailed instructions as to how those who are in need shall be cared for. We know from the scriptures exactly how to become a Christian, but we do not know from the scriptures exactly how to care for those less fortunate than ourselves. These matters evidently are left in the realm of expediency, left to the discretion of the individual Christian, and to the elders of congregations. The needs of people down through the various centuries of time have been so varied and different that it would have been impossible to spell out the exact details of providing for their needs.

We do find in the scriptures a few examples that give us some general guidelines as to how to proceed. As an example, take the case in Acts, chapter 6. In the Jerusalem church the widows of the Grecian Jews were being neglected in the daily ministration of food. The matter was called to the attention of the apostles and they worked out the problem beautifully in a relatively simple manner. They explained that they could not give up the more urgent work of teaching and guiding the church in order to dispense food, so they asked those who had brought the grievance to suggest the names of some wise and spiritually mature men to look after this matter. When the names were suggested, the apostles appointed these men to make sure that the widows in question were no longer neglected. This seems to be an application of the Golden Rule, as stated in Matthew 7:12, "All things therefore whatsoever ye would that men should do unto you, even so do ye also unto them: for this is the law and the prophets."

In the book of James, we find these words concerning the care of orphans and widows: "Pure religion and undefiled before our God and Father is this, to visit the fatherless and widows in their affliction, and to keep oneself unspotted from the world" (James 1:27). We are instructed to do the job; we are not told how to do it. In all these matters, where the scriptures do not spell out the exact method to be used, we must use our own good judgment. H. A. Dickson put it this way: "Until the Lord tells us *how* to care for widows and orphans, we will have to use our own best judgment."

Christ is our example of *unselfish service.* In Matthew 20:26-28, he said, "Whosoever would become great among you shall be your minister; and whosoever would be first among you shall be your servant: even as the Son of man came not to be ministered unto, but to minister, and to give his life a ransom for many." Surely, if we are Christians, we must follow in the Lord's steps, emphasizing that it is more important to render service to others who are in need than to receive such services ourselves. Jesus also said, "It is more blessed to give than to receive" (Acts 20:35).

A Special Reason

There is yet another reason for helping those in need: It opens closed doors and paves the way for the proclaiming of the gospel. A man does not listen well to the story of Jesus if he is wracked with pain or weak from hunger. Someone has said, "People do not care how much you know until they know how much you care." Caring for those in need often serves the purpose of evangelism. A cup of cold water may ultimately lead a person to the water of life . . . a loaf of bread may lead a family to the bread of life. ". . . be ready unto every good work. . ." (Titus 3:1).

CHAPTER ELEVEN

Government of the Church

In studying the organization and government of the New Testament church, it is necessary to make a distinction between *the church universal* and *a local congregation*. Each saved person is a member of the church universal. This is a designation for all Christians throughout all time and throughout the whole world. When one responds through obedient faith to the grace of God, as manifest in Christ, God saves him and adds him to his church (Acts 2:41, 47).

The New Testament church has no permanent world-wide organization. There is no *monolithic structure*. The New Testament does not provide for any brotherhood-wide machinery by which the church universal can be activated. The only influence is through teaching. After the apostles died there was neither a central authority nor a central location for the church. There are still no hierarchy, no central organization and no headquarters for the entire church. There is no authority but Christ and his word.

The local church, on the other hand, does have a form of government provided in the New Testament scriptures. For example, when the apostle Paul wrote to the church at Philippi, he began, "Paul and Timothy, servants of Christ Jesus, to all the saints in Christ Jesus that are at Philippi, with the bishops and deacons" (Philippians 1:1). Bishops, or elders, are the overseers in each local church. This is further borne out by a statement from Paul to Titus: "For this cause left I thee in Crete, that thou shouldest set in order the things that were wanting, and appoint elders in every city, as I gave thee charge" (Titus 1:5).

EACH CONGREGATION AUTONOMOUS

It is quite clear that the New Testament conception of the church is one of *autonomous congregations*, with no central organization linking these churches together. Instead of a vertical or monolithic structure such as the Roman Catholic Church, Christ's church has a horizontal organization. Congregations exist side by side, but independent of each other. They can cooperate with each other, assist each other, and encourage each other, but no one congregation (or its elders) has the right to control or dominate any other congregation.

In the eyes of men this seems a rather inadequate system, for men like big things, things that can be controlled from the top in an impressive and immediate manner. The Roman Empire, for example, was such an organization. Caesar could give a command and within a matter of a few days it would be carried out throughout the entire empire. Within a few centuries after the church began, the Roman Catholic Church evolved, following the organizational plan of the Roman Empire. This, however, was not the plan of government originally planned for the church and described in the scriptures.

On this point we can see the wisdom of God in using the autonomous system. With the monolithic structure of the Roman Catholic Church, it is possible by corrupting the head of the church—either doctrinally or morally—to contaminate the entire organization. On the other hand, if the elders of one local congregation become contaminated—either doctrinally or morally—it means only the loss of that one church. Each other congregation stands firmly in the path of right, unaffected by the digression of the neighboring church.

To put this in the form of an illustration, we might call attention to the oil fields of any of our oil producing states. Near the huge refineries which handle the crude oil there are often scores of large storage tanks. These are usually in neat rows separated from each other by a reasonable extent of open land. If lightning should strike one of these tanks and fire should destroy its contents, the other tanks would remain undamaged because they are separated by a protective area of open space. This is the reason the oil is not put into one great reservoir. It is a safeguard, a matter of security.

When God planned the organization of the church he planned it in such a way that it could not be swept into error in one quick stroke. The New Testament church is in some respects like a pontoon bridge. In such a bridge the destruction of one pontoon does not materially affect the other pontoons which support the bridge.

It is also interesting by way of comparison to remember that of the three major organizations ordained by God—the home, the church, and civil government—the home is also autonomous. Each family is independent under God from all of the other families in the neighborhood or in the city. The father and mother and the children make up a separate unit. The father is the head of his own family, not a score of families or a city of families.

The Lord's plan for each local congregation, therefore, is as follows: (1) Christ is the head of the church. (2) He rules through his inspired word, the Bible. (3) The elders, or bishops, or presbyters, or overseers, or pastors are Christ's administrators, operating under the Bible and under the headship of Christ. (4) Beneath the elders are deacons, evangelists and teachers. This is the total structure of the New Testament church.

THE LOCAL CONGREGATION

As we go back to study in some detail the original plan for Christ's

70

church as given by the inspired writers of the New Testament, we discover, first of all, that there was a plurality of elders in each congregation. This is shown by the fact that when Paul wrote his letter to the Philippians he referred to "the bishops and deacons" (Philippians 1:1). Similarly, when he wrote to Titus, as mentioned earlier in this chapter, he directed him to appoint *elders* in each city (Titus 1:5). Originally, then, there was a plurality of elders in each local church.

At this point we need to pause and demonstrate that the terms— elders, presbyters, bishops, overseers and pastors—are synonymous and are to be used interchangeably. The New Testament pictures a group of men, all of equal rank, ruling each congregation. The first major digression came when one of the elders was elevated to a superior level of authority and took the title of bishop, to designate a rank above the elders of the church. The New Testament teaches rather that bishops were simply elders. The Bible often shows that the Holy Spirit who guided the biblical writers anticipated erroneous doctrines and included special passages to refute false teachings even before they arose. Such is true in the case under consideration.

In the twentieth chapter of Acts we find a clear demonstration that all of these terms refer to the same group of men and that all of them were of equal rank. The apostle Paul came to the city of Miletus on his third missionary journey. We read, "And from Miletus he sent to Ephesus, and called to him the elders of the church" (Acts 20:17). The Greek word, translated into English here by the word elders, is the word *presbuteros*. It may be translated into English either by the word *elder* or *presbyter*. Obviously these two terms are synonymous since they come from the one Greek word.

When the elders or presbyters from Ephesus had come, Paul delivered to them a sermon in the midst of which he said, "Take heed unto yourselves, and to all the flock, in which the Holy Spirit hath made you bishops, to feed the church of the Lord which he purchased with his own blood" (Acts 20:28). The word translated here as bishops is from the Greek word *episkopos*. It may be translated into English either as *bishop* or *overseer*. Obviously bishop and overseer are interchangeable since both come from the same Greek word. *Now notice that Paul called the elders or presbyters to him and then addressed them as bishops or overseers.* Without question all four terms referred to the same group of men.

The New Testament also uses a third Greek word *poimen*, to refer to elders. It is usually translated as *pastor*, as in Ephesians 4:11, "And he gave some to be apostles; and some, prophets; and some, evangelists; and some, pastors and teachers." The work of *apostles* and *prophets* was an inspired work and after the first century, their work having been done, these two classes ceased to exist in the church. Evangelists, pastors (bishops, elders, presbyters, overseers) and teachers continue in the permanent organization of the church.

The Greek word *episkopos*, when translated into English as *bishop* or *overseer*, refers to a man charged with the duty of seeing that things done by others are done correctly. In the New Testament he is a "guardian of souls," one who watches over the welfare of others. The Greek word *presbuteros*, when translated into English as *elder* or *presbyter*, has reference to a person of mature age. It means a man advanced in life, an elder, a senior. The Greek word also can refer to rank or office. Among Christians it would designate those who preside over the assemblies. The Greek word *poimen* is translated as *pastor* in Ephesians 4:11. The word suggests the idea of a shepherd leading a flock of sheep in I Peter 2:25. In New Testament usage elders are older, more mature men, who direct and oversee the work of a local congregation. The emphasis is more on the work than on the office or title.

There were also *deacons* in the New Testament church. The general meaning of the Greek word *diakonos* is attendant, servant, or minister. This is the word from which we get our English word deacon. The word is used to include various ones who serve actively in the church, but it is also used in a special sense, or office, as indicated by the list of qualifications for deacons in I Timothy 3:8-13. This is also indicated from the association of the word with the office and work of the elders in the same passage and in the salutations of some of Paul's letters to churches. A deacon is a *helper*, *minister*, or *servant* in the church in contrast to the elder who is an *overseer*. Deacons work under the oversight of elders (Acts 6:1-6; I Timothy 3:8-13).

There are also *evangelists* in the New Testament church. The term evangelist comes from the Greek word *evangellion*, which means a *proclaimer of good news*. In Ephesians 4:11, as mentioned above, we find, "And he gave some to be apostles; and some, prophets; and some, evangelists; and some, pastors and teachers." In Acts 21:8 we read, "And on the morrow we departed, and came unto Caesarea: and entering into the house of Philip the evangelist, who was one of the seven, we abode with him." In II Timothy 4:5 we read further, "But be thou sober in all things, suffer hardship, do the work of an evangelist, fulfil thy ministry." The work of an evangelist is suggested in I and II Timothy and in Titus in an extended way. Evangelists are to preach the word, guard the faith, and build up the church, as indicated in these letters of Paul to younger men who were serving as evangelists.

There were also *teachers* in the New Testament church. These were people who had been taught by others and were capable of passing along the Christian faith to still others. The term is a very broad one, including both men and women. Women, in the early church, were not permitted to

72

preach or teach in the public assemblies, but were able to teach other women and, of course, to teach children. A case of private teaching, involving both a husband and wife, Aquila and Priscilla, is found in Acts 18:26.

In broad outline this is the organizational framework of the New Testament church. If this organization had been respected through the centuries, much of the religious division of our day would have been avoided. Also, many of the false doctrines that have splintered the religious world would not have been brought into the church. It is safe to conclude that if God's original plan for the organization of the church had been respected, millions more precious souls would have been saved.

CHAPTER TWELVE
Qualifications of Elders

In our effort to understand the church of the New Testament and to restore it in our time, it is important to study the manner in which the church was organized in apostolic times. As we have seen in the previous chapter, after the death of the apostles each congregation was autonomous, working side by side with other churches of the Lord, but organizationally independent of them. In all congregations Christ was the head, with the holy scriptures serving as guide in all matters. In each congregation elders were to rule. Deacons were to serve. Evangelists were to preach. Teachers were to teach.

QUALITY OF LEADERSHIP

One of the most important factors in the growth of any organization is the quality of its leadership. The same is true in the church. The elders of the church occupy a crucially important position. By their knowledge of God's word, their vision, their zeal, and their consecration to the Lord, they will largely determine the future growth and development of the church. The work of being an elder is one of the most important and most difficult of all works known to man. The responsibilities and the obligations are heavy; the opportunities and privileges are great. To be qualified to be an elder and to be appointed to that work is the greatest honor within the church—and the greatest honor which Christians can receive.

At three different places in the New Testament, the Holy Spirit guided the writers to set down the qualifications which are required for elders or bishops. Let us notice each of these passages:

I Timothy 3:1-7: Faithful is the saying, If a man seeketh the office of a bishop, he desireth a good work. The bishop therefore must be without reproach, the husband of one wife, temperate, sober-minded, orderly, given to hospitality, apt to teach; no brawler, no striker; but gentle, not contentious, no lover of money; one that ruleth well his own house, having his children in subjection with all gravity; (but if a man knoweth not how to rule his own house, how shall he take care of the church of God?) not a novice, lest being puffed up he fall into the condemnation of the devil. Moreover he must have good testimony from them that are without; lest he fall into reproach and the snare of the devil.

Titus 1:5-9: For this cause left I thee in Crete, that thou shouldest set in order the things that were wanting, and appoint elders in every city, as I gave thee charge; if any man is blameless, the husband of one wife, having children that believe, who are not accused of riot or unruly. For the bishop must be blameless, as God's steward; not self-willed, not soon angry, no brawler, no striker, not greedy of filthy lucre; but given to hospitality, a lover of good, sober-minded, just, holy, self-controlled; holding to the faithful word which is according to the teaching, that he may be able both to exhort in the sound doctrine, and to convict the gainsayers.

I Peter 5:1-4: The elders therefore among you I exhort, who am a fellow-elder, and a witness of the sufferings of Christ, who am also a partaker of the glory that shall be revealed: Tend the flock of God which is among you, exercising the oversight, not of constraint, but willingly, according to the will of God; nor yet for filthy lucre, but of a ready mind; neither as lording it over the charge allotted to you, but making yourselves ensamples to the flock. And when the chief Shepherd shall be manifested, ye shall receive the crown of glory that fadeth not away.

Groups of Qualifications

The three passages just read mention a number of qualifications, which fall into three groups; some are positive, some negative and some special. Notice first the *positive qualifications:*

1. "Blameless"—"without reproach." One so armed with righteousness that the barbs of criticism can find no weak places in his armour. One who cannot be justly accused of wrong doing. One against whom no nameable charge may legitimately be levied.
2. "Vigilant"—"alert and watchful." Always working energetically for the success of the church. Dead leaders mean a dead church. Fighting sin and Satan demands alertness.
3. "Sober"—"sober minded"—"one having a sound mind." There must be effective self-control before there can be successful direction of others.
4. "Of good behavior"—"orderly." Respectable and decent in both outward action and mind. The clownish and loud man is definitely disqualified. So is the cold and austere man. There must be great dignity and warm friendliness in the leaders of God's people.
5. "Given to hospitality." Neighborly even to strangers. This involves the sharing of one's home in Christian fellowship, but it also involves sharing of one's goods with those who are in need. Hebrews 13:1-2 teaches, "for thereby some have entertained angels unawares." In these impersonal times, Christian hospitality has often been replaced by commercial comfort.
6. "Patient"—"gentle." Contentious and quarrelsome leaders will inevitably wreck a congregation.
7. "One that ruleth well his own house." The reason given in I Timothy is that the ruling of one's own family successfully is a

75

concrete evidence that one has the ability to rule in God's family. If a brother cannot gain the respect of and the control over the small, intimate circle of his own family, it would seem impossible for him to obtain the respect of the entire congregation. Overseers must first oversee their own homes.

8. "Good report"—"good testimony from them that are without." The outside world will respect the church to whatever degree it is able to respect its leaders. It is a tragedy for a congregation to have leaders who are lacking in honesty and integrity. A person whose life has been under a cloud should not be put into the leadership of the church; certainly not until he has proved himself over a long period of time.

9. "Temperate." Self-control and self-denial are involved in this qualification. The elders must not be given to extreme habits. In administering justice, there must be mercy. Extreme and ill-considered measures must be avoided.

10. "Just." Elders must never be unfair, partial or prejudiced in making decisions relating to the work of the church.

11. "Holy." Pure in heart and life. Elders must be spiritually minded men.

Notice now some *negative qualifications:*

1. "Not given to wine." This includes any intoxicating drink. The Greek word here not only signifies the actual drinking, but also includes insolent and abusive behavior whether it comes from drinking or not.

2. "Not a striker." This word has taken on a new meaning since its inclusion in the scripture text. Originally, it referred to one who physically strikes another. In our time the word often suggests one who demonstrates against his employer because of dissatisfaction. In the text it means primarily a quarrelsome, belligerent person, one who strikes back at anyone who dares to disagree or who displeases him, one who lashes out at all who refuse to cater to him.

3. "Not greedy of filthy lucre"—"no lover of money." Men who desire the office of a bishop as a personal means of profit are unworthy. Men whose main interest is in material things are unworthy.

4. "Not a brawler"—"not contentious." The elder must not be a lover of strife. He must not be a trouble-maker.

5. "Not covetous." Leaders in the church must not covet any profits or advantages which the work of a bishop might bring. The service rendered should be the only reward desired.

6. "Not soon angry." Hot-tempered leaders are not qualified.

Elders should be deliberate and take action only after much consideration.

7. "Not self-willed." An elder must not insist on deciding every issue in his own way. He must be uncompromising in matters of faith, but not headstrong and unyielding in matters of judgment.

Now, let us notice some *special qualifications:*

1. "Husband of one wife." Originally this stipulation was against polygamy. In our day it would prohibit the appointment of a man as an elder who has more than one living wife. It does not prohibit a brother whose wife is dead and who has remarried from becoming an elder.

2. "Having believing children." Elders should be married and have faithful Christian children. While it is desirable for an elder to have more than one child, it does not appear to be an absolute requirement that he have a plurality of children. This scripture stipulation teaches that whatever number of children an elder may have, they must be Christians. It is not primarily a matter of how many children he may have.

3. "Apt to teach"—"holding to the faithful word"—"able to exhort in the sound doctrine." Teaching is defined as: "The process by which the person taught learns something he did not know or becomes something which he was not." This qualification does not require a fluent speaker, nor necessarily a man who can teach a large class. It does require that an elder be able to guide and direct others by his life and by his words.

4. "Not a novice." A man who is a new convert, or a person of little practical experience, should not be appointed as an elder. The reason given is that he is in danger of being puffed up by his new office and may fall into the snare of the devil.

Notice that some of these qualifications are matters of degree and involve growth. This would be true of such qualities as patience, temperance, and aptness to teach. On the other hand, some of the qualifications are absolute, such as being married to only one wife, and having believing children. It is well to point out that with the exception of the special qualifications which elders must have, all the other qualifications are qualities of life which every Christian should strive to achieve. It is reasonable, however, to expect that those appointed to the leadership will have these Christian qualities to a higher degree than other Christians may yet have achieved. All of these are qualities which young Christians should aspire to, with the hope that someday they may be qualified to be elders or wives of elders.

WORK OF ELDERS

The work of elders begins with a *general oversight of the local congrega-*

tion. Paul said to the elders of the church at Ephesus, "Take heed unto yourselves, and to all the flock, in which the Holy Spirit hath made you bishops, to feed the church of the Lord which he purchased with his own blood" (Acts 20:28). I Peter 5:1-4, quoted earlier in this chapter, describes the work which elders are to perform. I Timothy 5:17 refers to the work of teaching. I Thessalonians 5:12 speaks of admonition. Acts 11:29-30 indicates that elders have a part in benevolent work.

Elders also are to serve as *bulwarks against false teaching*. This is apparent in Paul's speech to the Ephesian elders as found in Acts 20:29-32. It is mentioned as a qualification of an elder in Titus 1:9. Also, elders are to have the *oversight in material things*, as mentioned in Acts 11:29-30. Still further, elders are to be *examples to the flock*. This is specifically mentioned in I Peter 5:3.

Most impressive of all is the fact mentioned in Hebrews 13:17: "Obey them that have the rule over you, and submit to them: for they watch in behalf of your souls, as they that shall give account; that they may do this with joy, and not with grief: for this were unprofitable for you."

The authority of elders is also a very important consideration. Elders have scriptural authority to do whatever is necessary to perform their God-given functions. This means that they can request assistance from members of the local congregation in the carrying out of their work. They may employ any outside help which the work requires. They can select definite helpers, such as deacons, or others. They are to supervise the work of the local evangelist. The preacher works under the authority and direction of the elders. He may suggest ideas and reason in behalf of certain matters, but ultimately the judgment of the elders is definitive. The elders employ preachers and also decide when preachers should move to other locations.

There are certain limitations upon the authority and work of elders. They have the oversight of their home congregations only. Congregational cooperation, which is highly desirable, must never harden into control or coercion by one eldership over other congregations. Each local congregation must remain independent, or autonomous, in order to remain scriptural. Elders are, of course, bound by the terms of the New Testament. Elders, in a sense, are like the administrators of an estate. They cannot change the provisions of the will, but are to carry out those provisions. In this case the will is the New Testament. They are examples to the congregation, as indicated in I Peter 5:3. They are not masters. Elders are servants of God and of the church.

According to Hebrews 13:7 and 17, elders have the responsibility of ruling in each congregation: "Remember them that had the rule over you. . . . Obey them that have the rule over you, and submit to them. . . ." They are compared to shepherds, caring for a flock of sheep. The shepherd is in complete charge of his flock, though he often guides and directs them simply by leading them. Elders, by their examples, can also accomplish a great deal as they lead in the work of the Lord. They do have, however, decision-making authority in the local congregation.

RESPECT FOR ELDERS

Congregations also have responsibilities. They are to love and respect their elders. They are to follow the instructions and examples of their elders. Paul wrote to Timothy, "Rebuke not an elder, but exhort him as a father; the younger men as brethren" (I Timothy 5:1). Later in the same chapter Paul said:

> Let the elders that rule well be counted worthy of double honor, especially those who labor in the word and in teaching. For the scripture saith, Thou shalt not muzzle the ox when he treadeth out the corn. And, The laborer is worthy of his hire. Against an elder receive not an accusation, except at the mouth of two or three witnesses. Them that sin reprove in the sight of all, that the rest also may be in fear.—I Timothy 5:17-20

When Paul told Timothy that elders are worthy of double honor, he was indicating that in addition to honor and respect they also may be paid, as they have need for such pay. The context of the passage indicates that it is speaking of financial help.

Concerning the matter of respect for elders the apostle Peter wrote, "Likewise, ye younger, be subject unto the elder" (I Peter 5:5). This statement is found in the passage in which he mentions the qualifications and work of elders. In a passage previously mentioned, the writer of the Hebrew letter spoke of the respect that Christians are to have for their elders: "Remember them that had the rule over you, men that spake unto you the word of God; and considering the issue of their life, imitate their faith" (Hebrews 13:7).

CHAPTER THIRTEEN
Qualifications of Deacons

In the New Testament plan of church organization, in addition to the elders, or bishops, who have the rule over the church, there are also deacons. These are thought to be younger men, less mature and less experienced in spiritual affairs than the elders under whom they serve. With more youth and vigor they are valuable assistants to the elders in the work of the church.

The qualifications of deacons are found only once in the New Testament. They were listed by the apostle Paul to the evangelist Timothy:

> *I Timothy 3:8-13:* Deacons in like manner must be grave, not double-tongued, not given to much wine, not greedy of filthy lucre; holding the mystery of the faith in a pure conscience. And let these also first be proved; then let them serve as deacons, if they be blameless. Women in like manner must be grave, not slanderers, temperate, faithful in all things. Let deacons be husbands of one wife, ruling their children and their own houses well. For they that have served well as deacons gain to themselves a good standing, and great boldness in the faith which is in Christ Jesus.

Deacons are to be "grave." This means that they are not to be giddy and light-minded, but are rather to be serious-minded. "Not double-tongued" means that they are to be firm and straightforward in speaking. They must not be two-faced, or changeable. "Not given to much wine" differs from the requirement for elders, "not given to wine," only by the inclusion of the word "much." However, Bible students generally feel that the two requirements are meant to be the same. Neither elders nor deacons are to be users of alcoholic beverages. "Not greedy of filthy lucre" simply means that deacons must not have their hearts set upon money or material things, but on spiritual matters. "Holding the faith in a pure conscience" implies that they are truly converted to Christ and that they are not selected hastily, but after careful observation of their lives. "Blameless," as in the case of elders, means that there must be no serious, nameable sins of which they are guilty.

"Women in like manner . . ." and "Even so must their wives . . ." indicates that deacons' wives must be grave, not gossipers, but temperate and faithful. The question arises, especially in our day, as to whether these two phrases refer to a separate office—that of the deaconess. Did the apostolic church have the office of elders, deacons and deaconesses? The interpretation of this passage as meaning qualifications to be possessed by deacons' wives seems to be a better interpretation than that these fragmentary phrases are meant to describe a distinct office.

It is true that there were women who served the early church, as is indicated in Romans 16:1, "I commend unto you Phoebe our sister, who is a servant of the church that is at Cenchreae." The word used here for servant is the same root word that is used for deacon. The generally accepted view down through the centuries has been that the church has only the offices of elders and deacons, though women and other men often serve the church in unofficial capacities.

The requirement of deacons that they be "husbands of one wife"— "ruling their children and their homes well" are essentially the same as the requirements for elders. Deacons must be heads of Christian families. There is one difference, however, for in the qualifications of elders it is required that they have believing children, while the qualification for deacons requires only that they rule their children and their homes well. Presumably, deacons will normally be younger men, whose children may not yet be old enough to be members of the church.

Selecting Elders and Deacons

No specific plan is outlined in the scriptures for the selection of elders and deacons. The matter is left to the judgment of the Christians in any local congregation. In the absence of a prescribed plan, it may be helpful to make a few general suggestions about a method that has been used extensively and does work well.

The *first step* is to choose a small group of men who are not themselves eligible to become elders or deacons. These men then become the "receiving body" to receive the names of those whom the congregation feels are qualified to serve either as elders or deacons. Of course, if the congregation already has elders and is seeking to appoint additional ones, the present elders would be this receiving group.

The *second step* is to instruct the congregation very carefully in the qualifications set down in the scriptures for both elders and deacons. Then, the members of the church are asked to look among themselves and to suggest the names of men who meet these scriptural qualifications. Their suggestions should be submitted in writing to the receiving group and the lists should be signed.

Step three is for the receiving group to contact each person put forward to see if he himself knows any scriptural reason why he should not serve, and also to see if he is willing to serve if appointed to the office.

Step four is to put the names of the men, thus nominated and cleared, before the congregation for a period of time so that their qualifications may be carefully analyzed and studied. Members of the congregation should be asked to submit in writing any scriptural objections to any person who has been put forward as a possible elder or deacon. If such scriptural objections are put forward, the receiving group must then investigate the charges, make a decision as to their validity, and then either leave the name on the list or remove it from the list.

Step five, after a reasonable length of time, is the public announcement that the men whose names have been put forward and who have passed careful examination are now to serve as elders or deacons of the congregation. Of course, it is possible for this entire process to be used in the appointment of elders only, or in the appointment of deacons only. In the actual appointment it is quite appropriate to have a service in which the responsibilities of elders and deacons are carefully delineated and the responsibilities of the congregation to the elders and deacons are also made clear. It goes without saying that this entire process must be done carefully and soberly, with much study of the scriptures, and much time spent in prayer.

THE DRINKING OF ALCOHOL

Since the matter of not drinking wine is mentioned in the qualifications of both elders and deacons, perhaps a few additional words on this subject are in order here. As we try to reconstruct the life-style of the early Christians, it appears to be relatively certain that at times Christians did drink a natural, light wine with their meals. When the grape harvest was new this drink would be unfermented, but as the months wore on until the next harvest approached there would be an increasing degree of natural fermentation.

If the early Christians did indeed drink wine with their meals, it should be recognized also that there were reasons for doing so which are not valid today. The water supply in the ancient villages, towns and cities of Palestine was not guaranteed pure, as is the case throughout our land today. The bacteria count in the cisterns, wells and streams is quite high even today in that part of the world. The drinking of a light wine would avoid the dangers of impure water, and seems to have been one of the reasons why many people did so.

Today, however, such a need does not exist. Our towns and cities have pure water supplies. Then, too, there is a very wide variety of other drinks which do not include any alcoholic content whatever—milk, tea, coffee, cocoa, soft drinks, and fruit juices, all of which were either non-existent or else limitedly available in apostolic times. In our day, the wisest course is for Christians to avoid any use of alcoholic-content beverages.

There are several solid, concrete reasons why Christians ought not to use alcoholic beverages. Among them are the following:

1. Social drinking is too dangerous to risk. In the United States today there are approximately 10,000,000 alcoholics, and another 10,000,000 problem drinkers. Most of these now blighted by the uncontrollable use of alcohol began as social drinkers.

82

One out of 11 social drinkers eventually becomes an alcoholic. The odds are too dangerous to trust, so total abstinence is the wisest policy.

2. *Drinking alcohol hurts one's influence.* The Christian has a great responsibility to protect his influence and to use it in behalf of the Lord's church. Among most people, even those who drink, the Christian's use of alcohol jeopardizes his Christian influence.

3. *Drinking alcohol hurts one's body.* It is generally accepted among medical people that the use of alcohol causes serious damage to the brain, to the circulatory system, to the liver and to other parts of the body. This is especially true if it is used in large amounts and over a long period of time. There is also a dulling effect upon the brain, with users of alcohol becoming muddled and confused if they continue to drink over a long period of years.

4. *Drinking alcohol endangers others.* According to the American Medical Association and the Bureau of Vital Statistics at least fifty percent of the highway deaths in America involves drinking drivers. Drinking is also involved in a great many of the crimes that are perpetrated against people and property in the United States each year. Many crimes are performed when the person is under the influence of alcohol.

5. *Drinking alcohol reduces willpower.* Alcohol tends to destroy a person's ability to make clear, accurate moral and ethical decisions. The use of alcohol contributes to the breaking up of homes, the losing of jobs, and the living of wasted lives.

6. *Drinking alcohol is costly in money.* The cost of liquor is high in dollars and cents, whether it is bought in the can or the bottle, or served in cocktails. It is a "luxury item" which most families cannot afford. The cost in money goes far beyond the original purchase of the product, however, reaching to the destruction of property, the loss of income, and the staggering costs which fall upon the taxpayer to clean up the mess that alcoholism leaves behind. This includes the cost of law enforcement, judicial action, and maintenance of jails and prisons for those who without the drinking of alcohol would not be involved in such activities. It is quite obvious that the Christian's money is needed for better purposes.

In view of these solid reasons, the only defensible position for a Christian is total abstinence. Even social drinking is too dangerous to try. There are no good reasons in favor of drinking; there are many good reasons against it.

CHAPTER FOURTEEN
Worship

Over the years it has been my privilege to know a great many young people of college age. From them I have gained insights of many kinds, often being greatly encouraged by the depth of their convictions, the devotion of their lives, and their sensitivity to spiritual things. Occasionally I have asked some of the more thoughtful students to tell me what worship has meant in their lives. The following responses have seemed to me especially meaningful:

> The time that I feel closer to God than any other is at dusk. I live on a farm and late in the afternoon, especially in the summer, I enjoy walking in the woods. When I first start, there is a hushed silence, but as I continue the air becomes cooler and the insects and small animals start to talk as if they were singing praise to their Creator. I feel peace and contentment enter into my heart and the cares of the day, no matter what they have been, are replaced by a wonderful feeling of being cared for and by a need to express thanks and praise to my Creator. So, with others of God's creation, I can join in praise of His name. Times like this make me stop and realize that nature herself can bring us closer to the meaning of true worship than any other single evidence of His presence and care for His creation. (Written by a young woman who was a senior in college.)

Another young person has written:

> The most wonderful devotional periods that I have ever experienced were on the nights in which my family gathered in the living room and worshipped God together. My father would read from God's word and we would then discuss the meaning of what he had read. I learned much of God's word in this manner and am greatly benefited from this knowledge today. After we had studied for half an hour or maybe more my father would suggest that we pray. All of us would kneel and each one of us would pray until my mother and then my father closed the prayer. These experiences were so meaningful to me that time will never erase them. My father has passed on now, but his and my mother's guidance through these devotions will always keep me nearer my God and my Savior.

Yet another college student has written:

> I was fortunate as a youngster to be "brought up" in the church by Christian parents. I developed the "habit" of attending church services, but this "habit" has now grown to be a very meaningful experience for me. I *enjoy* going to church. . . . At every service, I

84

try to understand and feel the words and music of the hymns which we sing. It seems to me that a glorious song sung from the heart is one of the best ways a Christian can express love and honor to the Lord. . . . It is easy for me to make the Lord's Supper an enriching and love-filled memorial. All I have to do is to turn in the Bible to the passages containing the trial and crucifixion of Christ, or open a hymnal to "Night With Ebon Pinion" and remember the Lord's prayer to God the night of his betrayal. . . . My worship is lacking in the areas of prayer and getting the most from the sermons. . . . After analyzing my worship participation, I can easily see that I *truly* worship only when I participate directly. Therefore I will make the prayer being led *my* prayer, and apply the sermon being preached to *my* life and decide how the ideas and thoughts expressed can best increase *my* service, and mold me into a more sincere, loving child of God.

WHAT IS WORSHIP?

It is not easy to put a definition of worship into words, so vast is the concept of worship. No definition seems adequate. Yet, we profit by trying. From many sources come the following meaningful definitions of worship:

(1) "Worship is the adoring reverence of the human spirit for the divine."

(2) "Worship is man's response to God's revelation of himself."

(3) "Worship is the outgoing of the human spirit toward God, recognizing in Him the source of all life and love and goodness and holiness and righteousness."

(4) "To worship is to feed the mind on the truths of God, to quicken the conscience by the holiness of God, to cleanse the conscience with the beauty of God, to open the heart to the love of God, and to devote the will to the purpose of God."

(5) "Worship is a group of specialized activities in which we draw near to and commune with God in an extra-ordinary manner."

(6) "Christian worship is communion with the true and living God, directions for which are given by the Holy Spirit. Jehovah, through all the ages from the time of Cain and Abel until now, has prescribed the exact means to be employed in acceptable worship. Any deviation from God's plan of worship has always been unacceptable."

(7) "The word worship means worth-ship—and is ascribing worth to God and from Him drawing worth into dependent souls. Worship is more than adoration and reverence; it is a response of the whole man to God's act, and includes praise and thanksgiving."

(8) "To worship is to quicken the conscience by the holiness of God, to feed the mind with the truth of God, to purge the imagination by the beauty of God, to open the heart to the love of God, to devote the will to the purpose of God."

85

IMPORTANT SCRIPTURES

There are certain key scriptures which come to mind when the subject of worship is mentioned. One of the first is found in the New Testament and contains the conversation between Christ and a woman by a well in Samaria. In the course of their conversation Jesus said, "But the hour cometh, and now is, when the true worshippers shall worship the Father in spirit and truth: for such doth the Father seek to be his worshippers. God is a Spirit: and they that worship him must worship in spirit and truth" (John 4:23-24). Jesus had just declared that neither Jerusalem nor Mt. Gerizim was the place where men must worship God, but that men could worship anywhere on earth. The emphasis was no longer to be where, but how. The primary concern was to be the worship of God *in spirit and in truth.*

The apostle Paul, in I Corinthians 14:15, emphasized this same point, as he said, "I will pray with the spirit, and I will pray with the understanding also: I will sing with the spirit, and I will sing with the understanding also." Our worship, in order to be acceptable to God, must be *in spirit*— with genuine feeling and sincere dedication. It must also be *in truth*— according to the instructions given in God's word and with understanding of what God wants us to do in worship. We are not at liberty to introduce our own desires, but must worship according to his instructions.

THE ESSENCE OF REAL WORSHIP

Read with me next a passage from the Old Testament which has in it a sublime description of worship:

> In the year that King Uzziah died I saw the Lord sitting upon a throne, high and lifted up; and his train filled the temple. Above him stood the seraphim: each one had six wings; with twain he covered his face, and with twain he covered his feet, and with twain he did fly. And one cried unto another, and said, Holy, holy, holy, is Jehovah of hosts: the whole earth is full of his glory. And the foundations of the thresholds shook at the voice of him that cried, and the house was filled with smoke.—Isaiah 6:1-4

The first emphasis in this passage is on *Jehovah God—high and lifted up.* Isaiah pictured Jehovah in the holy of holies of the temple with the two seraphim above him. The scene sounds familiar, because when we come to the fourth chapter of Revelation, we find in the picture of heaven which John was given a similar scene. There is the throne of God, and around it are thrones of the four and twenty elders, each of whom is dressed in white and wearing a crown of gold. The four and twenty elders bow down before the throne of God Almighty, saying, "Worthy art thou, our Lord and our God, to receive the glory and the honor and the power: for thou didst create all things, and because of thy will they were, and were created" (Revelation 4:11). From Isaiah or from John, from 750 years

86

before Christ or from nearly 100 years after Christ, the idea of God high and lifted up, transcendent, splendid beyond anything that man can conceive, is the beginning of worship. Real worship begins when man pauses to see his heavenly Father high and lifted up.

THE SINFULNESS OF MAN

While this is the beginning of worship, it is not the end. Having seen God, Isaiah next looked inward at himself: "Then said I, Woe is me! for I am undone; because I am a man of unclean lips, and I dwell in the midst of a people of unclean lips: for mine eyes have seen the King, Jehovah of hosts" (Isaiah 6:5). This is the antedote for man's pride. Man is proud of his buildings, his inventions, his income, his education, his skill. He thinks of the world as revolving around himself, until he lifts his eyes and sees the Lord God Jehovah, high and lifted up. When he compares himself with God he has the means of seeing himself as he really is, weak and inadequate, sinful and undone. In the long ago, it was only after he had seen his vision of Jehovah that Isaiah realized that he was a man of unclean lips. Until man can see God he does not know how weak and inadequate he himself is. Not until he beholds the pure righteousness of God does he recognize his own sin.

CLEANSED AND MADE HOLY

Then comes the next stage. "Then flew one of the seraphim unto me, having a live coal in his hand, which he had taken with the tongs from off the altar: and he touched my mouth with it, and said, Lo, this hath touched thy lips; and thine iniquity is taken away, and thy sin forgiven" (Isaiah 6:6-7). Our greatest need is to be cleansed and purified. We need to get rid of the hate, the greed, the selfishness, the lust and the other sins which drag us down. But the only way in which we can ever get rid of them is by bowing in humble submission before the majesty of God so that he may cleanse us. This is what Christianity is all about. Christ came that we might be clean, and that our hearts might be set on things that are holy instead of on things that are of the world. Christ came to take away the guilt of past sins so that we might go free.

Our initial cleansing begins when we become Christians. This was made possible by God's love and grace, which were revealed when Christ came to the earth and died for us on the cross. To God's grace we must respond in obedient faith, which involves our repentance from past sins, our confession of Christ as Lord and Savior, and our being baptized for the forgiveness of our sins. This is the way the New Testament scriptures explain the necessary response which we must make to God's offer of salvation. It is through Christ's blood that we are cleansed. After our initial cleansing—after we become Christians—then we are regularly cleansed anew by periods of worship in which we pray for forgiveness and rededicate our lives to the Lord. Isaiah spoke of his cleansing figuratively,

87

as a live coal from an altar burning out the dross.

FOR A PURPOSE

It is wonderful when we are cleansed, but even that is not the end. Listen again to Isaiah: "And I heard the voice of the Lord, saying, Whom shall I send, and who will go for us? Then I said, Here am I; send me. And he said, Go . . ." (Isaiah 6:8-9).

Some years ago Cleon Lyles told a delightful little story of an elderly lady who had been to worship. As she came away, she met someone who had arrived very late and who asked, "Is the sermon done?" meaning, "Is it finished?" The elderly woman responded, "The sermon has been preached, but it remains to be done." In our ongoing Christian lives, after we have been purified and cleansed by genuine worship, we go back to the busy thoroughfares of life, back to the people of the world, to help them find the vision of God, high and lifted up. We go back to lives of service to God and our fellowmen.

GOD—SERVANT OR LORD?

At this point let us go back and examine the worship of primitive times. For a moment let us think of ancient India, China, Africa, and the South Sea Islands. All of these civilizations, and many others as well, had similar qualities in their worship. While we do not wish to oversimplify the matter, the central element in primitive worship grew out of the fact that ancient man looked at the world about him and found it frightening and terrible. There were many elements in his world which he did not understand. As a result of his fear and uncertainty, he began to create in his own mind various gods to protect himself and his loved ones. Men tried to placate the gods through the offering of sacrifices and gifts. They worked out systems of magic and did all kinds of incantations to please these imaginary spirits and thus to protect themselves. Ancient man also felt that his gods were the means of satisfying his basic wants and needs. For protection and for the satisfaction of his needs, he devised elaborate means of worship.

For these gods men did not have much love, or adoration, or praise, or respect. Often the gods they believed in were evil, having villainous tendencies. Religion was merely the doing of the things that would keep harm from coming and that would bring blessings. Worship was primarily an effort to placate the gods, and to manipulate and control them for the good of man.

PRAISE AND ADORATION

How different is the motive behind the worship of the true and living God! The Psalmist David seemed to be more aware than most, of the majesty of God, as he wrote such great passages as this:

The heavens declare the glory of God;

And the firmament showeth his handiwork.
Day unto day uttereth speech,
And night unto night showeth knowledge.
There is no speech nor language;
Their voice is not heard.
Their line is gone out through all the earth,
And their words to the end of the world.—Psalm 19:1-4

There are two primary functions which worship serves. The first is *the glorification of God,* which is man's highest purpose in life. In the opening chapter of the Ephesian letter, the apostle Paul indicated man's highest purpose by the use of an expression three times in quick succession. In verse 6, he wrote, "to the praise of the glory of his grace," and in verse 12, "unto the praise of his glory," and in verse 14, "unto the praise of his glory." All three of these expressions emphasize the central purpose of man's existence.

As mentioned earlier, in one of the most magnificent scenes in all of the scriptures, the apostle John pictures for us heaven itself. There is a great sea of glass, upon which there is one central throne with God himself seated on the throne. He is surrounded by the four and twenty elders and by four great living creatures. The text reads:

And the four living creatures, having each one of them six wings, are full of eyes round about and within: and they have no rest day and night, saying, Holy, holy, holy, is the Lord God, the Almighty, who was and who is and who is to come. And when the living creatures shall give glory and honor and thanks to him that sitteth on the throne, to him that liveth for ever and ever, the four and twenty elders shall fall down before him that sitteth on the throne, and shall worship him that liveth for ever and ever, and shall cast their crowns before the throne, saying, Worthy art thou, our Lord and our God, to receive the glory and the honor and the power: for thou didst create all things, and because of thy will they were, and were created.—Revelation 4:8-11

It is in worship that man glorifies God in the purest and most complete sense possible.

There is a second significant purpose served by worship. It is *the satisfaction of the basic needs of man.* Among these needs we would name four: first, there is *man's desire to identify himself with something greater than himself.* Some time ago a camp counselor made a speech around the evening campfire, extolling the great accomplishments of man. Then he said, "But he can't even make one little leaf and make it grow," holding up a tiny leaf before his young audience. Ours is a day in which man often glories in his great accomplishments, but even in our day man cannot make even one little leaf and make it grow. Man is weak and ineffectual. He needs to identify himself with a power greater than himself.

This is why Augustine wrote, "Our souls are never at rest until they find rest in Thee." An unknown author has written:

Religion is the first thing and the last thing and until a man has found God and been found by God, he begins at no beginning, he works to no end. He may have his friendships, his partial loyalties, his scraps of honor. But all these things fall into place and life falls into place only with God. We exist for God.

In the second place, there is *man's desire to express gratitude and love.* Until we can express our appreciation for a gift or a kindness, even when it is a small gift or a little kindness from a friend, we feel off-balance and our equilibrium is upset. On a far deeper level, until we can express gratitude to God, which act is at the heart of worship, and until we can show him our love in return for his love, our lives are out of adjustment.

In the third place, there is *man's desire for something to soothe and calm his troubled spirit.* As civilization becomes more and more complex this need increases. Our generation seems to have more stress and strain than any previous generation, or at least we have more who have broken down under the pressures of day-to-day living. Ours is an age of tranquilizers, psychiatrists, and mental hospitals. Worship is a refuge in time of sorrow and trouble, a tremendous help to modern man in facing the complex pressure-filled existence of the twentieth century. We are reminded of the apostle Paul's statement, "In nothing be anxious; but in everything by prayer and supplication with thanksgiving let your requests be made known unto God. And the peace of God, which passeth all understanding, shall guard your hearts and your thoughts in Christ Jesus" (Philippians 4:6-7).

Finally, there is *man's desire for security and safety.* We live in a precarious world, a world of earthquakes, famines, tidal waves and illnesses. We are so weak and helpless. We need the security and safety of a loving heavenly Father who will care for us. We feel his presence and his strength as we worship him.

FIVE AVENUES

Even though we need to worship and even though we want to worship, we often find that worship is extremely difficult. We are so enmeshed in the affairs of our world that it is hard for us to worship God acceptably. We are so engrossed in buying and selling, going and coming, laughing and crying, being born and dying, and all the other activities of life, that it is hard for us to detach ourselves from this world of material things and enter into the spiritual activity of worship. It is not easy, for worship is the most important and the most difficult thing that we do.

In order to help us in our yearning to worship, God has given us helpful guidelines and instructions as to how he wishes us to worship him. As we read the New Testament, becoming acquainted with the full picture of Christianity, we discover that God has provided five avenues through which we may worship acceptably to God and meaningfully to

90

ourselves. These five avenues through which we are to offer up to God our adoration and praise are: (1) Listening while God teaches and guides and instructs, through his specially chosen spokesmen, as now found in the inspired scriptures. (2) Offering up the deep longings and petitions of the heart through prayer. (3) Praising and glorifying God in song. (4) Partaking of the Lord's Supper, as a memorial feast. And, (5) Giving of our means as we have been prospered. It shall be our purpose in succeeding chapters to discuss these avenues of worship which have been ordained of God.

CHAPTER FIFTEEN
Worship—Listening To God

When a person comes into a typical church building his eyes begin to explore the surroundings. He finds, first of all, that the building is of a relatively simple style. The early, apostle-guided Christians felt no need for images or elaborate ornamentation, nor does one find in the New Testament authorization for such. Each building provides protection from the elements for the worshipers, along with the other things that are necessary to enable the worshipers to concentrate upon the spiritual activities for which they have assembled—seats, lights, heating, cooling, and the like. There is a baptistry, implying that at each assembly there is the hope that one or more will want to become Christians. On Sundays the communion table is spread in anticipation of that time in the worship when the Lord's Supper will be served. Then, there is the pulpit. The pulpit is central. It is usually raised above the surrounding floor. It is prominent. The pulpit is for preaching, and preaching occupies from one-third to one-half of the total period of worship.

As one examines each of these New Testament avenues of worship, it is interesting to look at them in terms of the make-up of the human hand. Let each of the fingers represent one of the avenues: singing, prayer, the Lord's Supper, and giving. Then, let the thumb represent preaching. Just as in the make-up of the hand the thumb is different from the fingers, so preaching is different from the other acts of worship. When a congregation sings or prays or gives or eats the Lord's Supper, they are reaching up to God. When the preaching is done it is God reaching down to guide and direct his people. Just as the thumb is on a different plane from the fingers, so the preaching involves a different direction in worship. It is from God rather than to God.

THE RESPONSIBILITY OF LISTENING

Is preaching worship? The answer is yes. Ideally it is a period when a congregation reverently and responsively listens while the word of God is expounded. It is a time when God speaks to his people. While the congregation listens, they may appear to be passive, but actually they are worshiping actively through listening to the message of God.

For many generations in our educational system we have emphasized the development of such skills as reading, writing, figuring and speaking. Only in recent years, however, have we done very much to emphasize the importance of listening. Perhaps we have realized its importance all along, but only recently have we seriously undertaken to instruct the students in our schools in the skill of hearing what is said by their teachers.

Perhaps Christians should have their attention drawn to the responsibility of listening, for it plays a key role in God's plan. Those who will not hear the gospel of Christ have no chance of eternal salvation. Those who do listen with an open mind and with an understanding heart have the beginning of salvation. In this vein someone has said, "The most important part of the body is the ear." In the sense that the ear is a major doorway to the mind, the ear certainly is important. When Christ was on the earth there were many who did not "hear" him. Those who did were blessed; those who did not hear him robbed themselves. The same is true of Christians as they listen to God's message during periods of worship.

One of the great events in the earthly life of Christ was the transfiguration, which is described in the seventeenth chapter of Matthew. Peter, James, and John went up the mountian with Jesus, and there before their eyes he was transfigured. His face shone as the sun and his garments became white as the light. There then appeared with him Moses and Elijah. At this point Peter said, "Lord, it is good for us to be here: if thou wilt, I will make here three tabernacles; one for thee, and one for Moses, and one for Elijah." At this point one of the most significant sentences in the entire Bible unfolds. "While he was yet speaking, behold, a bright cloud overshadowed them: and behold, a voice out of the cloud, saying, This is my beloved Son, in whom I am well pleased; hear ye him" (Matthew 17:4-5). This was God's emphatic way of saying that we must heed the teachings of Christ.

Still another passage emphasizing the same vital responsibility is James 1:22, which reads, "But be ye doers of the word, and not hearers only, deluding your own selves." Yet another passage is Matthew 7:24-27, where Jesus said:

> Every one therefore that heareth these words of mine, and doeth them, shall be likened unto a wise man, who built his house upon the rock: and the rain descended, and the floods came, and the winds blew, and beat upon that house; and it fell not: for it was founded upon the rock. And every one that heareth these words of mine, and doeth them not, shall be likened unto a foolish man, who built his house upon the sand: and the rain descended, and the floods came, and the winds blew, and smote upon that house; and it fell: and great was the fall thereof.

The thirteenth chapter of Matthew contains a number of the great parables of Jesus concerning the kingdom. The first of these remarkable stories is generally known as the parable of the sower. Its theme emphasizes the vital role that the hearer has in the plan of salvation. It might also be called the parable of the soils, because the crucial element in the story is the way in which the various soils receive the seed. Christ closed his telling

93

of the story with the words, "He that hath ears, let him hear" (Matthew 13:9).

The Importance of Preaching

Phillips Brooks defined preaching as "the communication of truth by man to men. It has in it two essential elements, truth and personality. Neither of those can it spare and still be preaching." (*Lectures on Preaching*, p. 5) Preaching is the communication of God's truth by man to men. Preaching is a part of Christian worship.

The first of the two elements in preaching is *man*. When God created man in the beginning he made him a creature of choice and has, through the ages since, respected man's ability to choose. Man is never forced to do God's will. So, when man sinned against God and needed to be redeemed, God provided the way and communicated this blessing to man through his messengers. God has given us his inspired written word. However, a written page, necessary as it is for the permanence of God's inspired word, does not have the power nor influence that the spoken word has. God loved man enough that he arranged for his message to be presented with all of the life and vitality that comes through a living person. When a man believes God's message and feels deeply the value of this message he proclaims it with great power and influence.

As important as man is in the preaching process, however, he needs to remember that he is only the channel through which the word of God flows into the hearts of men. In the city of Nashville, as in other cities, there is a reservoir where the city keeps its water, so necessary for the life of its people. The huge reservoir of water, atop Reservoir Hill, contains the life-giving fluid that all must have or perish. However, it is necessary for this vital commodity to be brought to the people. From the reservoir there are great watermains which bring this source of water to all of the thousands of homes and hundreds of thousands of individuals in the area. There is nothing very exciting or sensational about black iron pipes, but they are essential in getting the water where it needs to go. A water pipe is a good water pipe if it gets the water to its destination free from dirt or rust or other impurities. Similarly, a preacher is a good preacher if he conveys God's message in its original purity. Preachers are essential in the same way that pipes are imperative, as means rather than ends in themselves.

The important element in preaching is the *message of God*. Paul wrote to the Romans, "For I am not ashamed of the gospel: for it is the power of God unto salvation to every one that believeth; to the Jew first, and also to the Greek" (Romans 1:16). The same apostle wrote to the Corinthians, "For seeing that in the wisdom of God the world through its wisdom knew not God, it was God's good pleasure through the foolishness of the preaching [literally through the thing preached], to save them that believe" (I Corinthians 1:21). Then, the same apostle said it even more directly in II Corinthians 4:7, in these words, "But we have this treasure in earthen vessels, that the exceeding greatness of the power may be of God, and not from ourselves." Man is a means through which the message comes, but the message itself is the absolutely essential element in preaching.

Two Objectives of Preaching

Preaching aims in two directions: first, it tries to bring the saving gospel of Christ to those who are lost, and, second, it edifies, encourages and instructs those who are already Christians. An example of this latter purpose is found in the opening verses of the book of Revelation. The book begins, "The Revelation of Jesus Christ, which God gave him to show unto his servants. . . ." Then a moment later there are the words, "Blessed is he that readeth, and they that hear the words of the prophecy, and keep the things which are written therein: for the time is at hand" (Revelation 1:1, 3).

The worship of Christians in the apostolic era included the reading of the various letters which God inspired his apostles and a few others to write. When these messages were read, the reader would often add a few words of explanation, or interpretation, so that the listeners might comprehend the message more fully. In this way preaching became an important element in the worship of the early church.

Preaching also had as its other purpose, the bringing of non-Christians to believe in Christ and to obey him. We are impressed by the fact that the Emperor Julian, when he observed that the pagan religions of the empire were declining as their temples were unvisited and their sacrifices unbought, called his pagan priests together and charged them to "preach every week as the Christians do." This is an unintended but very real compliment to the power of preaching.

William Paley, in his *Evidences of Christianity,* mentioned the coming of the early Christian preachers into the pagan cities of the Roman Empire. As they did so, they beheld elaborate and costly temples, numerous idols, hoards of priests; trades which depended upon idolatrous worship; theaters where sensual and religious spectacles were presented; arenas where bloody gladiatorial contests were held; teachers of the different mystery religions; philosophers; and the animosity of the Jews. The Christians came preaching the Cross of Christ, a symbol which to the Jew and to the pagan was the basest, most degrading instrument of death, reserved for the most heinous crimes and for the most wretched slave. Then Paley wrote:

> Yet to the Cross of Christ, men turned from deities in which were embodied every attribute of strength, power, and dignity; in an

incredibly short space of time multitudes gave up the splendor, the pride, and the power of paganism, to adore a Being who was thus humiliated beneath the meanest of mankind, who had become, according to the literal interpretation of the prophecy, *"A very scorn of men, and an outcast of the people."* (pp. 48-50, 51)

The power of the gospel is great when it is preached by dedicated Christians who believe that gospel and are living their lives in accordance with its directions.

PRESENT-DAY NEEDS

In our day there is an urgent need for more young men to give themselves to the work of preaching the gospel. There are hundreds and perhaps even a few thousand congregations already in existence which are needing qualified preachers. In addition there are multiplied thousands of towns and cities throughout the world where no New Testament church exists. Our Lord once said, "The harvest indeed is plenteous, but the laborers are few. Pray ye therefore the Lord of the harvest, that he send forth laborers into his harvest" (Matthew 9:37-38). The world has no greater need than to hear the gospel; man can do no greater work than to proclaim that gospel.

At the very end of his active life of proclaiming the gospel, the apostle Paul wrote to his beloved disciple Timothy, to give him this charge:

> I charge thee in the sight of God, and of Christ Jesus, who shall judge the living and the dead, and by his appearing and his kingdom: preach the word; be urgent in season, out of season; reprove, rebuke, exhort, with all longsuffering and teaching.—II Timothy 4:1-2

This is God's charge. We are to preach the word in all its fullness, with love and compassion, to those who are lost and also to those who are already within God's family.

TWO BASIC ATTITUDES

There are really just two basic attitudes in this whole matter of hearing. One is the attitude of the *closed mind.* It is an attitude of stubborness on many occasions, with man's pride closing the door of his heart. Often, it is also a matter of his being too busy. There is an interesting story about Robert Fulton, inventor of the steamboat. Napoleon, busy with his own plans, said that he could give Fulton only two minutes of his time. These two minutes were hardly enough time for Fulton to talk convincingly of the possiblity of the steamboat. Napoleon was not convinced. How different the outcome of his invasion of England might have been if he had only taken more time to hear Fulton talk of his strange invention. How different the lives of many might be and how different their eternal destiny, if they would only take more time to listen when God speaks.

The other attitude is that of the *open mind*. It is an attitude of willingness to consider whatever is presented. It is an attitude involving the willingness to take time for whatever one is called upon to examine. In I Thessalonians 5:21 the apostle Paul wrote, "Prove all things; hold fast that which is good." The best advice that we can give is to prove or examine all things and then accept that which is good.

Preaching involves a double responsibility. To the preacher, there is the responsibility to know God's word, to keep himself a fit channel for its proclamation, and to declare God's truth clearly and faithfully. There is also a responsibility on the part of the listener. To the hearer, the responsibility is to attend to the message carefully, to understand what God's will is, and then to obey God's commands. As Jesus said, "Not every one that saith unto me, Lord, Lord, shall enter into the kingdom of heaven; but he that doeth the will of my Father who is in heaven" (Matthew 7:21).

CHAPTER SIXTEEN

Worship—"The Prayer Of Faith"

As we have seen, it is a part of God's plan that his children should meet together each Lord's Day and at other times for the purpose of worship and study. These periods of worship and study not only bring fresh information to the Christian, but also added encouragement and inspiration to do the things which the Lord wants done. In such periods of worship prayer is especially meaningful. Prayer also is meaningful in individual lives, in families, and in small groups. Worship in prayer is essential to Christian living.

Unfortunately there are many in our modern world who do not believe that God hears and answers prayers. These skeptics consider prayer a delusion. Even among Christians there are many who do not make use of prayer as God intended. With them prayer is often infrequent and ineffective. While they say that they believe in prayer, they act as if they did not. Perhaps this is because they have never been taught from the scriptures the full significance of prayer and the major role that it can play in the life of the Christian. Perhaps they have never really been taught to pray.

Jesus Believed in Prayer

It is quite evident both in the teachings of Jesus and in the life which he lived that he believed in prayer. One day in Capernaum he had spent the day teaching and healing people. There was a continual press of people who wanted their loved ones healed. Jesus was tired when night came; he and the apostles slipped away for rest. "And in the morning, a great while before day, he rose up and went out, and departed into a desert place, and there prayed" (Mark 1:35). A little later when he was on the opposite side of the Sea of Galilee, we read, "And after he had taken leave of them, he departed into the mountain to pray" (Mark 6:46).

Concerning another occasion we read, "And it came to pass in these days, that he went out into the mountain to pray; and he continued all night in prayer to God" (Luke 6:12). When a person spends all night in prayer we may be sure that he believes in the value of prayer. On this particular occasion immediately after praying Jesus came down from the mountain and selected his twelve apostles. A little later we read, "And it came to pass about eight days after these sayings, that he took with him Peter and John and James, and went up into the mountain to pray" (Luke 9:28). While they were praying Christ was transfigured and the voice of God uttered the significant sentence, "This is my beloved Son, in whom I am well pleased; hear ye him" (Matthew 17:5).

On the night in which Jesus was betrayed he offered to God a prayer, which is found in the 17th chapter of John and which has come to be known as Christ's "intercessory prayer." Christ prayed for his disciples and then extended the prayer to include all of those who would believe on him through their word. He included this sentence in the prayer: "Neither for these only do I pray, but for them also that believe on me through their word; that they may all be one; even as thou, Father, art in me, and I in thee, that they also may be in us: that the world may believe that thou didst send me" (John 17:20-21).

In a fuller way Matthew described the final night of Christ's life before his crucifixion in these words:

> Then cometh Jesus with them unto a place called Gethsemane, and saith unto his disciples, Sit ye here, while I go yonder and pray. And he took with him Peter and the two sons of Zebedee, and began to be sorrowful and sore troubled. Then saith he unto them, My soul is exceeding sorrowful, even unto death: abide ye here, and watch with me. And he went forward a little, and fell on his face, and prayed, saying, My Father, if it be possible, let this cup pass away from me: nevertheless, not as I will, but as thou wilt. And he cometh unto the disciples, and findeth them sleeping, and saith unto Peter, What, could ye not watch with me one hour? Watch and pray, that ye enter not into temptation: the spirit indeed is willing, but the flesh is weak. Again a second time he went away, and prayed, saying, My Father, if this cannot pass away, except I drink it, thy will be done. And he came again and found them sleeping, for their eyes were heavy. And he left them again, and went away, and prayed a third time, saying again the same words.—Matthew 26:36-44

In this intimate glimpse into the life of Jesus, at the time of his agonizing anticipation of the cross, we find him praying to God. Jesus believed in prayer.

THE DISCIPLES BELIEVED IN PRAYER

The people whom Jesus left behind believed in prayer. In the beginning chapter of the book of Acts we read about Christ's ascension, then, after the names of the eleven faithful apostles, we read, "These all with one accord continued stedfastly in prayer, with the women, and Mary the mother of Jesus, and with his brethren" (Acts 1:14). It is good to know that Mary also believed in prayer. These remained in Jerusalem waiting for the beginning of the church. While they waited they continued stedfastly in prayer.

In that same chapter we read about the selection of the disciples to take the place of Judas after his death. The apostles named two men: Joseph Barsabbas and Matthias. The scripture says, "They prayed, and said, Thou, Lord, who knowest the hearts of all men, show of these two the one whom thou hast chosen" (Acts 1:24). They expected an answer to that prayer and we believe they got it. God chose Matthias to take the place of Judas.

After the church began and the three thousand had become Christians the scripture says, "They continued stedfastly in the apostles' teaching and fellowship, in the breaking of bread and the prayers" (Acts 2:42). A little later when a problem arose, the Grecian Jews were disturbed because their widows were neglected in the daily ministration of food. The apostles explained that they would allow the Grecian Jews to select seven people from among themselves to wait on tables, and then added, "But we will continue stedfastly in prayer, and in the ministry of the word" (Acts 6:4). The apostles believed that prayer was more important than the giving of food, even to people who were hungry.

Later on, in the same book of Acts the apostle Peter is described as being in prison, and the scripture says, "Peter therefore was kept in the prison: but prayer was made earnestly of the church unto God for him" (Acts 12:5). When Paul and Barnabas were sent out by the Christians at Antioch it was done in this manner: "Then, when they had fasted and prayed and laid their hands on them, they sent them away" (Acts 13:3). Still later, after Paul had gone into certain areas and established churches, the record says, "When they had appointed for them elders in every church, and had prayed with fasting, they commended them to the Lord, on whom they had believed" (Acts 14:23).

In the sixteenth chapter of Acts we learn that Paul and Silas were out by a riverside, where they supposed there was a place of prayer, in order to preach to Lydia and her household. In that same chapter we read about Paul and Silas at midnight in the prison praying and singing praises to God. After Paul had preached a great sermon to the elders of the congregation of Ephesus, the scripture says, "And when he had thus spoken, he kneeled down and prayed with them all" (Acts 20:36). Not only did Jesus believe in and practice prayer but his disciples also believed in it and practiced it.

Christ Taught His Disciples To Pray

Midway in the ministry of Jesus an incident occurred of which we read in the opening verse of the eleventh chapter of the gospel according to Luke: "And it came to pass, as he was praying in a certain place, that when he ceased, one of his disciples said unto him, Lord, teach us to pray, even as John also taught his disciples."

This is an interesting sentence, one which has rather far-reaching implications. First of all, John the Baptist, the forerunner of Christ, believed in prayer and taught his disciples to pray. In the second place, Christ's example of praying led the disciples to want to know more about prayer. This is quite suggestive for those who are parents. In the third place, it is surprising that mature men, products of the religious teaching of the Mosaic Law, and now especially chosen to be apostles of Christ,

100

should feel a need to be taught to pray. In view of the fact that they needed to be taught to pray, surely no one now should be embarrassed to ask to be taught how to pray.

It is in the sixth chapter of Matthew that we find a fuller explanation of Christ's instructions to his disciples concerning prayer. He began by telling them what not to do:

> And when ye pray, ye shall not be as the hypocrites: for they love to stand and pray in the synagogues and in the corners of the streets, that they may be seen of man. Verily I say unto you, They have received their reward. But thou, when thou prayest, enter into thine inner chamber, and having shut thy door, pray to thy Father who is in secret, and thy Father who seeth in secret shall recompense thee.—Matthew 6:5-6

Christ told his disciples, and us, not to pray to be seen of men. Even though our prayers are sometimes to be public, as was the case in New Testament times among the apostles and others, our concern is not being heard by human ears, but by God. We must not pray in order to be thought pious or eloquent, or for any other reason except that we have something about which we want to talk to our Father in heaven.

This text continues with a second negative recommendation:

> And in praying use not vain repetitions, as the Gentiles do: for they think that they shall be heard for their much speaking. Be not therefore like unto them: for your Father knoweth what things ye have need of, before ye ask him.—Matthew 6:7-8

This restriction tells us that God does not want us to be wordy or verbose. We do not give him information, since he knows all things. Rather, by our prayers we convey to him the attitudes of our hearts and the openness of our lives to his direction.

At this point the text continues, "After this manner therefore pray ye. . . ." Then follows what is often known as the "Lord's Prayer." More accurately it might well be called the "Model Prayer." It is a model in *brevity*. It contains only sixty-nine words and can be read in less than half a minute. It is a model in *scope*, since it presents both man's physical and spiritual needs. It is a model in *simplicity*, because it can easily be understood even by a child. It is a model in *directness*, in that it is not vague and indefinite but specific and vivid. The prayer is addressed to God. It contains three petitions concerning heavenly things and four petitions concerning earthly things. The prayer closes with a crescendo of praise to the Creator.

Note the sublime beauty and power in the simple prayer which Christ taught his disciples:

> Our Father who art in heaven, Hallowed be thy name. Thy kingdom come. Thy will be done, as in heaven, so on earth. Give us this day our daily bread. And forgive us our debts, as we also have forgiven our debtors. And bring us not into temptation, but

deliver us from the evil one. For thine is the kingdom, and the power, and the glory, for ever. Amen.—Matthew 6:9-13

CONTENTS OF ACCEPTABLE PRAYER

The scriptures teach us that *prayer should be addressed to God.* Also, there is in the scriptures the teaching that *we are to offer our prayers through Christ.* In John 14:14 we read Christ's statement, "If ye shall ask anything in my name, that will I do." Two chapters later, as he neared the time when he would leave his disciples, he added these words, "If ye shall ask anything of the Father, he will give it you in my name. Hitherto have ye asked nothing in my name: ask, and ye shall receive, that your joy may be made full. . . . In that day ye shall ask in my name" (John 16:23, 24, 26).

Our prayers should contain praise for God. There is a place for pure adoration and praise as we realize the majesty, the greatness, the generosity and the love of God. *Prayer ought also to include thanksgiving.* Our lives are filled with blessings which come from God. Surely we ought, in speaking to him, to express our gratitude for those blessings which mean so much to us. *Prayer also should contain confession of sin.* Not vague, generalized, omnibus expressions are meant, but specific admissions to God of various sins, asking his pardon and forgiveness. *Prayer ought also to contain requests for those things we need in our lives.* These needs are of many kinds, sometimes of a spiritual nature and sometimes of a physical nature. Nothing is too great and nothing too small to be included in our prayers to our Father who loves us.

REQUIREMENTS FOR ACCEPTABLE PRAYER

In order for our prayers to be heard they must be prayed in faith. Near the beginning of the book of James we read:

> But if any of you lacketh wisdom, let him ask of God, who giveth to all liberally and upbraideth not; and it shall be given him. But let him ask in faith, nothing doubting: for he that doubteth is like the surge of the sea driven by the wind and tossed.—James 1:5-6

Even more direct is Christ's statement in Matthew 21:22: "And all things, whatsoever ye shall ask in prayer, believing, ye shall receive." A faith in God's promise that he will hear our prayers is imperative. Without faith our prayers have no assurance of being heard.

A second basic requirement is that the one who prays must be living a life of humble obedience to God. In John 15:7 we read Jesus' statement, "If ye abide in me, and my words abide in you, ask whatsoever ye will, and it shall be done unto you." Notice how big an "if" is involved, If we abide in Christ and if his teachings abide in us, he promises to answer our prayers. This is essentially what the young Jewish man, who had been healed of his blindness, had said in John 9:31: "We know that God heareth not sinners: but if any man be a worshipper of God, and do his will, him he heareth." Another statement is found in James 5:16, where we read, "The supplication of a righteous man availeth much in its working." Effective prayer

102

comes from a man whose life is righteous.

The third requirement for an acceptable prayer is that it be offered according to the will of God. Our finest example is found in Christ's acceptance of God's will at the crucial moment of his facing the cross. As mentioned earlier, in Matthew 26:39, we find Jesus praying in the Garden of Gethsemane: "My Father, if it be possible, let this cup pass away from me: nevertheless, not as I will, but as thou wilt." This is essential. We may ask for whatever we feel is right but we ought always to desire that God's will be done. We often do not know all that is involved in our petitions. We ought to leave the final decision in his hands, with full submission to his will.

JAMES' INSTRUCTIONS ON PRAYER

In addition to the passages mentioned above there is a paragraph in the final chapter of the book of James which is very rich in its instructions concerning prayer. James wrote:

> Is any among you suffering? let him pray. Is any cheerful? let him sing praise. Is any among you sick? let him call for the elders of the church; and let them pray over him, anointing him with oil in the name of the Lord: and the prayer of faith shall save him that is sick, and the Lord shall raise him up; and if he have committed sins, it shall be forgiven him. Confess therefore your sins one to another, and pray one for another, that ye may be healed. The supplication of a righteous man availeth much in its working. Elijah was a man of like passions with us, and he prayed fervently that it might not rain; and it rained not on the earth for three years and six months. And he prayed again; and the heavens gave rain, and the earth brought forth her fruit.—James 5:13-18

In this passage there are seven important suggestions. In verse 13, we find the phrase, "Let him pray," which suggests *individual prayer.* In verse 14, we find, "Let him call for the elders of the church; and let them pray over him," which suggests *united prayer.* In verse 15, we read, "The prayer of faith shall save him," which suggests *believing prayer.* "Pray one for another," in verse 16, suggests *intercessory prayer.* Also, in verse 16, "The effective, fervent prayer of a righteous man," suggests *fervent prayer.* In verse 17, we have a reference that suggests *specific prayer,* in the words, "He prayed fervently that it might not rain." Finally, in verse 18, we read "And he prayed again," which suggests *repeated prayer.*

While it may not be possible to prove conclusively to a man who is a skeptic or a doubter that prayers are answered, when you turn to those who have every right to know, to Christ, to the apostles, and to the others mentioned in the inspired word of God, we have our assurance that prayers are answered. God has promised that when faithful Christians pray he will cause things to happen that would not have happened otherwise. He has promised to hear and to respond, according to his infinite wisdom, to the petitions of his children. God does not always say yes, but he does give an answer to every Christian's prayer.

103

CHAPTER SEVENTEEN

Worship—"Psalms, Hymns, and Spiritual Songs"

On the night in which Jesus was betrayed, just a few hours before he was to be crucified, he ate the Passover with his disciples for the last time and inaugurated the Lord's Supper. At the end of this memorable meeting the scriptures tell us: "And when they had sung a hymn, they went out unto the mount of Olives" (Matthew 26:30). We may wonder what hymn they sang, and who was the one who began the singing. The answer to these questions we may never know, but we do know that our Lord and his apostles sang.

Many years later the apostle Paul was a prisoner in Philippi. At midnight he and Silas were bound solidly in the stocks in the Roman prison. Undoubtedly many of the other prisoners were asleep when "about midnight Paul and Silas were praying and singing hymns unto God" (Acts 16:25). We wonder about the reaction of the other prisoners in their darkened dungeon when they heard the strains of Christian hymns at midnight. This we may never know, but we do know that Paul and Silas sang hymns under the most trying of conditions.

At a later time Paul wrote to the church at Corinth: "I will pray with the spirit, and I will pray with the understanding also: I will sing with the spirit, and I will sing with the understanding also" (I Corinthians 14:15). He also wrote to the church at Ephesus: ". . . speaking one to another in psalms and hymns and spiritual songs, singing and making melody with your heart to the Lord" (Ephesians 5:19). It is generally agreed that "psalms" refer to the actual psalms which we find in the Old Testament. "Hymns" are thought to be songs which are directed to God and Christ in praise and devotion. "Spiritual songs" are thought to be songs which are directed to fellow-Christians.

In his short epistle James, the Lord's brother, taught, "Is any among you suffering? let him pray. Is any cheerful? let him sing praise" (James 5:13). All of these passages indicate that the early Christians were a singing people. They sang as they walked on their journeys between the small towns of their ancient land. As they did their work, when circumstances permitted, they lifted their voices in song. In their assemblies they sang, as well as in small devotionals in homes and in caves. Singing was an important part of Christian worship.

At still another time the apostle Paul wrote, "Let the word of Christ

104

dwell in you richly; in all wisdom teaching and admonishing one another with psalms and hymns and spiritual songs, singing with grace in your hearts unto God" (Colossians 3:16). Singing was one of the five avenues of worship which were taught Christians in the beginning of the church era. The silence of the scriptures, or as we sometimes speak of it "the law of exclusion," permits no other acts of worship. For lack of authorization we have no lighting of candles, no burning of incense, no christening of babies, nor any other extra-biblical acts of worship today. We are pledged to do only that for which we find authority in the scriptures.

It is obvious from the reading of the scriptures that Christians are to be a singing people. Great blessings come to God's children as they engage in this act of worship. We recognize that singing was never meant to be meaningless nor perfunctory, nor merely habit. The early Christians sang meaningfully and worshipfully. Or to borrow the apostle Paul's expression, "with the spirit . . . and with the understanding also." There was always purpose behind their singing. Let us note some of the purposes behind the singing of our Christian hymns today.

TEACHING

One of the primary purposes for singing is teaching. As an example we might refer to that gem of a statement of our Lord in the Sermon on the Mount, which has been so beautifully set to music: "Consider the lilies of the field, how they grow; they toil not, neither do they spin: yet I say unto you, that even Solomon in all his glory was not arrayed like one of these" (Matthew 6:28-29). The message of this beautiful hymn is designed to encourage the Christian to believe that God will take care of him. He need not worry, he need not become a materialist, for God will provide.

Here is an example of a song which teaches the basic fundamentals concerning the church:

The Church's one foundation is Jesus Christ her Lord;
She is His new creation by water and the word;
From heav'n He came and sought her to be His holy bride;
With His own blood He bought her, and for her life He died.

Elect from ev'ry nation, yet one o'er all the earth;
Her charter of salvation, one Lord, one faith, one birth;
One holy name she blesses, partakes one holy food,
And to one hope she presses with ev'ry grace endued.

ADMONITION AND EXHORTATION

Other songs we sing admonish and encourage those who are Christians to do what they already know they should do. Here is an example:

Take time to be holy, speak oft with thy Lord;
Abide in Him always, and feed on His word;
Make friends of God's children; help those who are weak;
Forgetting in nothing His blessing to seek.

Take time to be holy, the world rushes on;

Spend much time in secret with Jesus alone;
By looking to Jesus, like Him thou shalt be;
Thy friends in thy conduct His likeness shall see.

Another song of exhortation says:

Work, for the night is coming,
Work thro' the morning hours;
Work while the dew is sparkling,
Work 'mid springing flowers;
Work when the day grows brighter,
Work in the glowing sun;
Work, for the night is coming,
When man's work is done.

How needed this admonition is in a day when so many other things crowd out the doing of the Lord's work. Hardly a Lord's Day passes but that we need to encourage each other to work while we have life and opportunity. Life is so fleeting and our opportunities are soon gone.

Yet another type of admonition song is the invitation. We often sing such words as:

While Jesus whispers to you, . . .
While we are praying for you, . . .
Now is the time to own Him, . . .
Now is the time to know Him,
Come sinner, come!

The effect of many voices saying these or similar words has led many a person outside of Christ to decide to respond to the Lord's invitation. There is definitely a place in our singing for songs whose purpose is admonition, encouragement and exhortation.

PRAISE, ADORATION AND THANKSGIVING

Yet another type of song is that in which we lift our voices in praise and adoration to God himself, or to Christ our Lord. One of the most meaningful is:

Holy, holy, holy! Lord God Almighty!
Early in the morning our song shall rise to Thee;
Holy, holy, holy! merciful and mighty!
God over all, and blest eternally.

Holy, holy, holy! Tho' the darkness hide Thee,
Tho' the eye of sinful man Thy glory may not see
Only Thou art holy! there is none beside Thee,
Perfect in pow'r, in love, and purity.

This is sheer praise and adoration. Another praise song has the words:

Fairest Lord Jesus! Ruler of all nature!
O Thou of God and man the Son!
Thee will I cherish, Thee will I honor,
Thou, my soul's glory, joy, and crown.

Fair are the meadows, fairer still the woodlands,

Robed in the blooming garb of spring;
Jesus is fairer, Jesus is purer,
Who makes the woeful heart to sing.

Such songs of praise, adoration and thanksgiving satisfy the inner urge to pay just tribute to the Creator of our universe and the Savior of our souls.

Personal Dedication

Other songs afford us an opportunity to reaffirm our commitment to Christ and to rededicate our lives to his Cause. One such song has the words:

Have Thine own way, Lord, Have Thine own way!
Thou art the Potter; I am the clay.
Mold me and make me; after Thy will,
While I am waiting, yielded and still.

Another favorite of submission to the Lord's will is:

I am Thine, O Lord, I have heard Thy voice,
And it told Thy love to me;
But I long to rise in the arms of faith,
And be closer drawn to Thee.

Consecrate me now to Thy service, Lord,
By the pow'r of grace divine;
Let my soul look up with a steadfast hope,
And my will be lost in Thine.

Petition to God and Christ

One final category is that of intimate, personal petition to God and Christ for strength and help. We often sing such words as:

Dear Lord and Father of mankind,
Forgive our foolish ways;
Reclothe us in our rightful mind,
In purer lives Thy service find,
In deeper reverence, praise.

Then, there is the beloved hymn:

Be with me, Lord—I cannot live without Thee,
I dare not try to take one step alone,
I cannot bear the loads of life, unaided,
I need Thy strength to lean myself upon.

Be with me, Lord, when loneliness o'ertakes me,
When I must weep amid the fires of pain,
And when shall come the hour of "my departure"
For "worlds unknown," O Lord, be with me then.

In this last hymn we are thinking about the time when life shall have run its course and we are getting ready to depart for the world beyond. How important it is to be with the Lord throughout life so that he will be with us at death.

There is unanimous testimony among music historians to the fact that the early Christians did not use mechanical instruments of music with their singing. Lyman Coleman, Presbyterian scholar and author of *The Apostolical and Primitive Church,* wrote:

> Both the Jews in their temple service, and the Greeks in their idol worship, were accustomed to sing with the accompaniment of instrumental music. The converts to Christianity accordingly must have been familiar with this mode of singing. . . .But it is generally admitted, that the primitive Christians employed no instrumental music in their religious worship. Neither Ambrose, nor Basil, nor Chrysostom, in the noble encomiums which they severally pronounce upon music, make any mention of instrumental music. Basil condemns it as ministering only to the depraved passions of men. (pp. 368-369)

Joseph Bingham, a member of the Church of England, in his book, *Antiquities of the Christian Church,* described the music in the early church in great detail, but made absolutely no mention of instrumental music. (Book XIV, Chapter I, p. 687f.)

Dr. Massey Shepherd, Jr., Professor of Liturgy in the Divinity School of the University of Chicago was asked, "Did the early church use instruments of music?" He replied:

> No. It was used in the Temple service but was not brought into the synagogue. The pagan cults used it in their worship. There were instruments then in the pagan worship, but not in the worship of the church. . . .This continued down to the middle ages. (Private interview with Dr. W. B. West, Jr.)

The Schaff-Herzog Encyclopedia of Religious Knowledge includes this paragraph:

> In the Greek church the organ never came into use, but after the eighth century it became common in the Latin church, not, however, without opposition from the side of the monks. . . .The reformed church discarded it; and though the church of Basil very early admitted it, it was in other places admitted only sparingly and after long hesitation. (Vol. II, p. 1702)

The American Encyclopedia says:

> Pope Vitilian is related to have introduced organs into some of the churches of Southern Europe first about A.D. 670, but the only trustworthy account is that of the one sent as a present by the Greek Emperor, Constantine Copronymus, to Peppin, King of the Franks in 775. (Vol. XII, p. 686)

John Calvin, the noted Presbyterian scholar, in his *Commentary on the Book of Psalms,* said,

> Musical instruments in celebrating the praises of God would be no more suitable than the burning of incense, the lighting up of the lamps, and the restoration of the other shadows of the law. . . .

Men who are fond of outward pomp may delight in that noise; but the simplicity which God recommends to us by the apostle is far more pleasing to him. (Vol. I, on the Thirty-Third Psalm, Eerdmans, p. 539.)

Adam Clarke, a Methodist distinguished for his *Commentary* on the entire Bible, wrote:

I am an old man, and an old minister; and I here declare that I never knew them [musical instruments] productive of any good in the worship of God; and have reason to believe that they were productive of much evil. Music, as a science, I esteem and admire; but instruments of music in the house of God I abominate and abhor.(*Commentary*, Vol. IV, p. 686.)

J. W. McGarvey, a gospel preacher of the Restoration Movement, wrote:

It is manifest that we cannot adopt the practice without abandoning the obvious and the only ground on which a restoration of primitive Christianity can be accomplished, or on which the plea for it can be maintained. (From his tract, "What Shall We Do About the Organ?", p. 10)

If It Is Argued . . .

If it is argued that the Greek word *psallo* (Ephesians 5:19) actually contains the idea of instrumental accompaniment, we reply, "Let us understand *psallo* as the apostle Paul, who used the word, practiced it." According to music historians he and the other apostles did not use instruments, so he must not have considered the word to include the instrument.

If it is argued that the early Christians did not have instruments to use, we reply, "They had castanets, cornets, cymbals, flutes, harps, lutes, pipes, psalteries, sackbuts, tabarets, trumpets, and viols." Even this list of available instruments may not be complete, but the fact is they did have instruments to use if they had felt it appropriate and proper.

If it is argued that we now use other things not mentioned in the New Testament, such as buildings, benches, lights, song books, and the like, we reply, "*Whatever is absolutely necessary to carry out a command of God is authorized.* On the basis of this authorization, we do provide meeting-houses and those things that are necessary for a congregation to assemble and have the opportunity to worship." Under this principle we supply a public address system when the room is too large for people to hear adequately without it. We supply lights in order that they may see and participate in the singing or the reading of God's word. We supply benches on which they may sit, for we know that standing is not possible for many over a long period of time, without completely nullifying their ability to worship meaningfully.

On this basis, we do not include instruments to accompany the singing, for we do not consider instruments necessary. On the contrary, the finest singing is *a cappella*, when sincere worshipers offer up the "fruit of their lips" to God in praise. Many of the finest choral groups in America demonstrate that singing at its best is unaccompanied by instruments, though their motivation for doing so is not that of religious conviction, as ours is.

The basic reason why we do not believe in the use of mechanical instruments to accompany the singing in Christian worship is that we find no authorization for such usage in the New Testament. We genuinely love God and want to do his will. Therefore we want to be very sure that we stay within the bounds of his authorization when we worship him. We can be sure that worshiping without instruments is approved because that is the way the apostles worshiped. This is the safe, sure way. We do not feel that we have the right to authorize that which might be pleasing to our own tastes, but that for which we cannot find scriptural authorization.

As we look back we have seen that the early Christians often sang psalms, hymns and spiritual songs in praise to God and in admonition to one another. There are great blessings to be had in singing, which none of us must permit himself to miss. Singing is one of God's ways of lifting us to a higher plane of devotion. Let us pray and let us work that our worship in song may be a blessing to us and an acceptable offering to our Father in heaven.

CHAPTER EIGHTEEN
Worship—Supper Of The Lord

For nearly two thousand years Christians have assembled each Lord's Day to worship God in the manner described in the New Testament. Eating the Lord's Supper is one of the five avenues of worship taught in the sacred scriptures. The eating of this memorial meal is for many of us the most meaningful part of the worship on the Lord's Day. By its very nature it is more intimate and more personal than some of the other acts of worship. The Lord's Supper is a very special time when Christians commune with their Lord and with each other.

One of the most interesting of the writings of the early church leaders concerning the Lord's Supper is that from the pen of Justin the Martyr, who lived in the second century, possibly from around 100 to 165 A.D. In his *Apology I*, sections LXV-LXVII, he wrote these words:

> Then is brought to the president of the brethren bread and a cup of water and wine. And he takes them and offers up praise and glory to the Father of all things, through the name of his Son and of the Holy Ghost, and gives thanks at length that we are deemed worthy of these things at his hand. When he has completed the prayers and thanksgiving all the people present assent by saying *Amen. Amen* in the Hebrew tongue signifies "So be it." When the president has given thanks and all the people have assented, those who are called deacons with us give to those present a portion of the Eucharistic bread and wine and water, and carry it away to those who are absent.

> This food is called with us the Eucharist, and of it none is allowed to partake but he that believes that our teachings are true, and has been washed with the washing for the remission of sins and unto regeneration, and who so lives as Christ directed. For we do not receive them as ordinary food or ordinary drink. . . . For the Apostles in the memoirs made by them, which are called gospels, have thus narrated that the command was given; that Jesus took bread, gave thanks, and said, "This do ye in remembrance of me; this is my body." And he took the cup likewise and said "This is my blood," and gave it to them alone. . . .

> And on the day which is called the day of the sun there is an assembly of all who live in the towns or in the country; and the memoirs of the Apostles or the writings of the prophets are read, as long as time permits. Then the reader ceases and the president speaks, admonishing us and exhorting us to imitate these excellent examples. Then we arise all together and offer prayers; and, as we said before, when we have concluded our prayer, bread is brought, and wine and water, and the president in like manner

111

offers up prayers and thanksgivings with all his might; and the people assent with *Amen;* and there is the distribution and partaking by all of the Eucharistic elements; and to them that are not present they are sent by the hand of the deacons. And they that are prosperous and wish to do so give what they will, each after his choice. What is collected is deposited with the president, who gives aid to the orphans and widows and such as are in want by reason of sickness or other cause; and to those also that are in prison, and to strangers from abroad, in fact to all that are in need he is a protector. (Taken from Bettenson, *Documents of the Christian Church,* pp. 93-95.)

THE SCRIPTURES SPEAK

While these paragraphs from Justin Martyr are interesting, as reflecting the practices of the very early church, it is to the inspired, sacred scriptures that we go for the most meaningful information and instruction. In the gospel according to Mark we read of events which happened during the final week of Christ's life. Beginning with verse 12 of Mark 14, we read:

And on the first day of unleavened bread, when they sacrificed the passover, his disciples say unto him, Where wilt thou that we go and make ready that thou mayest eat the passover? And he sendeth two of his disciples, and saith unto them, Go into the city, and there shall meet you a man bearing a pitcher of water: follow him; and wheresoever he shall enter in, say to the master of the house, The Teacher saith, Where is my guest-chamber, where I shall eat the passover with my disciples? And he will himself show you a large upper room furnished and ready: and there make ready for us. And the disciples went forth, and came into the city, and found as he had said unto them: and they made ready the passover.—Mark 14:12-16

We are all aware, perhaps, that the passover was a very special time for the Jews. Faithful Israelites from all over the world came to Jerusalem and, in order that they might have a place to eat the passover feast, the local residents made rooms available to them for this purpose. These rooms were furnished with a table and on that table there were provided the elements of the passover meal—a lamb roasted in its entirety, unleavened bread, bitter herbs, and fruit of the vine. So, Christ's disciples found the room designated and procured the necessary elements for the passover supper.

Continuing to read, beginning in verse 22:

And as they were eating, he took bread, and when he had blessed, he brake it, and gave to them, and said, Take ye: this is my body. And he took a cup, and when he had given thanks, he gave to them: and they all drank of it. And he said unto them, This is my blood of the covenant, which is poured out for many. Verily I say unto you, I shall no more drink of the fruit of the vine, until that day when I drink it new in the kingdom of God.—Mark 14:22-25

This was the setting and this was the manner in which Jesus instituted the Lord's Supper.

THE ELEMENTS

In the verses just read we have a clear indication that the Lord's Supper consisted of two elements and only two. First, there was *unleavened bread*. This means simply bread without yeast. A generation ago a Christian woman wrote this interesting paragraph concerning her manner of preparing the unleavened bread:

> Taking the best white flour, I mix it with pure sweet milk, with the cream still on, putting in nothing else whatever. The cream that is in the milk is sufficient shortening to prevent toughness, yet it is not greasy and does not bake so hard as when lard and water are used. It should be baked rather slowly and should not remain in the oven long enough to become hard. (*Gospel Advocate*, 1886.)

In the second place, there is the *fruit of the vine*. Since the scriptures do not specify either fresh grape juice or fermented wine, but rather use the expression "fruit of the vine," it is permissible to use either. Justin Martyr in his *Apology I*, p. 65, mentioned earlier, indicated that it was customary to mix water with the wine. In our day it seems wisest to use grape juice, especially when we remember that some of our young people, should we use fermented wine, might be encouraged to acquire a taste for something which would be harmful to them.

We are deeply impressed with the *simplicity* of the elements which make up the Lord's Supper. We are also impressed with the *beauty* of this memorial meal. What else could possibly convey so beautifully the fact we are to take our Lord into our very beings? We become what we eat in the physical world. Spiritually, this memorial meal suggests the same intimacy in taking Christ into our very beings. We are also deeply impressed with the *availability* of these elements. They are available to the poor as well as to the rich; they are available, with some thought and planning, in every part of the world.

TO THE CORINTHIANS

Perhaps the most meaningful of all of the passages in the New Testament concerning the Lord's Supper is found in I Corinthians 11:23-30. After having established the church at Corinth and having given the Christians oral instructions concerning this memorial meal, the apostle Paul wrote back to them these words:

> For I received of the Lord that which also I delivered unto you, that the Lord Jesus in the night in which he was betrayed took bread; and when he had given thanks, he brake it, and said, This is my body, which is for you: this do in remembrance of me. In like manner also the cup, after supper, saying, This cup is the new covenant in my blood: this do, as often as ye drink it, in remembrance of me. For as often as ye eat this bread, and drink the cup, ye proclaim the Lord's death till he come.

First, there is *the retrospective look*: "This do in remembrance of me." Human beings forget. The Lord's Supper is a period of several minutes each Lord's Day in which we Christians look back to the life of our Lord and contemplate his love and sacrifice for us. It is a time in which we contemplate the very center of our religion. In the Lord's Supper the heart of Christian doctrine is enacted in visible form. As we remember our Lord our hearts are cleansed and purified and we are lifted up to a higher plane of life.

The Lord's Supper is a living monument. It contrasts with the monuments of stone that have been so impressively built to honor the world's great leaders. In Washington one is impressed by the beauty and grandeur of the Lincoln Memorial, the Jefferson Memorial, and the Washington Monument. In New York the outstanding monument is Grant's Tomb. When one moves across the Atlantic to the old world, in London he sees the monument of Lord Nelson atop the spire in Trafalgar Square. He finds in the city of Paris the Arch of Triumph, a memorial to the victories of Napoleon. He visits the Brandenburg Gate in the heart of Berlin. He is impressed by the Victor Immanuel Monument in the center of Rome. He examines the remains of the ancient Parthenon atop the Acropolis in Athens. Finally, he marvels at the oldest monuments of all, the pyramids of ancient Egypt. These monuments of men are tied to one place, whereas Christ's memorial is available wherever a band of Christians chooses to meet for worship.

In the second place, there is *the prospective look:* "Ye proclaim the Lord's death till he come." The Lord's Supper is to be eaten by Christians, those who not only remember that their Lord died to make possible their salvation, but who also look forward to his eventual coming again. It is a declaration of faith in the future. If this memorial meal only looked back to the cross and the tomb, it would be sad and sorrowful. However, the fact that it is an announcement of Christian faith for all to see, and a constant declaration of faith that the Lord is living and will come again, makes it a joyous meal.

The Lord's Supper is also a marvelous means of teaching the young. As a child in his early years watches his father and mother partake of these emblems, he has a curosity which leads him to ask what they mean. This affords an opportunity for father or mother to explain Christ's great redemptive love and leads the child to look forward to the time when he is old enough to be a Christian and to partake of the Lord's Supper as his parents do.

In A Worthy Manner

Our text continues:

Wherefore whosoever shall eat the bread or drink the cup of the Lord in an unworthy manner, shall be guilty of the body and the

114

blood of the Lord. But let a man prove himself, and so let him eat of the bread, and drink of the cup. For he that eateth and drinketh, eateth and drinketh judgment unto himself, if he discern not the body. For this cause many among you are weak and sickly, and not a few sleep.

The words of warning were written to cause each Christian to realize the seriousness which attends the eating of this memorial meal. It is to be done reverently and thoughtfully, never carelessly and idly. The leader of this portion of the worship should prepare himself carefully in advance. First of all, he should be a good man, lest his life cause others to be disturbed when he leads the worship. He should then spend some hours during the week prior to this important responsibility tuning his mind and heart to this great and important opportunity. He should pray thoughtfully, spiritually and specifically for each element of the Lord's Supper as he offers thanks. First, he offers thanks for the bread, and when it has been served he offers thanks for the fruit of the vine. He should do so in a manner designed to lead each participant to partake spiritually. While leading others, he should make sure that he himself also worships.

During the time of the eating of the Lord's Supper every Christian should make a supreme effort to be sure that he is worshiping acceptably. Before coming to the house of the Lord, each should prepare his heart and mind for the activities of worship in which he is to engage. During the time of eating he should meditate quietly on the life and love of his Lord. It is a time in which one can pray for strength to meet the temptations of the ensuing week. It is a time for parents to ask help in the rearing of their children. It is a time for children to pray for proper respect for parental authority. Hearts are mellowed, cleansed, and strengthened as they assemble around the Lord's Table. Some like to spend these minutes in the reading of appropriate scriptures. Others like to meditate upon some appropriate hymn. Others like simply, with closed eyes, to meditate upon the Lord and what he means in their lives.

Focus for a moment on the expression "in an unworthy manner. . . ." Our text tells us that whoever eats of the bread and drinks of the cup in an unworthy manner is guilty of the body and the blood of the Lord. This is indeed a serious charge. What does it mean? Some have thought that the passage refers to a person who has lived an unworthy or sinful life during the recent past, and that he should not partake of the Lord's Supper. This passage does not have reference to the life of the one partaking, but to the manner of the actual eating of the supper itself. Not to discern or think of Christ and his death for us while eating his supper is the sin being warned against. It is true, however, that the Christian who has fallen into sin does need to repent genuinely and pray for God's forgiveness before he comes to the Lord's Table. When he has repented and prayed for forgiveness, he especially needs to come to the Lord's Table and to eat. He above all needs the spiritual strength that this supper provides.

THE FIRST DAY OF THE WEEK

In Acts 20:7, we read, "And upon the first day of the week, when we were gathered together to break bread, Paul discoursed with them. . . ." This passage is the only passage in the New Testament which tells us with absolute certainty that the early Christians ate the Lord's Supper on the Lord's Day. The setting is this: The apostle Paul was hurrying back to Jerusalem from his second missionary journey, hoping to arrive at Jerusalem by Pentecost (Acts 20:16). Even though he was in a hurry he remained in Troas for several days in order to meet with the brethren and to eat the Lord's Supper. If it could properly have been eaten earlier, presumably he would have done so and been on his way to his destination. But, it seems quite clear, he waited because it was not proper to do so until the Lord's Day—the first day of the week.

Those of us who are committed to following the New Testament in its silences as well as in its pronouncements find no authority anywhere in God's inspired word for eating the Lord's Supper on any day except the Lord's Day. In the final week of Christ's life on the earth he told his apostles, "I have yet many things to say unto you, but ye cannot bear them now. Howbeit when he, the Spirit of truth, is come, he shall guide you into all the truth . . ." (John 16:12-13). When Christ left the earth he left the Holy Spirit to guide the disciples into all truth. How did the Holy Spirit guide the apostles in regard to the time when the Lord's Supper was to be eaten? We have our answer in Acts 20:7: "And upon the first day of the week, when we were gathered together to break bread. . . ."

Sometimes we hear it said that the Lord's Supper is the most important of the five avenues of Christian worship. The only ground in the New Testament on which this belief could be based is Acts 20:7. The argument is made that they came together primarily for the breaking of the bread, the Lord's Supper. We believe that to base the doctrine that the Lord's Supper is more important than the other avenues of worship on this phrase is unwarranted. In connection with what was said in the preceding paragraphs, Paul and others could pray and sing on other days in the week, but the Lord's Supper was exclusively reserved for the first day of the week. Therefore this statement would be quite understandable in that context.

To single the Lord's Supper out as the most important act of worship is unwise and unwarranted. The truth of the matter is that all of the acts of worship are necessary and therefore vitally important. They are important because each is commanded by the Lord. It would be unfortunate to single out the act of singing and say it is more important than the other avenues of worship, and similarly the matter of praying, or the matter of

116

giving. Is the Lord's Supper more important than God's speaking to us in the reading of his word, or the proclaiming of his gospel? No, the avenues of worship are distinctive and each one is supremely important in its own place.

The situation is much like that of our physical bodies. Are we to say that the heart muscle is more important than any other part of the body? Is it really more important than the brain? Is it more important than the circulatory system? Is it more important than the nervous system? The fact is that all are important and that life cannot go on without all of them. We cannot be spiritually acceptable to God in our worship without all of the avenues of worship performed genuinely in spirit and in truth. Let us not diminish the importance of any act of worship by referring to some other as more important.

During the last few years I have asked more than 500 college students to evaluate their own activities in worship. It has been especially interesting to notice that a vast majority of the students indicate that their worship is most meaningful in the eating of the Lord's Supper. In this activity they feel a higher degree of personal dedication to God, and a greater degree of intimacy with God than in any other act. Perhaps many of us share something of their feeling. All of us feel the spiritual uplift of this special act of communion with God. It is more personal, more intimate, than some of the other acts. However, this is not to say that it is more important. It is different, but not more important.

Sacred history bears out the fact that the early Christians ate the Lord's Supper each Lord's Day. Justin Martyr, Tertullian, Pliny and others tell us that the supper was eaten weekly during the second century. This weekly observance is a part of the truth into which the Holy Spirit guided the apostles. They therefore set the example of eating the Lord's Supper on each first day of the week. *Erskine's Dissertations* tell us that the Greek church continued this weekly observance until the seventh century. John Calvin and other reformers lamented the decline in the weekly observance of the Lord's Supper as late as the sixteenth century. Surely we need this spiritual meal each seven days. It is a wise, safe course to do it as the early Christians did, not annually, not semi-annually, not quarterly, not monthly, but on each Lord's Day.

The Lord's Supper calls us back each week to the central facts of the Christian religion. In the Lord's Supper the heart of Christian doctrine is enacted in visible form. As we assemble around this table the Lord gives us spiritual strength and cleanses away the evil that has crept into our lives. This sacred meal provides for us the spiritual food which our souls need. We should resolve never to miss an opportunity of eating this spiritual feast. The Lord's Supper is for Christians only. All are invited to the feast, but only those who are willing to accept Christ as Savior and obey his commands are permitted to eat.

CHAPTER NINETEEN
Giving—Stewardship

As we explore the avenues of Christian worship, we come to the act of giving. Each Sunday there comes a time in the hour of worship when Christians give of their means to the Lord. Is this worship? Some have felt that while giving is appropriate at the time of worship, that it in itself is not an act of worship. Is giving worship?

In answering this question it may be helpful to look back through the centuries and think briefly of the things which man has done in his worship of God. He has built temples and erected altars. He has made pilgrimages, as the ancient Hebrews did annually to Jerusalem. He has listened respectfully and responsively as God has spoken, as the Hebrews did at the foot of Mt. Sinai when God gave his law through Moses. Man has prayed. Man has sung hymns. Man has eaten religious meals, as in the Passover and the Lord's Supper. Man has also fasted. Then, in addition to all of these, man has given gifts. The sacrifices of the Old Testament were gifts. Animals and food were given for the purpose of offering sacrifices unto Jehovah. In fact, one of the most important and most consistent acts of worship has been that of giving.

There is a very deep significance behind the giving of gifts in worship. Man cannot give himself, or even a part of himself, in worship to God, so instinctively he wants to give some token or symbol of himself. This is what he does when he gives a gift to God. This is quite obvious in the Old Testament Law of Moses. The firstborn was to be redeemed by the offering of a lamb, or in cases of less affluence, the offering of a pair of turtle doves or a pair of pigeons (Exodus 13:1, 2, 13; Leviticus 12:8). The firstborn belonged to God but was to be redeemed through the offering of a gift. So today, Christians give the products of their hands, or the income from hours of their labor, as an evidence of their love for God. Giving is worship.

In the New Testament we find these words, "I beseech you therefore, brethren, by the mercies of God, to present your bodies a living sacrifice, holy, acceptable to God, which is your spiritual service" (Romans 12:1). God does not want human sacrifice to be offered on altars. Dead human sacrifices would be a mockery to God, since man is a spirit made in the image of God. Rather, God wants man to be a "living sacrifice," working during his lifetime for the Cause of Christ. In I Corinthians 6:19-20, Paul emphasized this same point: "Ye are not your own; for ye were bought with a price: glorify God therefore in your body." In II Corinthians 8:5,

Paul commended the people of Macedonia because "first they gave their own selves to the Lord."

RIGHT ATTITUDES

The achieving of right attitudes is often one of the most difficult aspects of the Christian life. Right attitudes toward people, toward self, toward certain activities, and toward material things are so difficult to achieve that they often constitute the work of a lifetime. It is especially difficult to achieve proper attitudes toward our material possessions, for there is a great temptation to let these occupy a central place in our lives. Our lives are often dominated by things. Of all the areas where attitudes are important, none is more difficult than the area of material possessions.

The Lord's teaching concerning the proper attitude toward material possessions is plainly declared in the Sermon on the Mount, as we find it in Matthew 6:19-33, which reads in part:

> Lay not up for yourselves treasures upon the earth, where moth and rust consume, and where thieves break through and steal: but lay up for yourselves treasures in heaven, where neither moth nor rust doth consume, and where thieves do not break through nor steal: for where thy treasure is, there will thy heart be also.- . . . Be not anxious for your life, what ye shall eat, or what ye shall drink; nor yet for your body, what ye shall put on. Is not the life more than the food, and the body than the raiment? . . . But if God doth so clothe the grass of the field, which today is, and to-morrow is cast into the oven, shall he not much more clothe you, O ye of little faith? Be not therefore anxious, saying, What shall we eat? or, What shall we drink? or, Wherewithal shall we be clothed? For after all these things do the Gentiles seek; for your heavenly Father knoweth that ye have need of all these things. But seek ye first his kingdom, and his righteousness; and all these things shall be added unto you.

Our attitude toward material things comes to its severest test when we face the matter of giving. Many otherwise good people fail to give enough to the Lord. There are primarily two reasons: (1) We do not fully understand Christ's teachings concerning possessions. We do not comprehend that we are merely stewards of God's bounty, and that all our material possessions are not really ours but his. (2) The second difficulty is in overcoming our own innate selfishness. It is so easy to think of our own desires and to disregard the needs of the Lord's work and of others.

GOD'S PLAN OF GIVING

The teaching of the New Testament on the subject of giving can be briefly summarized by referring to a few sentences in the writings of the apostle Paul. First, notice I Corinthians 16:2, which reads: "Upon the first day of the week let each one of you lay by him in store, as he may prosper, that no collections be made when I come." A careful analysis of this passage indicates that the Christian's giving should be *periodic*—"Upon the first day of the week;" that it should be *personal*—"let each one of you lay by him in store;" that it should be *proportionate*—"as he may prosper;" and that it should be *preventive*—"that no collection be made when I come."

A second passage from the pen of the apostle Paul is II Corinthians 9:7, which reads: "Let each man do according as he hath purposed in his heart; not grudgingly, or of necessity: for God loveth a cheerful giver." Notice that this passage indicates that the Christian's giving should be *purposeful*—"as he has purposed in his heart." One's gift should not be an afterthought or a casual matter, but should be planned and given cheerfully. These five words constitute a quick summary of the teaching of the Lord concerning giving: *periodic, personal, proportionate, preventive,* and *purposeful.*

Under the Old Law

In discussing our responsibilities to God in regard to giving, we need to pause and remember how generously God has given to us. Think of the world about us, with all of its beauties and blessings. Think of the productivity of the soil which makes possible our food, clothing and shelter, along with all of the luxuries of life. Think, too, of the blessings that come through our relationships with family and friends. Then, add to these the spiritual blessings which are uniquely ours as children of God. We need to begin by remembering that, as James put it, "Every good gift and every perfect gift is from above, coming down from the Father of lights, with whom can be no variation, neither shadow that is cast by turning" (James 1:17). God has been so very generous in loving and caring for us. Our part, in return, is to give of ourselves and our means to God and to his Cause. This is suggested in Christ's statement, "Freely ye received, freely give" (Matthew 10:8).

In further considering our responsibilities to God, it is helpful to review the giving of God's servants in the Old Testament period. They began by giving a tithe, or ten percent, of everything they received. That means ten percent of the increase of their flocks, ten percent of their grain, and ten percent of everything else they had. In addition there was the regular giving of animals for certain special sacrifices. Still further was the giving for special feasts and pilgrimages to Jerusalem. They were also required to leave their land idle one year out of every seven and to forgive all their debts each fiftieth year, a year of jubilee. When all of the things which they were required to give because of their religion are added up, it appears that from twenty-five to forty percent of everything that came into a loyal Jew's hands was to be returned to God.

The Early Christians

As we move from the Old Testament period to the New Testament

120

era let us examine a few verses which show the remarkable attitude which the early Christians had toward material things. In the second chapter of the book of Acts we read about the beginning of the church. After reading about the three thousand who became Christians on the Day of Pentecost, we read about the worship of the early church. Then soon there is the sentence: "And all that believed were together, and had all things common; and they sold their possessions and goods, and parted them to all, according as any man had need" (Acts 2:44-45). This is an amazing thing when we realize that this great number of people had been Christians only a few days, yet their faith was so deep that they were willing to contribute whatever they had in order that certain ones in their midst could be cared for. A few pages later in the same book we find:

> And the multitude of them that believed were of one heart and soul: and not one of them said that aught of the things which he possessed was his own; but they had all things common. . . .For neither was there among them any that lacked:for as many as were possessors of lands or houses sold them, and brought the prices of the things that were sold, and laid them at the apostles' feet: and distribution was made unto each, according as any one had need.—Acts 4:32, 34, 35.

It is true that this was an emergency situation in the early church. On the day of Pentecost there were people from at least sixteen different nations gathered at Jerusalem who heard the gospel preached. Three thousand people from the four corners of the then-populated earth became Christians. Many had heard little or nothing of Christ and his church before. Yet their pilgrimage to Jerusalem had already run its course and it was time for them to go home. Their funds had been exhausted, yet they needed to stay at Jerusalem longer in order to learn more of Christianity. In that emergency situation the Jerusalem Christians simply opened their hearts and cared for their newly-made brethren. They sold their lands and houses and put the funds into a common treasury. Then they cared for those who were in need. This was an emergency situation and their generous response was not taught as a permanent requirement for all Christians down through the centuries. However, behind their action in that emergency situation there is a principle which is still binding upon all Christians: *When Christians are in need, if there are other Christians who can supply that need, they are obligated to do so.* In the letter which Paul wrote to the Galatians, there are these words: "Bear ye one another's burdens, and so fulfil the law of Christ." Then later on: "So then, as we have opportunity, let us work that which is good toward all men, and especially toward them that are of the household of the faith" (Galatians 6:2, 10).

UNDER THE NEW LAW

In the Christian dispensation God's children live under the law of

121

liberty, the law of love. As a clear indication of what this involves in relation to giving, the apostle Paul wrote extensively to the church at Corinth. In the second letter which Paul wrote there are these words:

> Moreover, brethren, we make known to you the grace of God which hath been given in the churches of Macedonia; how that in much proof of affliction the abundance of their joy and their deep poverty abounded unto the riches of their liberality. For according to their power, I bear witness, yea and beyond their power, they gave of their own accord, beseeching us with much entreaty in regard of this grace and the fellowship in the ministering to the saints. . . .But as ye abound in everything, in faith, and utterance, and knowledge, and in all earnestness, and in your love to us, see that ye abound in this grace also. I speak not by way of commandment, but as proving through the earnestness of others the sincerity also of your love. For ye know the grace of our Lord Jesus Christ, that, though he was rich, yet for your sakes he became poor, that ye through his poverty might become rich. . . . For if the readiness is there, it is acceptable according as a man hath, not according as he hath not. . . .—II Corinthians 8:1-5, 7-9, 12

The following chapter adds these impressive words:

> But this I say, He that soweth sparingly shall reap also sparingly; and he that soweth bountifully shall reap also bountifully. Let each man do according as he hath purposed in his heart; not grudgingly, or of necessity: for God loveth a cheerful giver. And God is able to make all grace abound unto you; that ye, having always all sufficiency in everything, may abound unto every good work. . . .And he that supplieth seed to the sower and bread for food, shall supply and multiply your seed for sowing, and increase the fruits of your righteousness. . . .—II Corinthians 9:6-8, 10

This is the essence of the teaching of the New Testament on giving. God has poured out his wonderful store of blessings upon us, and out of our love and gratitude to him we give generously to support his Cause and to help our fellowmen.

Two Basic Attitudes

There are basically two attitudes which Christians can have toward material things. The first of these attitudes is this: *They are mine. I have earned my possessions by my own intelligence and my own industry. They are mine, and now as a Christian I will give part of what is mine to the Lord.* This attitude flies in the teeth of everything that we read in the scriptures. There are no passages which teach that the material resources which we control are ours.

There is a second attitude toward material possessions. A man with this attitude says, *They are thine.* He goes on to say, *God has blessed me with these material possessions. They are a trust from God. I will use a necessary portion for myself and my family, but I am mindful all the while that they really belong to God.* It is a basic difference in attitude. This second attitude is the one which we find taught in the scriptures. The one word which conveys the idea is the word *stewardship*. The idea is that God created the world and owns it. We are his stewards. He gives us certain talents—mental and physical. He opens to us certain opportunities; we have the insight to see them; we have the industry to make capital of them; but God gives us the ability to begin with. The total of our possessions really belongs to God. David had this idea in mind when he wrote, "The earth is Jehovah's and the fulness thereof; The world, and they that dwell therein" (Psalm 24:1). We and all that we have belong to God.

It may be a bit surprising to learn that the subject of stewardship is presented in the New Testament more often than the teaching on baptism. It may be a little surprising to know that the idea of Christian stewardship is more fully taught in the New Testament than the Lord's Supper. Half of the parables teach the idea of stewardship. To a significant degree our success or failure in living the Christian life will be determined by the way we use the material possessions which the Lord has entrusted to our care.

WHILE WE LIVE AND WHEN WE DIE

The Christian must not only be a faithful steward during his lifetime, through giving generously to the Lord on the first day of each week, and as other needs may arise, but he should also continue to be a good steward at the time of his death. By the very nature of our civilization, it is likely that each of us will leave behind at death some kind of estate. During the thirty or forty or fifty years in which we are gainfully employed it is right and proper for each of us to remember oncoming old age and to save something for the retirement years. Since we cannot possibly know how long those retirement years will last, it is often true that we save back more than is actually needed to take care of us. Consequently, we leave part of our savings behind when we die.

In the second place, an estate is often established through the purchase of a dwelling place. During our working years we buy a home and continue to use that home until the time of death. This means that at death a valuable piece of property is left behind, thus becoming an important part of our estate. Still another contribution to our estate comes in the form of life insurance of the type which is paid only at the end of life. All of this means that the Christian while facing the uncertainity of an extended old age is not in a position to give all that he has to the Lord, but at death finds himself in possession of a considerable estate. Each of us needs to think forward toward that time and to make certain plans to include the Lord in the distribution of this accumulated wealth.

Roger Babson, the noted economist once said, "Nothing but trouble follows when you die without a will; don't be foolish, see a lawyer." He then pointed out five reasons for the making of a will: (1) A will is the only instrument that speaks with authority after you are gone. (2) It insures that your estate is to be distributed according to your desires. (3) It prevents misunderstandings among your heirs. (4) It permits you to say who will have charge of the handling of your estate. (5) It often reduces the expenses of probating the estate and may reduce the estate tax. A Christian booklet adds these impressive suggestions:

> As a steward of God you are responsible for the distribution of your estate after your death as well as its handling while you live. God made all, owns all, and gives all. As Christian stewards we are responsible to God for everything that comes into our hands. God requires an accounting of our stewardship. That obligation continues to the final disposition of your estate—all of which is God's property and over which you are merely a steward. A Christian should make his legal will thoughtfully and prayerfully to see that those he loves are properly protected. Seek to know the will of God regarding the final disposition of your estate. Write the will of God into your will so that the causes you hold dear will continue to be supported. No man can tell you the will of God regarding the final disposition of your property. Only by prayerfully seeking God's leadership can you know what he wants you to do.

The acceptance of this idea would mean that each Christian would make a list of all his assets and the names of the persons or causes which he wanted to participate in his estate at his death. He would then take this list to his attorney, telling him what he wanted to accomplish in the disposition of his estate. In his will there would be a paragraph such as the following:

> I hereby give, devise, and bequeath to the_____
> _____Church of Christ (or some other worthy cause),
> at _____, the sum of $_____or the following
> properties, to wit:_____to be used in promoting the
> work of the church and the Cause of Christ. I hereby appoint and
> designate the elders of the church, or their successors, whoever
> they may be, as the executors of this my last will and testament, to
> serve without bond.

If his estate is an extensive or complicated one, it is quite possible that it would be wiser to use a bank or some other professional executor. In any case, it is fitting and proper for each Christian to remember the Cause of Christ in the disposition of his estate at the time of his death.

When we remember the Lord in our wills nothing happens at the moment, but after we are gone, it will mean that missionaries are supported who otherwise would not have support, that old people and orphans will receive care who otherwise would not have that care, that young people will be taught the Bible who otherwise would not get a Christian education, that church buildings will be built that otherwise might not be built, and that the Cause of Christ in general will be advanced beyond what would have been possible otherwise. Surely these are worthy ends and surely this is a Christian disposition of our estate. This is responsible stewardship while we live and when we die.

A fitting conclusion to this entire discussion might well be Christ's statement in Luke 6:38 which reads: ". . . give, and it shall be given unto you; good measure, pressed down, shaken together, running over, shall they give into your bosom. For with what measure ye mete it shall be measured to you again."

Gen. 1:26
plurality word us

Comforter, Counselor

2 times to apostles that they be able
to teach + spread the gospel so could
through miraclous measures

United Pentecostal Church
A person (not a thing)
spiritual being

CHAPTER TWENTY
House of Cornelius
that they are able to
teach the Gentiles
The Holy Spirit

One of the most important teachings of the Bible, yet one of the least understood, is that which pertains to the Holy Spirit. In the Old Testament the Holy Spirit is referred to some eighty-eight times; in the New Testament some two hundred and sixty-four times. Different names are also used, for sometimes he is called the Holy Spirit, sometimes the Spirit of God, and sometimes just the Spirit. Also, he sometimes is referred to as the Paraclete, the Comforter, the Helper and the Advocate. When all of these are added together there are well over four hundred references to this third person of the Godhead. Obviously, this subject is important. The number of references suggests its importance, but far more significant is the nature of the Holy Spirit.

WHO IS THE HOLY SPIRIT?

Actually, we might well begin our study with the question "Who," or, as some would say, "What is the Holy Spirit?" The answer is that he is a spiritual being, a personality like God and like Christ. He is the third person of the Godhead, which is a term used only occasionally in the New Testament. For example, the apostle Paul used this term when he addressed the ancient Athenians: ". . . we ought not to think that the Godhead is like unto gold, or silver, or stone, graven by art and device of man" (Acts 17:29). The same author also used the word in speaking of Christ when he said, ". . . in him dwelleth all the fulness of the Godhead bodily . . ." (Colossians 2:9). The scriptures indicate that the Godhead is made up of three separate personalities—God, Christ and the Holy Spirit. Each one is a part of the one divine nature or substance. The word is equivalent to the Latin word divinity, and also means the same as deity.

We find a reference to the three divine personalities who make up divinity in Matthew's statement of the great commission, where he quoted Jesus as saying, "Go ye therefore, and make disciples of all the nations, baptizing them into the name of the Father and of the Son and of the Holy Spirit" (Matthew 28:19). Another passage which links these three names in such a way as to show that they are all divine is I Corinthians 12:4-6, where we read, "Now there are diversities of gifts, but the same Spirit. And there are diversities of ministrations, and the same Lord. And there are diversities of workings, but the same God. . . ." Notice: the same Spirit, the same Lord and the same God. Still another such passage is the final sentence of the second letter that Paul wrote to the Corinthians. There we

126

Matt. 10 Limited Commission
Acts 1-2 Baptism of HS given, only to Apostles Jews + Gentile
show Authority - Only God does it water
remission of sin

read, "The grace of the Lord Jesus Christ, and the love of God, and the
communion of the Holy Spirit, be with you all" (II Corinthians 13:14).
These three separate and distinct personalities are one in the deep sense
of being divine. They make up the Godhead.

THE HOLY SPIRIT GUIDING GOD'S SPOKESMEN

As Christ prepared to leave the earth he promised to send the Holy
Spirit to guide the apostles. It was his plan to leave the apostles to establish
his kingdom and to proclaim his gospel to the whole world, but he did not
leave them alone. He sent the Holy Spirit to guide them in what they said,
what they did, and what they wrote. The gospel of John is most explicit in
making known Christ's plan. For example in John 14:16-17, Jesus was
quoted as saying:

> And I will pray the Father, and he shall give you another Comfor-
> ter, that he may be with you for ever, even the Spirit of truth:
> whom the world cannot receive; for it beholdeth him not, neither
> knoweth him: ye know him; for he abideth with you, and shall be
> in you.

Further on in this same chapter Jesus added:

> These things have I spoken unto you, while yet abiding with you.
> But the Comforter, even the Holy Spirit, whom the Father will
> send in my name, he shall teach you all things, and bring to your
> remembrance all that I said unto you.—John 14:25-26

Two chapters later Jesus was further quoted as he gave instructions to his
apostles about the coming of the Holy Spirit:

> Nevertheless I tell you the truth: It is expedient for you that I go
> away; for if I go not away, the Comforter will not come unto you;
> but if I go, I will send him unto you. And he, when he is come, will
> convict the world in respect of sin, and of righteousness, and of
> judgment.—John 16:7-8

A little later in the same chapter he added:

> I have yet many things to say unto you, but ye cannot bear them
> now. Howbeit when he, the Spirit of truth, is come, he shall guide
> you into all the truth: for he shall not speak from himself; but
> what things soever he shall hear, these shall he speak: and he shall
> declare unto you the things that are to come.—John 16:12-13

Earlier in Jesus' ministry he had told his apostles how they would be
God's spokesmen, as recorded in Matthew 10:19-20:

> But when they deliver you up, be not anxious how or what ye shall
> speak: for it shall be given you in that hour what ye shall speak.
> For it is not ye that speak, but the Spirit of your Father that
> speaketh in you.

We find numerous references in the New Testament to the fact that
the Holy Spirit guided the apostles and a certain select number of others
when they spoke. Near the close of John's gospel are the words, "And

127

when he had said this, he breathed on them, and saith unto them, Receive ye the Holy Spirit" (John 20:22). A short time later on Pentecost Sunday, the Holy Spirit guided the apostles extensively. We read:

> And suddenly there came from heaven a sound as of the rushing of a mighty wind, and it filled all the house where they were sitting. And there appeared unto them tongues parting asunder, like as of fire; and it sat upon each one of them. And they were all filled with the Holy Spirit, and began to speak with other tongues, as the Spirit gave them utterance.—Acts 2:2-4

A little later we read, "Then Peter, filled with the Holy Spirit, said unto them . . ." (Acts 4:8). Paul referred to the Holy Spirit in this manner: "But the Spirit saith expressly, that in later times some shall fall away from the faith, giving heed to seducing spirits and doctrines of demons" (I Timothy 4:1).

Notice also the apostle Peter's statement: "For no prophecy ever came by the will of man: but men spake from God, being moved by the Holy Spirit" (II Peter 1:21). Let us add a statement from Paul concerning the matter of the Holy Spirit's guidance of the writers of the scriptures. In the first Corinthian letter Paul wrote:

> But we received, not the spirit of the world, but the spirit which is from God; that we might know the things that were freely given to us of God. Which things also we speak, not in words which man's wisdom teacheth, but which the Spirit teacheth; combining spiritual things with spiritual words.—I Corinthians 2:12, 13

From these and other scriptures, we can be very sure of the work of the Holy Spirit in guiding God's spokesmen to deliver God's message. This was the most prominent work of the Holy Spirit mentioned in the scriptures.

DIFFERENT MEASURES OF THE SPIRIT

As one reads the New Testament he finds that four different measures of the power of the Holy Spirit are described. *First of all, Christ possessed the Spirit Without Measure, or without limit.* In John 3:34, 35, we read, "For he whom God hath sent speaketh the words of God: for he giveth not the Spirit by measure. The Father loveth the Son, and hath given all things into his hand." In contrast to the lesser measures of the Spirit which others had, the pioneer preacher Walter Scott described Christ's unique possession of the Spirit:

> . . . our Lord Jesus Christ had the Spirit of God . . . without measure; so that his spiritual operations were not like those of some of God's servants, limited to a single miracle, or to any number of miracles in one department of being, but were spread over every department of life—nature, society, science, art, and religion; to expel a legion of demons, or evoke a legion of angels, was the same to him. He could open the human understanding, or shut the heart; create bread, or blast a tree; subdue a colt, or

open the blind eyes, unloose the dumb tongue, or recall the dead; stay the wind, calm the storm, walk the deep, impart his power to others, and work all wonders either in person or by proxy. Every department of existence felt his power, and responded to his word; heaven and hades, the sick bed and the grave itself; the air, vegetable and animal, disease and death, men and devils, recognized in this resplendent personage, the power of the Spirit of God, and were ready to exclaim "John did no miracle, but this man does all things well." (Walter Scott, *The Messiahship Or Great Demonstration*, p. 280.)

The second manifestation of the Holy Spirit's power is that known as the Baptismal Measure, an experience which the New Testament mentions as happening on only two occasions. The first of these two occasions was that of the apostles on Pentecost. Christ "charged them not to depart from Jerusalem, but to wait for the promise of the Father . . . ye shall be baptized in the Holy Spirit not many days hence" (Acts 1:4-5). A moment later Jesus said to these same apostles, "But ye shall receive power, when the Holy Spirit is come upon you . . ." (Acts 1:8). A chapter later the Holy Spirit is described as coming upon the apostles:

And suddenly there came from heaven a sound as of the rushing of a mighty wind, and it filled all the house where they were sitting. And there appeared unto them tongues parting asunder, like as of fire; and it sat upon each one of them. And they were all filled with the Holy Spirit, and began to speak with other tongues, as the Spirit gave them utterance.—Acts 2:2-4

The scene is described in some detail, indicating that there were strangers in Jerusalem from sixteen different geographic locations, and that the Holy Spirit gave the apostles the miraculous power of speaking in such a way that every one heard them in his own native language. These visitors to Jerusalem commented, ". . . we hear them speaking in our tongues the mighty works of God" (Acts 2:11). The Holy Spirit, then, came upon the apostles, and enabled them to speak in languages which they had not previously known but which were known to various ones in their audience.

Notice that they did not speak in "unknown tongues" but in real languages which were known to their hearers. No one, if we may anticipate something that we shall want to say again later, is able to do that today. This striking miracle on Pentecost served two purposes: first, it was an authentication or endorsement from God showing that these men were his spokesmen and that what they said was his message. In the second place, their speaking in unlearned languages overcame the difficult problem of the language barrier.

The only other place in the New Testament where we read of the Baptismal Measure of the Holy Spirit is in the case of the conversion of the Roman centurion, Cornelius, a Gentile. This man and his family became

Eph. 1:13-14
guarantee of our inheritance

129

Christians in the usual way, as described in Acts 10:44-47, but in the telling of the story Luke indicated that the Holy Spirit fell upon them, again showing God's endorsement, again authenticating what occurred. On Pentecost the Jews had spoken other languages. In the case of the conversion of Cornelius, Gentiles spoke other languages. The outpouring or baptism of the Holy Spirit on the second occasion was to show to the Jews, to whom such a thing was unthinkable, that Gentiles also were welcome in God's kingdom, the church. It took this spectacular miracle to settle for all time the fact that God is not a respecter of persons but that all men are welcome. Never in all of the New Testament do we read of another outpouring or Baptismal Measure of the Holy Spirit.

The third measure of the power of the Holy Spirit is the Miraculous Measure, which was given to a select and limited number of people. The Lord needed messengers to proclaim his gospel and he needed to help make their message believable, so he gave them special powers through the laying on of the apostles' hands. In Acts 8:18, we read, "Now when Simon saw that through the laying on of the apostles' hands the Holy Spirit was given, he offered them money. . . ." In Acts 19:6, we find this additional statement, "And when Paul [an apostle] had laid his hands upon them, the Holy Spirit came on them; and they spake with tongues, and prophesied." We find still another example in II Timothy 1:6, where the apostle Paul wrote to Timothy, ". . . I put thee in remembrance that thou stir up the gift of God, which is in thee through the laying on of my hands."

We would make two special observations at this point. First, this miracle-working power of the Holy Spirit was needed during the first century, when the church was not yet fully formed and when the inspired New Testament was not yet complete, in order to authenticate the message that was being preached. We do not have the same conditions or needs today, so it is logical to believe that this miraculous working of the Holy Spirit has not been extended to our time. The apostle Paul, guided by the Holy Spirit, wrote to the Corinthian church concerning the termination of these special miraculous gifts: "Love never faileth: but whether there be prophecies, they shall be done away; whether there be tongues, they shall cease; whether there be knowledge it shall be done away." Then, in contrast to these miraculous acts which were temporary, he spoke of the things that would be permanent during the Christian regime: "But now abideth faith, hope, love, these three; and the greatest of these is love" (I Corinthians 13:8, 13).

Our second observation is that since these special miraculous powers of the Holy Spirit were given by the laying on of apostolic hands, it follows that these gifts would last only until the death of the last apostle and the death of those upon whom the apostles had laid their hands. We have no scriptural evidence that this miracle-working power of the Holy Spirit continued beyond the apostolic age. The need for these miraculous powers no longer existed. The apostles who could convey this power no longer were alive. So, gradually, as these specially chosen human instruments of God died, these miraculous powers ceased, just as the need for them had passed away.

Finally, the fourth measure of the Holy Spirit's power is that which we may call the Ordinary or Normal Measure. This was promised to the early Christians on Pentecost in these words: "Repent ye, and be baptized every one of you in the name of Jesus Christ unto the remission of your sins; and ye shall receive the gift of the Holy Spirit" (Acts 2:38). J. W. McGarvey, an outstanding Bible scholar of the last century, said concerning this passage, "The expression means the Holy Spirit as a gift; and the reference is to that indwelling of the Holy Spirit by which we bring forth the fruits of the Spirit, and without which we are not of Christ." (*Commentary on Acts*, p. 39.) There are other plain passages which indicate that the Holy Spirit is to dwell within all faithful Christians. Acts 5:32 reads, "And we are witnesses of these things; and so is the Holy Spirit, whom God hath given to them that obey him." The Holy Spirit, then, comes as a gift to all those who obey the Lord's commands. To this agrees Paul's statement, "Or know ye not that your body is a temple of the Holy Spirit which is in you, which ye have from God? and ye are not your own; for ye were bought with a price: glorify God therefore in your body" (I Corinthians 6:19-20).

How the Holy Spirit Dwells in Christians

Many other scriptures indicate that the Holy Spirit in the Normal or Ordinary Measure dwells within all faithful Christians. In fact, the Holy Spirit dwells in the Christian just as God and Christ dwell in the Christian. We see this, for example, in the Roman letter, chapter 8, where we read:

> But ye are not in the flesh but in the Spirit, if so be that the Spirit of God dwelleth in you. But if any man hath not the Spirit of Christ, he is none of his. . . . But if the Spirit of him that raised up Jesus from the dead dwelleth in you, he that raised up Christ Jesus from the dead shall give life also to your mortal bodies through his Spirit that dwelleth in you.—Romans 8:9, 11

To the Thessalonians Paul wrote, "Therefore he that rejecteth, rejecteth not man, but God, who giveth his Holy Spirit unto you" (I Thessalonians 4:8). To the Ephesians the same apostle wrote:

> . . . in whom ye also, having heard the word of the truth, the gospel of your salvation,—in whom, having also believed, ye were sealed with the Holy Spirit of promise, which is an earnest of our inheritance, unto the redemption of God's own possession, unto the praise of his glory.—Ephesians 1:13, 14

In this same letter there are these additional words: "And grieve not the Holy Spirit of God, in whom ye were sealed unto the day of redemption" (Ephesians 4:30).

131

In our day there are sometimes heated discussions about just how the Holy Spirit dwells in Christians. We like the words of the fine Biblical scholar, Gus Nichols:

> I see no reason for disturbance among us over this question so long as all believe and teach that the Holy Spirit **does** dwell in faithful and obedient children of God in some way. The honest but misguided interpretations which may be made in trying to show how the Spirit dwells in us should not by those on either side, disrupt brotherly love and unity . . . to all who obey the gospel from the heart, the promise will be fulfilled as God planned it, whether or not we understand "how" the Spirit dwells in us. (*Lectures on the Holy Spirit*, pp. 155-156.)

The same writer added:

> Some say they cannot comprehend the Holy Spirit's being in all faithful Christians. It is a matter of faith. I cannot comprehend the soul, or spirit, which dwells in me, anymore than I can the idea of any such Being as the Holy Spirit—but I believe it. I cannot comprehend the infinity of space, nor gravity, atoms, the wind, a thought, and other things invisible. But I believe! (pp. 165-166.)

WHAT DOES THE HOLY SPIRIT DO FOR CHRISTIANS TODAY?

John Banister, in his fine lecture, "The Indwelling of the Holy Spirit," pointed out some of the significance of the fact that the Holy Spirit dwells in Christians. *(Abilene Christian College Bible Lectures*, 1957, pp. 60-70.) Here are some of the points which he presents in enumerating the results of that indwelling:

(1) *The indwelling of the Holy Spirit is an evidence of our sonship.* "The Spirit himself beareth witness with our spirit, that we are children of God . . ." (Romans 8:16). "And because ye are sons, God sent forth the Spirit of his Son into our hearts . . ." (Galatians 4:6). "And hereby we know that he abideth in us, by the Spirit which he gave us" (I John 3:24). The apostle Paul in the Ephesian letter wrote, ". . . ye were sealed with the Holy Spirit of promise . . ." (Ephesians 1:13). This word "sealed" may be interpreted to mean something like the word "trademark"—a sign of ownership. In ancient times jars of wine were sealed with the seal of the owner of the vineyard. The seal of the Holy Spirit is a guarantee that a person belongs to God.

(2) *The indwelling of the Holy Spirit gives strength and help in our Christian living.* In Ephesians 3:14-16, there is this language: "For this cause I bow my knees unto the Father . . . that ye may be strengthened with power through his Spirit in the inward man. . . ." Paul also wrote, "For I know that this shall turn out to my salvation, through your supplication and the supply of the Spirit of Jesus Christ . . . ." (Philippians 1:19.) Then, there is this statement, ". . . if by the Spirit ye put to death the deeds of the body, ye shall live" (Romans 8:13). Obviously, we receive strength and help from the Holy Spirit in our desire to live the Christian life.

132

(3) *The indwelling of the Holy Spirit means that the Holy Spirit helps us in our prayers.* We read:

> And in like manner the Spirit also helpeth our infirmity: for we know not how to pray as we ought; but the Spirit himself maketh intercession for us with groanings which cannot be uttered; and he that searcheth the hearts knoweth what is the mind of the Spirit, because he maketh intercession for the saints according to the will of God.—Romans 8:26-27

The Holy Spirit helps us in our prayers, rather than praying for us apart from our own prayers.

(4) *The indwelling of the Holy Spirit produces good fruit in us.* Paul wrote to the Galatians, "But the fruit of the Spirit is love, joy, peace, longsuffering, kindness, goodness, faithfulness, meekness, self-control; against such there is no law" (Galatians 5:22-23). All of us have known people who had special spiritual qualities and we refer to them as "spiritually minded people." This means that God's word, which the Spirit brings, had entered into their hearts and lives and had produced the fruit of which we have just read. The Holy Spirit dwells in such a person to a greater degree than in others. This faithful Christian does not work miracles, but in the normal, ordinary affairs of life he shows that the Spirit has come into his life.

(5) *The indwelling of the Holy Spirit is an incentive to holiness.* When we pause to realize the rich significance of the statement, "Know ye not that ye are a temple of God, and that the Spirit of God dwelleth in you?" (I Corinthians 3:16), we are encouraged to so use our bodies as not to disgrace ourselves and disappoint God. We are encouraged to live clean, pure lives by the realization that God's Spirit dwells within us.

(6) *The indwelling of the Holy Spirit inspires hope in us.* Again, we notice Paul's words to the Romans: "Now the God of hope fill you with all joy and peace in believing, that ye may abound in hope, in the power of the Holy Spirit" (Romans 15:13).

(7) *The indwelling of the Holy Spirit is a guarantee or pledge of eternal life.* "Now he that wrought us for this very thing is God, who gave unto us the earnest of the Spirit" (II Corinthians 5:5). The word used here is the Greek word *arrabon* and can be translated as pledge, or earnest, or seal. It is the regular Greek word of business for the first installment of a price or fee, as a token guarantee that a full payment will follow. Paul is telling us that the indwelling of the Holy Spirit is an advance payment, or a foretaste, or a guarantee that God will fulfill his promise to his faithful followers and that they will one day live in his presence in heaven.

With these very real blessings coming into our lives as a result of the Holy Spirit dwelling within us, what should be our attitude toward this great blessing? Negatively, it should be an attitude which leads us not to indulge the flesh, nor to quench, nor to grieve, the Holy Spirit within us.

133

In Ephesians 4:30, there are these words, "Grieve not the Holy Spirit of God, in whom ye were sealed unto the day of redemption." Positively, our attitude should be that we will "Walk by the Spirit," be "led by the Spirit," bear "the fruit of the Spirit," and "live by the Spirit," to borrow expressions from Paul. (Galatians 5:16, 18, 22, 25.)

CONCLUSION

During this study we have discovered that the Lord himself possessed the Holy Spirit *Without Measure*, that on two occasions the Holy Spirit was poured out in the *Baptismal Measure*, that on numerous occasions the apostles laid their hands on a certain select few who were empowered with the *Miraculous Measure* of the Holy Spirit, and then, most meaningful to us, we have discovered that the Holy Spirit was promised to all Christians in the *Ordinary* or *Normal Measure*. What this means is that after the apostolic era, which ended during the first century, we do not find the Baptismal Measure, nor the Miraculous Measure of the Holy Spirit. We do have promised to Christians of all times the Normal or Ordinary Measure of the Spirit.

Barton W. Stone wrote concerning this:

> It is this Spirit in Christians that supports them in all the ills of life, and causes them to triumph in death. It not only helps our infirmities, for we know not what we should pray for as we ought, but the Spirit maketh intercession for us with groanings which cannot be uttered. As this Spirit in us begets the holy temper of love, joy, peace, so it begets the disposition and spirit of prayer. (*Christian Messenger*, June 1842, p. 249.)

Moses E. Lard wrote, "We need the Holy Spirit, then, to strengthen us with might in the inner man; we need it to help our infirmities, we need it to intercede for us. . . ." He said that there is "no just ground on which to deny the literal indwelliing of the Spirit." (*Lard's Quarterly*, March 1864, pp. 239, 241.) Alexander Campbell wrote:

> Christians are, therefore, clearly and unequivocally temples of the Holy Spirit; and they are quickened, animated, encouraged, and sanctified by the power and influence of the Spirit of God, working in them through the truth. . . . To those, then, who believe, repent, and obey the gospel, he actually communicates of his Good Spirit. (*Christian System*, pp. 49-50.)

CHAPTER TWENTY-ONE
The Gifts of the Holy Spirit

Because of the special interest in the gifts of the Holy Spirit in our time, and because a significant number of people claim to possess one or another of these gifts, it is important that we examine the scriptures to see what they teach about these miraculous powers. They are listed in I Corinthians 12:4-11. Since all of these gifts are miraculous gifts, it is important that we spend a few moments in studying the subject of miracles, as revealed in the New Testament.

Exactly what is a miracle? *Webster's New Collegiate Dictionary* defines a miracle as "An event or effect in the physical world deviating from the known laws of nature, or transcending our knowledge of these laws; . . . a wonder or wonderful thing; a marvel" (p. 536). This definition is in keeping with the average man's use of the word in normal conversation. He speaks of man's landing on the moon and safe return to earth as a miracle. Earlier he called radio and television miracles. This, however, is not at all the meaning of the word miracle as used in the scriptures.

C. S. Lewis of Oxford in his book, *Miracles,* defines a miracle as "an interference with Nature by supernatural power" (p. 15). While this is a good definition, a more complete definition is to be found in *The Westminster Dictionary of the Bible:* ". . . miracles are events in the external world, wrought by the immediate power of God and intended as a sign or attestation. They are possible because God sustains, controls, and guides all things, and is personal and omnipotent" (p. 399). This definition suggests that supernatural power (God) occasionally does something beyond the ordinary. This is the Biblical explanation of miracles.

PURPOSE OF MIRACLES

The primary purpose of the miracles performed by the people mentioned in the Bible is to create faith. For example, the American Standard Version of the gospel according to John refers to miracles as signs. This was a careful choice of words, for they were signs pointing toward something—the divinity of Christ. Near the end of his account of the life of Christ, John stated in an unmistakable way the real purpose behind miracles: "Many other signs therefore did Jesus in the presence of the disciples, which are not written in this book: but these are written, that ye may believe that Jesus is the Christ, the Son of God; and that believing ye may have life in his name" (John 20:30-31). The primary purpose of miracles, in both Old and New Testaments, was to create faith.

In the New Testament we discover that there are two sources of miraculous power: (1) The baptism of the Holy Spirit, which is mentioned as happening only twice, as indicated in the preceding chapter. And (2) The laying on of the apostles' hands, as mentioned in Acts 8:14-19. When the last apostle died, it would follow, this power to convey miracle-working power upon others became extinct.

MIRACLES TO CEASE

No single passage of scripture has been discussed more often in connection with the end of the miracle-working period of the church than I Corinthians 13:8-11. Chapter twelve of this book lists the nine miraculous gifts of the Holy Spirit; chapter fourteen continues the discussion. Chapter thirteen contains the apostle Paul's beautiful tribute to love, placed in the book to quiet the jealousy over spiritual gifts among the Corinthian Christians. These gifts at Corinth can be traced back to the apostle Paul (II Corinthians 12:12).

In understanding this important passage, we should begin by recognizing the two opposing positions. (1) One view holds that I Corinthians 13:8-11 refers to the end of time when Christ shall return to call the righteous to heaven. (2) The other view holds that the passage refers to the time when the New Testament church had been completely formed and the New Tesament completely written. It is the second view which we believe to be taught clearly in this passage. With all of the teachings concerning how one becomes a Christian, how the church is to be organized and governed, and how Christians are to live and worship clearly set forth in the scriptures, it can be said that the church and its divine blueprint are fully formed, complete and perfect.

Notice the text:

Love never faileth: but whether there be prophecies, they shall be done away; whether there be tongues, they shall cease; whether there be knowledge, it shall be done away. For we know in part, and we prophesy in part; but when that which is perfect is come, that which is in part shall be done away. When I was a child, I spake as a child, I felt as a child, I thought as a child: now that I am become a man, I have put away childish things. For now we see in a mirror, darkly; but then face to face: now I know in part; but then shall I know fully even as also I was fully known. But now abideth faith, hope, love, these three; and the greatest of these is love.—I Corinthians 13:8-13

If this passage does refer to the end of time, why does it single out only the miraculous acts of prophecies, tongues, knowledge, and not the other gifts of the Holy Spirit? If it refers to the end of time, then all things that pertain to this earth will end. Why mention only these miraculous acts? Evidently, therefore, the passage is saying that there will come a time when the gifts of the Holy Spirit will terminate, and other Christian activities continue.

136

A look at the expression "that which is perfect" in verse ten is also helpful. The original Greek *to telion* which is translated into English as "that which is perfect" literally means "to bring to completion, finish, carry through, make perfect," according to standard lexicons. Abbott-Smith's *Manual Greek Lexicon of the New Testament* defines *teleios* as "*having reached its end, finished, mature, complete, perfect. 1. Of persons, primarily of physical development. 2. Of things, complete, perfect.*" *The Analytical Greek Lexicon* defines the word under consideration as "*brought to completion, fully accomplished, fully developed, . . . complete, entire,* as opposed to what is partial and limited [I Corinthians 13:10] . . ." (p. 400). Now a question: Do these definitions sound like the fullgrown church and the completed New Testament scriptures, or do they sound like the end of time and Christ's return? Richard Trench in his *Synonyms of the New Testament,* wrote, "In a natural sense the *teleioi* are the adult (sic), who, having attained the full limits of stature, strength and mental power . . ." (p. 75). A. T. Robertson, commenting on I Corinthians 13:10, indicated the meaning to be "the perfect, the full-grown . . . , the mature." (*Word Pictures in the New Testament,* p. 179.)

Hence, we can conclude with confidence that the passage is saying that while life goes on here on the earth the miraculous gifts of the Holy Spirit will cease. When the church and the New Testament are complete, fully formed, and in that sense perfect, the miracles will no longer be needed. The final sentence of the passage seems to indicate this also. After the complete or perfect is come, there is the indication that faith and hope and love will still continue. Faith will end at the end of time, for in the life beyond, faith will be sight. Hope will end with the end of time, for in the life to come, hope will be realization. The gifts of the Holy Spirit will have ceased while there are yet faith and hope, meaning while time yet continues here on the earth.

A simple illustration will convey what we believe the scriptures teach. When a large and important building is constructed there is an imperative need for extensive scaffolding. When the building is complete, however, the scaffolding is removed and the building stands free. In the construction period of the Lord's church there was a need for miracles to authenticate the messengers and the message. However, when the church was fully formed and when the New Testament was fully written, the scaffolding (the miraculous) was no longer needed and was removed.

WHAT ABOUT SPEAKING IN TONGUES?

Because this particular manifestation has been especially interesting to people of our time, let us examine modern-day speaking in tongues, or *glossolalia.* Tongue-speaking is a phenomenon mentioned in only three New Testament books: Mark, Acts, and I Corinthians. The Greek word *glossa* occurs fifty times in the New Testament with various usages, and in twenty-five of these cases it describes the phenomenon of speaking in tongues. This miraculous act was evidence of the presence and activity of the Holy Spirit on the day of Pentecost when the church began (Acts 2:1-4). The Holy Spirit manifested himself through speaking in tongues at the household of Cornelius, thus indicating that Gentiles were also welcome in Christ's church (Acts 10:44-48). Spiritual gifts, including speaking in tongues, were also exercised through the power of the Holy Spirit by certain members of the Corinthian church (I Corinthians 12-14). There is no question but that this was a genuine phenomenon in the apostolic period of the church.

Let us examine the New Testament to see if we can determine exactly what was meant by speaking in tongues in apostolic times. It is significant that the glossolalia of Biblical history, a gift of the Holy Spirit, produced in men the ability to speak words that were readily understood and which evoked the question from their hearers, ". . . are not all these that speak Galilaeans? And how hear we, every man in our own language wherein we were born?" (Acts 2:7, 8). On the other hand, the tongue-speaking of our own day grows out of an intense excitement whereby a peculiar ecstatic and completely unintelligible utterance pours forth from the person who is highly and emotionally charged. Points of difference between the original Pentecostal tongue-speaking and modern-day glossolalia are rather marked. The apostolic variety was characterized by clarity and intelligibility, while the modern variety is characterized by random syllables which carry no rational message.

It is generally agreed by almost all Biblical scholars that the tongue-speaking of Pentecost, described in Acts 2, was a case in which the apostles spoke languages which they had not learned, but which were understood by the different groups in their audience. When Christ commissioned his apostles to go into all the world and preach the gospel to every creature, they needed help along two very important lines. First, they could not, without divine help, carry out the commission to preach to all men when they did not understand the languages of the many different national and racial groups. So Christ promised them that the Holy Spirit would enable them to "speak with new tongues" (Mark 16:15-20). The Lord did not want to wait forty or fifty years after Pentecost till the New Testament would be written, and have it translated into all languages before getting the gospel started to all nations in their own tongues. The barrier in the way was overcome by the baptism of the Holy Spirit, enabling the apostles to speak in other tongues or languages (Acts 2:1-11). The apostles were also given the power to lay their hands on others and thus enable them to speak with tongues (Acts 8:18; 19:6). This miraculous gift enabled these specially selected men to convey the precious gospel message to those who spoke and understood only other languages.

The second need was for some kind of authentication or endorsement of the message which would prove that it was truly from God. This miraculous gift, speaking in unlearned languages, certainly was an evidence that the men who spoke had been given a divine gift. Such gifts proved to unbelieving men that God was back of the truth being taught (I Corinthians 14:21-25).

That speaking in tongues was not intended as a prominent and permanent part of Christian activity was pointed out quite convincingly by the perceptive Biblical scholar, H. Leo Boles, who wrote:

> There are eight writers of the New Testament—Matthew, Mark, Luke, Peter, Paul, James, John and Jude. There are twenty-seven books of the New Testament; there are twenty-one books or letters written to individual Christians, churches, and groups of churches. Paul wrote thirteen or fourteen of these letters. There are twenty-seven churches mentioned by name in the New Testament. Paul is the only writer who discussed the gift of speaking with other tongues. He wrote not a word on the subject of tongues to the church at Rome, Ephesus, Colosse, Thessalonica, Philippi or the churches in Galatia. He wrote a letter or letters to all of these churches, but said nothing about the gift of speaking in tongues. Neither did he mention the subject in his Epistles to Timothy, Titus, or Philemon. James did not mention the speaking of tongues in his general Epistle; John, who wrote five books of the New Testament, does not mention the subject. Even Peter, the spokesman on the day of Pentecost, who evidently had the gift of speaking with tongues, did not mention the subject in writing his two letters. It is a strange omission indeed if the gift of tongues was an essential part of the Christian experience or if it was to be perpetuated in the church of the Lord's people. (*The Holy Spirit*, pp. 179-180.)

What Is This Present-Day Phenomenon?

If modern glossolalia is not the same phenomenon as that found in the scriptures, then what is it? Dr. Stuart Bergsma, a graduate of Rush Medical College of the University of Chicago, a medical missionary in Ethiopia and later India, now Superintendent of a hospital for the mentally ill and disturbed, a respected medical doctor and a psychiatrist, has written:

> I wish to reiterate my division of glossolalia into two categories: (1) Authentic, miraculous, Pentecost-day, apostle-Paul endorsed glossolalia in which a revelation from God is uttered in an authentic, recognizable, verifiable language not previously consciously known to the glossolalist speaker; and (2) Later, modern glossolalia, a secular unintelligible, devoid-of-any message type glossolalia, which for brevity's sake I call 'modern glossolalia.'

Bergsma then summarized:

> . . . Almost without exception authors writing on modern glossolalia and psychologists studying glossolalists, regard the phe-

nomenon as a neurotic manifestation, another neurosis of our modern age following, in general, a pattern laid down long before and during the psychoneurotic hysterical middle ages. (*Speaking With Tongues,* pp. 14-15.)

We would summarize what we believe to be the right position on this whole matter by asking: If miraculous spiritual gifts are still available today, why are not all of them available? Why did the New Testament writers not mention the gift of tongues more often and teach about it more widely? Why do devout missionaries (who need to speak in foreign languages) not have this gift? Why do modern glossolalists seek the least valuable gift? Why pray for this gift when the scriptures indicate that spiritual gifts were to cease? Why do the best informed Bible students and the more spiritually mature Christians not have this gift?

As we have seen in the previous chapter, the Normal or Ordinary Measure of the Holy Spirit, the indwelling of the Holy Spirit, is real. One should not allow an extreme claim on the part of some to cause him to deny the value or the reality of the Holy Spirit in his life. This leads us to say again that those who are Christians are greatly blessed, not only by the promises of an eternal life to come, but by the great encouragement and strength which the Holy Spirit provides in our lives here and now.

CHAPTER TWENTY-TWO

Fellowship

The theme of love, fellowship and unity among Christians occupies a very prominent place in the New Testament. On the night of his betrayal, Jesus prayed fervently for the apostles and then broadened the circle of his concern in these words:

> Neither for these only do I pray, but for them also that believe on me through their word; that they may all be one; even as thou, Father, art in me, and I in thee, that they also may be in us: that the world may believe that thou didst send me.—John 17:20-21

A little earlier Jesus had said, "A new commandment I give unto you, that ye love one another; even as I have loved you, that ye also love one another. By this shall all men know that ye are my disciples, if ye have love one to another" (John 13:34-35). These statements from the Lord, late in his ministry, indicate very clearly the closeness which he desired among his disciples. Christian fellowship is one of the clearest indications that a congregation and the individuals who make up that congregation are truly Christian. Whenever there are schisms, rivalries and divisions the essential spirit of Christianity has been forgotten.

The apostle Paul, like the apostle John just quoted, wrote extensively on this theme, using a significant portion of one of his letters, I Corinthians 12:12-27, to point out that the church is like a body. Just as there are many members in our physical bodies, each having its own particular function and responsibility, so in the body of Christ there are many members who must cooperate together in order for the body to function properly. As in our physical body, no member is unimportant, no member is unneeded. Each contributes to the well-being of the entire body.

This emphasis was continued in Paul's letter to the Galatians, where he said, "Bear ye one another's burdens, and so fulfill the law of Christ." A moment later he added, "So then, as we have opportunity, let us work that which is good toward all men, and especially toward them that are of the household of the faith" (Galatians 6:2, 10). A little earlier in the same book he had written, "There can be neither Jew nor Greek, there can be neither bond nor free, there can be no male and female; for ye all are one man in Christ Jesus" (Galatians 3:28).

The apostle Peter added, "Finally, be ye all likeminded, compassionate, loving as brethren, tenderhearted, humbleminded . . . ." (I Peter 3:8). A chapter later we find, ". . . above all things being fervent in your love among yourselves; for love covereth a multitude of sins: using hospitality one to another without murmuring . . ." (I Peter 4:8-9).

This was also a favorite emphasis of the apostle John who wrote:

> Beloved, let us love one another: for love is of God; and every one that loveth is begotten of God, and knoweth God. . . . Beloved, if God so loved us, we also ought to love one another. . . . If a man say, I love God, and hateth his brother, he is a liar: for he that loveth not his brother whom he hath seen, cannot love God whom he hath not seen. And this commandment have we from him, that he who loveth God love his brother also.—I John 4:7, 11, 20, 21

All of these passages help to convey the picture of the family of God, living and working together in such a manner that each is strengthened by the others. Just as a fine Christian family shares both burdens and joys, so the members of God's family share each other's joys and sorrows. The strong help the weak. The older and more mature contribute to the younger and less mature, but the reverse is also true, for the younger sustain and strengthen the older. The rich help the poor. Love and fellowship are among the greatest blessings that man can know on earth and these are to be found in the Lord's church to a degree found nowhere else.

BROKEN FELLOWSHIP

Tragically, there are times when this ideal Christian fellowship is broken. Always when such is the case there is sorrow. Something has gone wrong. Someone has forgotten the Lord's instructions.

Sometimes the break in fellowship is a result of a Christian's abandonment of the faith. Paul referred to such a case when he said, "Demas forsook me, having loved this present world, and went to Thessalonica . . . ." (II Timothy 4:10). The temptations of the flesh caused some to fall away. Persecution caused still others to abandon their first love. Jesus had anticipated this, as indicated in his parable of the sower in which he warned of the dangers of "tribulation or persecution" and "the care of the world, and the deceitfulness of riches" (Matthew 13:21-22). Peter also warned against apostasy, as he wrote, "Be sober, be watchful: your adversary the devil, as a roaring lion, walketh about, seeking whom he may devour" (I Peter 5:8). In the final book of the Bible is this charge from the Lord himself, "Be thou faithful unto death, and I will give thee the crown of life" (Revelation 2:10). In succeeding centuries the problem became a serious one in times of heavy persecution. While many Christians remained faithful until death, there were others who let their religion lapse, denying under pressure that they were Christians. They came to be known as the "Lapsis."

In the pagan city of Corinth, after the church was established, the apostle Paul singled out a Christian who had slipped back from Christian morality into pagan immorality. It was a case of incest, and Paul recommended severe discipline as he wrote, "to deliver such a one unto Satan for the destruction of the flesh, that the spirit may be saved in the day of the Lord Jesus." He went on to say, "Know ye not that a little leaven leaventh the whole lump? Purge out the old leaven, that ye may be a new lump . . ." (I Corinthians 5:5-7).

Sometimes the apostasy was a departure from Christian doctrine, rather than a departure from Christian morals. There are numerous warnings throughout the New Testament against false teachers. One of the clearest examples of serious erroneous teaching is that referred to in II John. Notice the severity of the discipline, a complete disfellowshiping of the false teachers:

> Whosoever goeth onward and abideth not in the teaching of Christ, hath not God: he that abideth in the teaching, the same hath both the Father and the Son. If any one cometh unto you, and bringeth not this teaching, receive him not into your house, and give him no greeting: for he that giveth him greeting partaketh in his evil works.—II John 9-11

In this case the heresy was the doctrine that Jesus had not come in the flesh, or in human form. John branded this doctrine as heresy and taught that those who held it should be disfellowshipped.

CHURCH DISCIPLINE

There is only one method of church discipline. It is the *withdrawal of fellowship*. Perhaps the clearest case found in the New Testament is that referred to above—the man at Corinth who was guilty of incest. In addition to the text already cited, we find this recommendation of the apostle Paul:

> . . . I wrote unto you not to keep company, if any man that is named a brother be a fornicator, or covetous, or an idolator, or a reviler, or a drunkard, or an extortioner; with such a one no, not to eat. . . . Put away the wicked man from among yourselves.—I Corinthians 5:11, 13

The primary motive for this withdrawal of fellowship—not eating with the sinful Christian—is to save the sinner. In II Corinthians 2:5-11, we find the apostle Paul writing about the man of whom he had spoken in the earlier letter, saying, ". . . ye should rather forgive him and comfort him, lest by any means such a one should be swallowed up with his overmuch sorrow. Wherefore I beseech you to confirm your love toward him." In other words, the man had been led to repentance and now it was time to restore fellowship with him.

II Thessalonians 3:6, 14-15, adds emphasis:

> Now we command you, brethren, in the name of our Lord Jesus Christ, that ye withdraw yourselves from every brother that walketh disorderly, and not after the tradition which they received of

us. . . . And if any man obeyeth not our word by this epistle, note that man, that ye have no company with him, to the end that he may be ashamed. And yet count him not as an enemy, but admonish him as a brother.

To this add Galatians 6:1, "Brethren, even if a man be overtaken in any trespass, ye who are spiritual, restore such a one in a spirit of gentleness; looking to thyself, lest thou also be tempted." Finally, on this point James said, "My brethren, if any among you err from the truth, and one convert him; let him know, that he who converteth a sinner from the error of his way shall save a soul from death, and shall cover a multitude of sins" (James 5:19-20).

There is yet another motive for administering church discipline. It is to protect the church. Discipline is often needed because there are hypocrites in the church. Negligent Christians undermine the influence of the Lord in his church and therefore need to be disciplined. Inadequately taught Christians may leave the wrong impression on those outside the body of Christ and thereby hinder the church. They need admonition and teaching. We find this emphasis in Romans 16:17-18:

Now I beseech you, brethren, mark them that are causing the divisions and occasions of stumbling, contrary to the doctrine which ye learned: and turn away from them. For they that are such serve not our Lord Christ, but their own belly; and by their smooth and fair speech they beguile the hearts of the innocent.

We might well remember, though the circumstances were vastly different, that because of the damage being done to the model church at Jerusalem severe punishment was administered to Ananias and Sapphira. God, who knew their hearts and lives as no mere man can know the heart and life of another man, simply caused them to fall down dead, because they had lied to the Holy Spirit (Acts 5). This is not a type of discipline that could be administered by anyone other than God himself, but it does demonstrate that there are times when discipline must be meted out because of the damage being done to the church itself.

It is difficult to understand why in the church today there is so little discipline administered. One wonders why. The answer may lie in the fact that it is extremely difficult to know *what* to do and also *how* to do it. We cannot be unsympathetic to elders who find it difficult to take the lead in this extremely perilous undertaking. Also, it is likely true that the most godly men feel unworthy to correct others. Their humility leads them to turn away from the condemnation of others who really need some kind of discipline. And, of course, men who are not good cannot administer discipline because of the impediment of their own lives. Still further, there is little teaching either from the pulpit or in classes on this subject of discipline. All of these combine to lead the church today to be relatively inactive in the important sphere of administering discipline. Let all of us resolve to be more concerned in our homes and in the church to love those who are violating God's rules enough to administer the discipline which they need in order to help them be saved.

SUMMARY

Fellowship is love, trust and devotion built upon agreement upon the basic principles of the Christian faith (I Corinthians 15:1-4; 1 John 1:1-4). The New Testament abounds in pictures of full fellowship among Christians. This was true at the very beginning of the church (Acts 2:43-47), when they "had all things common." The ideal is pictured in I Corinthians 1:10, when Christians are in full agreement with each other. Submission to the Lord and his teachings is the key to fellowship, for when all are following the Lord, they will find that they are in step with each other. The absence of fellowship is also described in the scriptures. I Corinthians 1:10-13 gives a sad picture of the beginning of the fractioning of the church at Corinth, which down through the centuries has come to its full flower in the multiple denominations which exist today. Galatians 1:6-9 and II John 9-11 also reflect the absence of Christian fellowship.

It is possible to describe Christian fellowship as full, partial, or none at all. An example of full fellowship would be that of the early Jerusalem church (Acts 2:42). An example of partial fellowship is found in the case of John Mark, over whom Paul and Barnabas had a division of judgment (Acts 15:37-41). Paul felt that Mark was unworthy to be taken as a companion on his second journey, because of his failure to complete the earlier journey. Barnabas felt differently, so the two great leaders went separate ways. There was no disfellowshiping in the full sense of considering each other displeasing to Christ or teaching and practicing false doctrine, but simply a sharp difference in judgment. An example of the absence of any fellowship at all is that recommended by the apostle John in II John 9-11.

Christians should work diligently "to keep the unity of the Spirit in the bond of peace" (Ephesians 4:3), as expressed by the apostle Paul to the Ephesians. The love of God and the love of one's fellow Christians provides the motivation for Christian fellowship. As Christians love God they learn his will and follow that will, thus walking in step with each other. As they love their fellowmen, they are too concerned for each other to allow quarrels and divisions to arise.

SUGGESTIONS RELATED TO CHRISTIAN FELLOWSHIP
To STIMULATE THOUGHT AND DISCUSSION

1. The Christian must love all men sincerely. Matthew 5:43-44; Mark 12:29-31; John 13:34-35; Romans 13:8.
2. The Christian should seek agreement and fellowship with everyone with whom he can scripturally do so. Matthew 5:25; Romans 12:9-10; Romans 14:19.

3. The Christian should approach fellowship with humility. Matthew 23.
4. The Christian should be willing to "search the scriptures" to be certain that what he himself believes is right, realizing that all human beings can be wrong. John 5:39; Acts 17:11; Acts 23:1; Acts 26:9; I Corinthians 10:12; II Timothy 2:15; I Peter 3:15.
5. The Christian should have a longing to know the truth and to teach the truth. John 8:32; Ephesians 4:15.
6. The Christian should be willing to discuss religious differences with anyone. Colossians 4:6; I Thessalonians 5:21; I Peter 3:15.
7. The Christian should carefully listen to and have respect for other people's views, and then evaluate them according to the scriptures.
8. The Christian may go along with any man who is in the right, stay with him as long as he is right, and leave him when he goes wrong. I Thessalonians 5:21-22; Titus 3:9.
9. The Christian must not judge others—only God can judge. Matthew 7:1-2; John 7:24; Romans 14:4.
10. The Christian should not extend fellowship which will encourage religious error. Romans 16:17; II Corinthians 6:14-18; I Thessalonians 5:22; II Thessalonians 3:6, II John 9-11.
11. The Christian should not extend fellowship which will undermine his ultimate influence for the Lord.
12. In order to have fellowship we must ask ourselves: do we violate any principles of the Bible? Will this improve or destroy our Christian influence in the community? And will it be for the good or betterment of others? The disfellowshiping of others should be motivated either by a desire for the good of the person disfellowshiped or the good of the church. Acts 5:1-11; I Corinthians 5:5-7.
13. The Christian should be careful not to bind on others that which is in the realm of opinion. Matthew 23:1-5; I Corinthians 8:1-10; Galatians 2:1-5.
14. The basic principles on which fellowship is to be determined are whether or not a person believes in God, the divinity of Christ, and the inspiration of the Bible, and has been baptized for the remission of sins as described in the New Testament.
15. Merely being overcome with sin does not remove one from the church.
16. The Christian should rely heavily upon prayer and the study of God's word.

CHAPTER TWENTY-THREE
That They May Be One

Because of its great importance let us read again that portion of Christ's prayer on the night before his crucifixion which deals with his earnest longing for unity among the apostles and among his disciples in the ages to come:

> Neither for these only do I pray, but for them also that believe on me through their word; that they may all be one; even as thou, Father, art in me, and I in thee, that they also may be in us: that the world may believe that thou didst send me.—John 17:20-21

APOSTOLIC WARNINGS AGAINST APOSTASY

Let us read a few passages in which the apostles warned of the falling away which they could foresee. We begin with a passage from the apostle Paul, who went out of his way on one occasion to talk with the elders of the church at Ephesus. When he had brought them together he delivered one of the great sermons of the New Testament. Toward the end of that sermon are these words:

> Take heed unto yourselves, and to all the flock, in which the Holy Spirit hath made you bishops, to feed the church of the Lord which he purchased with his own blood. I know that after my departing grievous wolves shall enter in among you, not sparing the flock; and from among your own selves shall men arise, speaking perverse things, to draw away the disciples after them.—Acts 20:28-30

The same apostle wrote a letter to the Galatians, in the opening chapter of which he spoke again of holding fast the things that had been taught. Here is the language of the scriptures:

> But though we, or an angel from heaven, should preach unto you any gospel other than that which we preached unto you, let him be anathema. As we have said before, so say I now again, If any man preacheth unto you any gospel other than that which ye received, let him be anathema.—Galatians 1:8-9

The curse of God is upon those who would change the original teachings of Christ and the apostles into different teachings.

The apostle Paul also wrote to the young man Timothy:

> But the Spirit saith expressly, that in later times some shall fall away from the faith, giving heed to seducing spirits and doctrines of demons, through the hypocrisy of men that speak lies, branded in their own conscience as with a hot iron; forbidding to

147

marry [celibacy], and commanding to abstain from meats [fast-
ing], which God created to be received with thanksgiving by them
that believe and know the truth.—I Timothy 4:1-3

Not only did the apostle Paul warn against changing Christ's
teachings, but the apostle Peter also in the second chapter of II Peter
included this warning:

But there arose false prophets also among the people, as among
you also there shall be false teachers, who shall privily bring in
destructive heresies, denying even the Master that bought them,
bringing upon themselves swift destruction.—II Peter 2:1

From Paul we go to Peter and from Peter we go to John. In I John 4, the
opening verse reads, "Beloved, believe not every spirit, but prove the
spirits, whether they are of God; because many false prophets are gone
out into the world." These warnings against apostasy from the apostles
are typical, clear, forceful warnings against leaving the doctrines of
Christ.

The Falling Away

As we turn the pages of history, however, we find that men did just
what Christ and the apostles warned them not to do. In the early centuries
of the church there were six major departures from the teachings of the
New Testament:

1. *Change in the Form of Church Government.*
   Instead of a plurality of elders or bishops in each local congregation, there developed the practice of exalting one of the
   elders above the rest and calling him "the bishop." As time
   went by, he became more and more prominent and more and
   more powerful until he had authority not only in his home
   congregation, but also among the congregations in an entire
   area. He became known as a "diocesan bishop." This happened especially in the main population centers, such as
   Rome, Alexandria, Carthage, Ephesus, Constantinople, Antioch and Jerusalem. As time passed the bishops of these major
   areas contested with each other for prominence until ultimately the bishop of Rome became the pope. This whole process—
   the bishop's elevation over a congregation, the consolidation
   of several congregations under a single bishop, the making of
   a distinction between clergy and laity, and the organizing of
   conventions to enact regulations and laws—was a major departure from the form of government found in the New
   Testament.
2. *Change in the Name by Which the Church Was Known.*
   Originally the designation most commonly used for Christians
   was the "church." As time went by it was referred to as "the
   catholic church," simply meaning that it was universal, ap-
   plying to all people everywhere. Later, it became known as the
   "Holy Catholic Church" and still later as the "Holy Roman
   Catholic Church." This move also paved the way for the use of
   other human names.

148

3. *Change in the Subject of Baptism.*

Early in the third century some began to advocate the baptism of little children. The argument was made that infants were born in sin and therefore needed to be cleansed immediately. Originally only those old enough to hear and understand the gospel were proper subjects for baptism, but the false presupposition that infants are born with inherited sin led to the practice of infant baptism. The first writer to mention the subject was Tertullian, who lived from about 160 to 240 A.D. He opposed the practice, but Origen, born sixteen years later, advocated infant baptism. Agitation for it grew and ultimately it began to be practiced widely.

4. *Change in the Form of Baptism.*

Originally in the New Testament baptism was, as its name requires, immersion—the total submerging of a person in water. Sprinkling and pouring began to be substituted for immersion, as early as the third century. The first recorded instance was that of Novatian in 251 A.D., who had water poured upon his body. It was called "clinic baptism." The Council of Ravenna, Italy, in 1311 officially approved sprinkling and pouring as valid baptism in the Roman Catholic Church.

5. *Change in the Creed.*

The word creed simply refers to what one believes. The creed of the New Testament centers in the person of Jesus Christ. The inspired New Testament is a statement of the creed which God wishes his children to believe and to practice. Early, however, men began to write their own human creeds. A summary of the many facts about Christ were included in the so-called "Apostles' Creed," written sometime in the second century. The Nicene Creed, adopted in 325 A.D., subsequently became the basis for most human creeds in the "so-called Christian world." Thus, human documents became the standard of faith and displaced the inspired New Testament scriptures as the only authority.

6. *Change in the Form of Worship.*

In addition to the five avenues or acts of worship found in the New Testament, the lighting of candles, the honoring of images, the burning of incense, and the celebration of special days and seasons were introduced. The addition of instrumental music to accompany singing made its appearance in the form of an organ as early as the seventh century A.D. These innovations in worship became more and more popular as time passed and have become almost universal today.

Along with these six major departures in the early years of the church, there have been many others down through the centuries, such as the canonization of saints and praying to saints, the adoration of Mary, monasticism, the use of relics in religion, the seven sacraments, compulsory celibacy for church leaders, and the doctrine of purgatory. All of these are departures from New Testament teaching and practice.

THE REFORMATION

From time to time there have been efforts to get back to original New Testament ground. Among the most prominent was the *Reformation Movement* led by John Huss, Girolamo Savonarola, and Huldreich Zwingli, the prereformers, who paid with their lives for calling men to go back to the old ways that one reads about in the Bible. After them, Martin Luther was persecuted almost beyond human endurance. Then there were John Calvin, John Knox and a host of others. They, too, were calling for a return to the old paths. While in their generation they did not reach all the way back to the Bible, the sixteenth century was a great century. There was a feeling on the part of many people that the church had drifted away from God's pattern. The Bible was read, for it was translated into the language of the people. Widespread distribution of the Bible resulted. At times it was a crime to translate the Bible, to print it, to sell it, or to own it, but the people had the courage to do it anyway. The free use of the Bible today is a result.

THE RESTORATION

At the beginning of the nineteenth century there was another movement, largely here in America, in which men advocated going all the way back to the Bible. This movement was known as the *Restoration Movement* and was quite welcome in early America as an antidote to all the religious division and disunity. "Why can't we go back to the old paths and stand where the early Christians stood?" they asked. These efforts to return to New Testament Christianity emphasized such teachings as how to become a Christian, how to worship, and how to govern the church. The emphasis was ancient and apostolic. The book of Acts, with its clear instructions on how to become a Christian, was preached again. The original instructions on worship, with none of the innovations, were again taught. The same thing was true about New Testament living. There was an emphasis upon spiritual matters rather than upon material things, and an emphasis upon purity of morals. The restoration of New Testament Christianity was appealing to the masses.

Little groups of people began to say, "What we need is the kind of religion that men had back when the apostles were still on the earth guiding them." They began to talk in homes and in small groups about returning to the Bible, about speaking where it speaks and being silent where it is silent and about uniting in one church. This *Restoration Movement*—the reason for its being called such is obvious—had no formal organization. It was just an attitude in the minds of the people. They found that they were saying about the same thing, up and down the Atlantic coast and out through the frontier states of Kentucky, Tennessee, Pennsylvania, and Ohio.

What they were saying was, "Our *objective* is unity of all believers in Christ." On the night that he was betrayed, less than twenty-four hours before he was killed on the cross, Jesus prayed that all his disciples "might be one" (John 17:20-21). It was important to Christ that those who follow him should all be united. The *basis* on which they conceived it possible to achieve this unity was the New Testament: in other words, no creed but the New Testament. Nothing written later that the New Testament would be binding in religion. The *method* of achieving this unity was restoration.

These men began to preach this emphasis in their communities and people liked the sound of it. The movement appealed to thousands of people who became Christians in the pure, New Testament fashion. One of their slogans was, "Where the Bible speaks, we speak; where the Bible is silent, we are silent." There is no improvement on that yet. If God's word says it, we can say it; if God's word does not say it, we had better not say it either. This movement back to the Bible is an undenominational movement. What is wanted is not any man's church, but the Lord's church. How to become a Christian, how to worship, and how to live are determined by what the apostles wrote 1900 years ago. God did not give us a make-shift church in the beginning that needed to be improved by the ingenuity of men; God gave us a church that was perfect. Man's changes and modifications have lessened its perfection. What we need to do is go back to the old paths and stand where the apostles stood.

How Did It Begin?

One of the beginnings was in a person by the name of James O'Kelly, who lived and worked in North Carolina and Virginia. He was a member of the Methodist Episcopal Church. He had read his Bible for years and had become concerned about some of the things his creed required which were not in the Bible. He went to the Baltimore conference of his church in 1793 and called on the delegates to go back and take the Bible as their only creed. His proposal was not accepted by the conference, but a little later, he and a group of 7,000 communicants of that church decided to move back toward the Bible. At first they were known as Republican Methodists; later they took the name Christian and wore only that. They took the Bible as their only creed and tried to call things by Bible names. It was a movement back toward the old paths.

In 1802 there was a similar movement in New England. It was independent of this first movement for the men involved did not even know each other. They just happened to see the same problems and to arrive at the same conclusions. There was a man by the name of Abner Jones and another by the name of Elias Smith, both Baptists, who spoke out for the undenominational, New Testament church in New England. They "were disturbed in regard to sectarian names and creeds." These circuit-riding preachers decided that the name Christian was the name men ought to

151

wear, so they began to wear only that name. The churches they served dropped every other name but the name Christian. They established congregations patterned after the New Testament, with no additions or deletions, in Linden and Bradford, Vermont, and in Hanover, Piedmont and Portsmouth, New Hampshire.

Next, we move to the frontier state of Kentucky in the year 1804. You will remember that the Louisiana Purchase came in 1803, extending United States territory beyond the Mississippi. Things were still primitive in Kentucky in 1804, but a man by the name of Barton Stone, without knowing of these other movements, stood on the same ground. Stone, along with several other preachers of the Presbyterian Church, Robert Marshall, John Dunlavy, Richard McNemar, John Thompson and David Purviance, was disturbed about the creed he had promised to preach. More and more these men felt an urgency to use the New Testament and nothing more. In the year 1804 they withdrew from the Springfield Presbytery of which they had been a part, taking "the Bible as the only sure guide to heaven." They wore only the name Christian.

The Response

The response of the people to this new plea was so widespread that Barton Stone's biographer could say that for sixteen consecutive years he baptized more than one thousand people a year. That would be a very large percentage of the people who came to hear him preach. Even in populous times like these that would be most unusual, but there in frontier America in 1804 it was phenomenal. The idea of going back to the Bible, with no creed but the Bible itself and no organization except that of which we read in the Bible, appealed mightily to the people. In the first fifty years of this movement half a million people decided they wanted to be New Testament Christians, and dedicated themselves to go back and restore primitive Christianity.

In 1809, two other names came into the story: Thomas Campbell, and his son, Alexander Campbell. They were not first, but they became more illustrious as the movement developed. Alexander Campbell is one of the few preachers who ever had the privilege of speaking to both houses of the Congress of the United States in joint session. He preached to them, from John 3:16, a sermon on "God so loved the world." When he came to Washington to preach, the President of the United States would often attend the services. He, however, did not lead in this movement. James O'Kelly, Abner Jones, Elias Smith, Barton Stone, and others had for a dozen years and more been active in it before he announced his convictions along this line. The odd thing is that these men did not even know of each other. There was a groundswell feeling that all believers in Christ needed to be united and that the only way to achieve this was by taking the Bible as the only creed.

152

The father, Thomas Campbell, wrote a "Declaration and Address" in which he said:

> Nothing ought to be admitted, as of divine obligation, in the constitution and management of the church but what is expressly enjoined by the authority of our Lord Jesus Christ and His apostles upon the New Testament church, either in express terms or by approved precedent. . . . Nothing ought to be received into the faith or worship of the church, or be made a term of communion among Christians, that is not as old as the New Testament.

That is solid ground. We do not speak; we only listen while the Lord speaks. Nothing that is not in God's word ought to be bound upon God's children.

BACK TO CHRIST

This *Restoration Movement* grew out of a general grass-roots desire for unity in Christ. It stretched across our continent. Today, it is also known in England, Scotland, and in more than fifty nations of the world. At its center is the desire to erase the barriers which separate honest, sincere believers in Christ, a desire that we should all walk one way and stand in one solid rank. We need this as badly today as it was needed a century and a half ago.

We do not go back to Barton Stone, or Alexander Campbell, or James O'Kelly, just as we do not go back to John Wesley, or Martin Luther, or John Calvin. We go back to Christ! These men advocated leaving all the things which men had brought into the church, and returning to the old paths. We do not go back to Rome; we do not go back to Constantinople; we go back to Jerusalem. It is not "my church," nor "your church," but our Lord's church that we must be concerned about. Let us pray that we may be undenominational in our faith and practice.

This is the only hope of real unity in our religious world; it is the only possibility of saving the souls of the billions of earth. Our world is still divided after some seventy-five generations of Christianity. Our only hope of a Christian world is for all believers in Christ to walk faithfully in the old paths, following in the steps of our Lord. As we become more completely united with him we will be united with each other. This must begin on an individual basis. It can start nowhere else.

May we have the courage to follow the advice of God's great prophet Jeremiah who wrote, "Thus saith Jehovah, Stand ye in the ways and see, and ask for the old paths, where is the good way; and walk therein, and ye shall find rest for your souls . . . ." (Jeremiah 6:16).

CHAPTER TWENTY-FOUR
Will the Good People
of all Churches be Saved?

Sometime ago I received an invitation to speak on a lectureship on the theme, "Will the Good People of All Churches Be Saved?" Because of the vital importance of this subject I want to review at least a part of that message.

As a beginning point I would like to remind you of an incident in the Old Testament, which we find in the final chapter of the book of Genesis. The last seventeen years of Jacob's life were spent in Egypt, where he and his elder sons were guests of his more illustrious son Joseph. After Jacob died these older sons, who had sold Joseph into Egyptian bondage many years earlier, feared for their lives. They thought that perhaps now that their father was dead Joseph would take his revenge upon them, so they came, cringing in fear, to beg for their lives at the hands of Joseph who was governor of Egypt. When he heard their plea Joseph said, "Fear not: for am I in the place of God?" (Genesis 50:19). Joseph had the keen insight to realize that he was not their judge.

In Romans 14:4, the apostle Paul, in an entirely different kind of situation, asked a very meaningful question, "Who art thou that judgest the servant of another? to his own lord he standeth or falleth." The Pharisees of Jesus' day left the impression that they thought that they were better than everyone else, and that they were so good that they could climb up on God's throne and judge everyone else. How wrong such an attitude is! God is the judge and all of us will be judged when the final judgment comes. The self-righteous, holier-than-thou attitude is certainly foreign to the teaching and the spirit of Christ.

Only God Knows

When we come to the question of who will be saved and who will be lost, fortunately, we are not left to grope in blindness. God has told us plainly in his inspired book, the Bible, how we will be judged when all of us stand before him in that great last day. First of all, we know with absolute certainty that only those who love God will be eternally saved. Jesus stated the greatest commandment of all as follows: "Hear, O Israel; the Lord our God, the Lord is one: and thou shalt love the Lord thy God with all thy heart, and with all thy soul, and with all thy mind, and with all thy strength" (Mark 12:29-30). In the second place, we know that only those who obey the Lord's commands will enter heaven, for Jesus said, "Not every one that saith unto me, Lord, Lord, shall enter into the kingdom of heaven; but he that doeth the will of my Father who is in heaven" (Matthew 7:21). Jesus also said, "If ye love me, ye will keep my commandments" (John 14:15). Only those who love God and keep his commandments can expect to be saved.

No man has the right to judge other men, but when some loved one or friend appears not to know the Lord's will, or is careless in obeying some plain teaching of our Lord, each of us has the responsibility of going to him, making certain that he understands the will of God on the point in question, and urging him to obey God's command.

As an example, if some friend of mine is not a believer in Christ, it is not my place to pass judgment upon him, for God has already passed judgment on those who do not believe. "Without faith it is impossible to be well-pleasing unto him; for he that cometh to God must believe that he is, and that he is a rewarder of them that seek after him" (Hebrews 11:6). It is my place to talk with my friend in such a way that he may come to have faith in God and in Christ the Son of God.

Or again, if some person whom I know and respect has never come to realize the necessity of being baptized, it is my place to read with him such passages as the Lord's statement, "Verily, verily, I say unto thee, Except one be born of water and the Spirit, he cannot enter into the kingdom of God" (John 3:5). Our attitude toward all men should take into consideration the fact that all of us stand on exactly the same ground before God. That is, that no man can be saved who does not love God and his fellowmen, and that loving God must make itself manifest in obedience to the Lord's commands. Those who do not love God and who do not obey him stand condemned—not by us, but by God. We gladly leave the judging to God, for "Am I in the place of God?"

CHRIST'S DESIRE FOR UNITY

Directly related to the theme which we are discussing is the very apparent teaching of the New Testament that God desires for all his people to be one. Notice that Jesus spoke of his church in the singular, giving no hint that he approved of the idea that his kingdom would be divided into many different groups. Just a few hours before he was betrayed by Judas Iscariot, in John 17:20-21, we find him praying, "Neither for these only do I pray, but for them also that believe on me through their word; that they may all be one; . . ." Tragically, this fervent appeal in the final night of our Lord's life, has largely gone unheeded even by those who have called themselves Christians.

Not only did our Lord teach the idea of a single, united church, but we find that his apostles also echoed the same teaching in vigorous language. For example, in writing to the Ephesians, Paul said, "There is

155

one body, and one Spirit, even as also ye were called in one hope of your calling; one Lord, one faith, one baptism, one God and Father of all" (Ephesians 4:4-6). In the same book he had already defined the one body as the church, in these words, "And he put all things in subjection under his feet, and gave him to be head over all things to the church, which is his body" (Ephesians 1:22-23). Just as there is one Lord, one Holy Spirit, and one God, there is also one body, the church.

Too Many Churches

Today, nearly 2,000 years after the beginning of the Lord's church on Pentecost, the modern religious world is woefully divided. The last religious survey listed some 308 different religious groups professing to be followers of Christ. In view of the emphasis of the New Testament on unity, it seems strange that there should be those who advocate that a multiplicity of churches is actually an asset rather than a tragic liability. There are many who defend the *idea* of denominationalism, though, of course, they do not defend the antagonisms that have existed between the denominations. The argument goes something like this: "Men differ widely in educational, economic, cultural, social and emotional backgrounds. It is good to have a multiplicity of churches, so that each man may choose a church of his choice." This statement is completely foreign to the New Testament, where the Lord is pictured as the one to determine what the church should be like and man is pictured as needing to accept the Lord's wishes rather than to provide a church conforming to his own desires.

The idea of a multiplicity of churches with many divergent doctrines is intellectually indefensible. We live in an age when a premium is placed upon truth. In thousands of laboratories countless workers spend millions of hours in the quest for facts. Ours is a scientific age in which the search for truth in every realm goes on relentlessly. Ours is an age in which the flag of truth has flown from the very top of the mast-head. Because of this insistence on finding the facts, man has been able to go to the moon and to build airplanes that span a continent in a matter of a few hours, to invent means of communicating instantly with his neighbors around the world by television, radio, and telephone, and to extend the years of his own life through the development of medical techniques and wonder drugs of many kinds. The progress of the twentieth century has been achieved because man waged a relentless war on ignorance and thereby discovered fact after fact which in turn enabled him to lift himself to the present high plane of living. A sentence from the pen of Solomon might well be chosen as the slogan of our time, "Buy the truth, and sell it not" (Proverbs 23:23.)

156

However, when we move into the realm of religion, modern man hauls down the flag of truth and raises in its stead the flag of sincerity, honesty of purpose, and depth of feeling. No matter what faith one may hold, if a man is honest and sincere in his religion, he is judged to be all right. No matter how divergent the doctrines, modern man feels that everyone is on his way to heaven, simply traveling by a different road from that of his neighbor. In other fields the facts count. In the field of religion the facts are no longer sought, but are buried under an avalanche of tolerance and of generosity of feeling toward one's fellowmen. The motive behind this generosity of feeling is admirable and fine, but the disregard of truth is tragic!

Who would think of allowing his child to continue in a school where the teacher of arithmetic taught that two plus two equals five, or nine, or thirteen? Or what teacher of geography could get by even for a single day, teaching that the world is either round or flat, depending upon the wish of the student?

In order that you may feel the full impact of what I am saying, let me speak in specific terms. Just a few blocks from the building in which I have worshipped for years, there is another assembly of sincere people, and in this second assembly there is a general agreement that Christ is not divine but merely an enlightened leader of the past. The emphasis of all my preaching is that Jesus is the divine Son of God. Now, either one or the other of these two views is wrong. Both cannot be right. It must be one or the other.

Three blocks away in a slightly different direction there is a church building that is empty on Sundays. Those who worship in that building assemble on Saturday, believing that it is the day on which God desires his children to worship him. Our convictions are that it is the first day of the week, the Lord's day, when men ought to worship God. Again, both cannot be right. Either Saturday is the day of worship or it is Sunday. It cannot be either, or.

Yet again, approximately three blocks in still a different direction there is a large and very zealous body of people who believe that baptism is not essential to salvation. In contrast, my preaching emphasizes it as one of the necessary things that man must do in order to be saved. Such passages as Mark 16:16, "He that believeth and is baptized shall be saved," lead us to the conviction that this act is necessary. Both of these views cannot be correct; either baptism is necessary for salvation or it is not necessary. It cannot be both.

TRUTH CAN MAKE US FREE

Truth does not lie on opposite sides of the same fence. Truth is narrow and cannot be described in terms of anything that man might

157

wish. It was Christ who emphasized the importance of truth when he said, "Ye shall know the truth, and the truth shall make you free" (John 8:32). As to why modern man has this "blind spot" in regard to his religion, we know no adequate explanation. We only know that this "winking" at truth is costly to the ongoing of the Christian religion. Many modern intellectuals see the absurity of "everything is all right, just so long as a man is sincere." This is not true in any other realm and it is not true in the realm of religion.

This playing fast and loose with the truth in the realm of religion has led many thinking people to feel that religion must be a kind of fairy tale, since it can be either round or flat, depending upon the wishes of those who play the game. It is also no wonder that godless Communism looks to the Western world with a quizzical eye when the subject of religion comes up. Hardheaded Communists find it hard to believe that truth can be so lightly handled and that anything that men believe can pass for that which is truth. It is unlikely that this kind of Christianity will ever conquer the minds of those who presently are without faith in God, or Christ, or the Bible.

The idea of a multiplicity of churches, all of which are right, destroys faith in the Bible as the final authority in the realm of religion. When a man reads, "He that believeth and is baptized shall be saved" (Mark 16:16), and then preaches from his pulpit, "He that believeth and is not baptized shall be saved," it does something to the respect that men have for the Bible. When men have spent several generations explaining that the Bible does not mean what it says on baptism, on the one church, on the name, on falling from grace, and on many other religious themes, it is no wonder that people get the idea that maybe the Bible does not mean what it says on marriage and divorce, on basic morality, and on the importance of being Christians at all.

The idea of a multiplicity of churches with their divergent doctrines all equally correct has led many to end their lives in infidelity. The prayer that Christ prayed in the Garden of Gethsemane on his betrayal night had in it the phrase, "that the world may believe." The unity for which Christ prayed was for the purpose of creating belief in the hearts of the unbelieving masses of humanity. Many a man would like to become a Christian, but he is confused when good men give him such different answers to his earnest questions about what to do to become a Christian, about how to worship God acceptably, and about how to live a Christian life.

After seventy-five generations of Christianity the world is still not Christian and only slightly above half of the population within this so-called Christian nation is church-affiliated. Denominationalism leaves many a person thinking he is saved, when he has not yet obeyed all the Lord's commands. It leaves many another bewildered and content to do nothing, since he has no certainty about what he must do. Satan has long used the tool of divide and conquer as one of his most valuable weapons.

A Ray of Hope

When they asked me the question, "Will the good people of all churches be saved?" they asked the wrong person. Only God knows who will be saved; only God can answer this question. In the second place, when they asked the question, "Will the good people of all churches be saved?" they asked the wrong question. The question really ought to be, "How can all mankind come to be members of the Lord's church?" It is the only church in which there is the promise of eternal salvation. Man has blundered badly in fractioning the body of Christ into hundreds of pieces. The only real solution to the problem of a multiplicity of churches is to return to the pattern of the church that our Lord died to establish as set forth in the New Testament. Salvation is to be found in his church and in his church alone. Our concern must be to leave off everything else and to become New Testament Christians. This, and this alone, is solid ground.

In the midst of the dark and discouraging picture of vast destructive division, there is a ray of hope. It is an ever-widening emphasis upon a return to New Testament Christianity. The slogans are ever sounding forth in wider and wider circles, "Let us speak where the Bible speaks and be silent where the Bible is silent." "Let us have a 'Thus saith the Lord' for everything that we do in our religious faith and practice." "Let us go back to the Bible." If each of us is willing to leave his own preconceived ideas and return to the teachings of God's inspired book, laying aside all human creeds and doctrines of men, then it will be possible for all of us to march in one great army under the banner of our Savior, Jesus Christ. May each one of us, as did our Lord nearly 2,000 years ago, pray fervently, "That they may all be one."

CHAPTER TWENTY-FIVE

Where Was—And Is—The Church?

From time to time we study the book of Daniel. The book is a very interesting book, because of the significant events which it describes in the life of Daniel and his three young Hebrew companions. It is also an interesting book because of the prophecies which it contains. In the second chapter there is the combination of an interesting experience and also a meaningful prophecy.

Nebuchadnezzar, king of Babylon, dreamed of a great image. The head was of gold, the breast and arms were of silver, the belly and thighs were of brass, the legs were of iron, and the feet were of iron mixed with clay. With God's help Daniel was able to interpret the dream. The head of gold referred to Nebuchadnezzar's Babylonian kingdom. The silver referred to another worldwide empire that would follow. This, we later recognize as the Persian Empire. The brass represented still another world-wide kingdom, which turned out to be the Grecian Empire. The iron in the image stood for still another world-wide empire, which history revealed to be the Roman Empire. The story comes to its climax in the words:

> And in the days of those kings shall the God of heaven set up a kingdom which shall never be destroyed, nor shall the sovereignty thereof be left to another people; but it shall break in pieces and consume all these kingdoms, and it shall stand forever.— Daniel 2:44

In the dream this last kingdom was described not as a part of the image, but as a stone cut out of the mountain without hands. The stone then rolled down the mountain and struck the image and destroyed all of the other parts.

This final kingdom, the spiritual kingdom of God, was different from the other empires and was to outlive all of them. This spiritual kingdom is described in the New Testament. The book of Acts tells of the beginning of the Lord's kingdom, or church, on Pentecost in the year A.D. 30, and of its growth during the remaining decades of that first century of the Christian era. It was this kingdom which the prophet Daniel predicted would never be destroyed and would stand forever.

At this point in our study of Daniel and his prophecy concerning the church, it is quite common for someone to ask, "Down through the centuries, particularly through the Dark Ages, where was the church?" It is a good question and deserves a thoughtful answer.

There are two answers which we wish to suggest. First, let us remember Christ's parable concerning the sower, as we read it in Matthew 13. As you will recall Christ tells of a farmer who sowed seed in his field, with the result that some fell by the wayside, some upon the rocky ground, some upon the thorny ground, and some upon the good ground. As the parable unfolds it is obvious that the seed is the word of God and that the soil represents the hearts of men and women. God's word when planted in human hearts brings forth a harvest. This is the whole import of this familiar parable of the sower. God's word is the seed, and that seed is planted when the gospel is preached.

Each of us possesses a copy of God's inspired word. This is the seed. This seed has existed through all the centuries, during the Dark Ages and all other ages. Whenever men have read it and studied it, it has brought forth Christians. It has created congregations of the Lord's church. In that sense, God's kingdom has existed from the day of Pentecost down to this present hour. As long as the seed exists, the church exists.

We might illustrate this by something which happened in the life of one of America's political greats of another generation. William Jennings Bryan visited Egypt and went into one of the Pyramids. When he came out he had a few grains of wheat in his hands. In one of his speeches he referred to these as being centuries old, or even perhaps thousands of years old. Yet in the seed there was still life. More recently, in an article in the *National Geographic* magazine we read of lotus seeds unearthed in Japan. When measured by one of the latest scientific methods of estimating age, the Carbon-14 technique, they were found to be more than 3,000 years old. Yet, when planted, they brought forth lotus plants. Similarly, the seed of God's word continues to perpetuate the church. As long as the seed exists the church exists. There has never been a time when the church, in seed form, has ceased to exist.

In History, Too

In the second place, we have the faith to believe that the church has also existed through all these centuries, in visible, outward form. Remember how the church began on Pentecost with visitors present in Jerusalem from many different nations. Three thousand people became Christians and then a few weeks later they went home. Some of them went to Africa, some went to Rome, some went east toward the orient. They scattered everywhere. We have in the Bible just a fragmentary story of the spread of the early church. We read in Acts of only a few of the apostles. We cannot trace the preaching activities of the others, yet we know that they were devout Christians, and we can be sure that they went about preaching. Most of the story of the early church was never recorded.

161

There is another fact that we need to consider. Recorded history tells only a fragmentary story of the events of the ancient past. Recorded history tells of only a few of the most prominent persons—kings, generals, tyrants and the like. It tells of only a few of the most spectacular events—wars, catastrophies, and the rise and fall of empires. The meetings of little bands of dedicated Christians for the purpose of worship would hardly appear noteworthy. What historian would have recorded the simple activities of the New Testament church? In our day, too, the activities of the church seldom appear in the news pages. Even church history was primarily concerned with the major doctrinal controversies, the meetings of special councils and the struggles for ecclesiastical power and position—none of which was a part of the Lord's church.

It is my faith that through these sparsely reported centuries bands of faithful Christians read God's word and passed it on from generation to generation. That faith is supported by the fact that today we regularly discover new groups of Christians in various parts of the world. For example, after the second World War in France and in Germany bands of New Testament Christians were discovered of which we had never known before. More recently several congregations of devout Christians have been discovered in Spain. Other groups have been discovered in Ethiopia. These studied their Bibles and began to be Christians in the New Testament way. Still others have been found in Italy. We have also discovered several hundred New Testament Christians in India. They have also been discovered behind the Iron Curtain in the Russian part of the world.

IDENTITY OF THE CHURCH

In our 20th century as we seek to establish the identity of the New Testament church we suggest the taking of the New Testament as the blueprint or pattern and then coming across the centuries to our own day. Let us find a church that is most like the pattern. That is the plea that we make. Let us go back and be the New Testament church. Let us respect the authority of the Bible, adding nothing to the pattern and taking nothing from it.

How does one become a member of Christ's church? In the Bible the pattern states that the gospel is to be preached. When people believe it, they are to confess the name of Christ, repent of their sins, and be baptized. In every recorded instance the baptism was immersion. There was no place in the early church for infant baptism or for sprinkling. These have been added by men since the pattern was completed by God's inspired writers.

Take the matter of worship. In the early church they gave of their means, they sang hymns, they prayed, they ate the Lord's Supper, and they preached God's word. There were only these five avenues of worship. Of these we read in the pattern. The lighting of candles, the burning of incense, the use of musical instruments and the use of images are not found in the New Testament scriptures, hence, we must leave them off.

Next, we examine the early church in its organization. It was made up of independent congregations, each ruled by a plurality of elders. There was no hierarchy or elaborate organizational system in the pattern. When we look for the Lord's church, we find it in independent congregations under elders, who in turn are under the Lord as the only head of the church. If we are trying to identify the church we need simply to take God's book and read to see what his church was like. Then we need to find a body of people who are living and worshipping in the way which he prescribed. At this point we have found the Lord's church.

CHAPTER TWENTY-SIX

"Maranatha"—"Our Lord, Come"

Nineteen centuries ago, in the early days of the church, Christians used an expression which we seldom hear today. It was the Aramaic word, *"Maranatha,"* which means "Our Lord, come." It was often spoken orally; it was used at the end of written documents; it was inscribed on the walls of the catacombs and elsewhere. It was constantly in the hearts and on the tongues of early Christians. It was a kind of prayer, "Our Lord, come."

Christianity began in the pagan Roman world, where there were many persecutions and much uncertainty. These negative conditions encouraged the desire for the Lord to come speedily. In the second place, the early Christians lived in a rather meager world. They did not know the comforts and luxuries of life which we know today, but rather the bare necessities of life. There were privations common to all men in that day that we of our day would find intolerable. Add to this the fact that many of the early Christians were slaves and we can see still another reason why the early Christians were quite willing to give up this world for a better world to come. We can further understand the longing of the early Christians for Christ to come when we realize that they had a very real conception of the blessings of the future life in heaven. Having heard from Christ and the apostles something of the untarnished joys of heaven, they looked forward to eternity with enthusiasm.

Today, in our twentieth century, we have less fear, less persecution, and less suffering than did the early Christians. It certainly goes without saying that our lives are also filled with more temporal blessings than were theirs, for we have not only the necessities of life but an abundance of luxuries. The contrast between this world and heaven is not as sharp as it was in the minds of the early Christians. As a result of all of these factors, the modern Christian does not really long for the coming of the day of the Lord. Hence, he seldom says, *"Maranatha,"* or "Our Lord, come." Because we Christians of modern times need to think more often and more seriously of the life to come, with its wondrous blessings for the redeemed and its terrible tragedies for the lost, we need to read some of the passages which we find in the New Testament about the coming of the Lord. A clearer vision of heaven will afford joy to the Christian and will encourage all of us to make more careful preparation so that we may be ready when the Lord comes.

164

Throughout the length and breadth of the New Testament there are numerous references to the fact that Christ will come again. Many of these are woven in an incidental manner into portions of the scriptures which deal primarily with other subjects. For example, in I Corinthians 11:23-26, we are reading about the Lord's Supper, but we find an emphasis upon the coming of the Lord also. Here is the passage:

> For I received of the Lord that which also I delivered unto you, that the Lord Jesus in the night in which he was betrayed took bread; and when he had given thanks, he brake it, and said, This is my body, which is for you: this do in remembrance of me. In like manner also the cup, after supper, saying, This cup is the new covenant in my blood: this do, as often as ye drink it, in remembrance of me.

Having pointed out that one of the primary purposes of the Lord's Supper was the remembrance of Christ, Paul then pointed out a second reason for eating the supper: "For as often as ye eat this bread, and drink the cup, ye proclaim the Lord's death till he come."

A similar incidental emphasis is found in II Timothy 4:7-8, where the apostle Paul summarized his own life as follows:

> I have fought the good fight, I have finished the course, I have kept the faith: henceforth there is laid up for me the crown of righteousness, which the Lord, the righteous judge, shall give to me at that day; and not to me only, but also to all them that have loved his appearing.

Those who will be saved are those who have looked forward to the coming of the Lord.

In addition to these brief indications that the early Christians expected Christ's return, there are more extended passages whose central message is the coming of the Lord. Matthew 25 is such a passage. It begins with the parable of the ten virgins, five of whom were foolish in that they made no preparation for the return of the bridegroom, and five of whom were wise in that they did make preparation for his return. The passage ends, "Watch therefore, for ye know not the day nor the hour" (Matthew 25:13).

The second section of Matthew 25 presents the parable of the talents. The men who received five and two talents were rewarded because they had used their Lord's money wisely, whereas the man who received one talent and did nothing with it was cast out into the outer darkness.

The final section of Matthew 25 is the extended picture of the final judgment, the most complete such picture in the entire Bible. It begins:

> But when the Son of man shall come in his glory, and all the angels with him, then shall he sit on the throne of his glory: and

before him shall be gathered all the nations: and he shall separate them one from another, as the shepherd separateth the sheep from the goats; and he shall set the sheep on his right hand, but the goats on the left. Then shall the King say unto them on his right hand, Come, ye blessed of my Father, inherit the kingdom prepared for you from the foundation of the world. . . . Then shall he say also unto them on the left hand, Depart from me, ye cursed, into the eternal fire which is prepared for the devil and his angels. . . . And these shall go away into eternal punishment: but the righteous into eternal life.—Matthew 25:31-34, 41, 46

In the previous chapter of Matthew our Lord had said:

Heaven and earth shall pass away, but my words shall not pass away. But of that day and hour knoweth no one, not even the angels of heaven, neither the Son, but the Father only. And as were the days of Noah, so shall be the coming of the Son of man. For as in those days which were before the flood they were eating and drinking, marrying and giving in marriage, until the day that Noah entered into the ark, and they knew not until the flood came, and took them all away; so shall be the coming of the Son of man. Then shall two men be in the field; one is taken, and one is left: two women shall be grinding at the mill; one is taken, and one is left. Watch therefore: for ye know not on what day your Lord cometh.—Matthew 24:35-42

The emphasis here is upon the unexpectedness of Christ's return.

A Heavenly Home

Perhaps the dearest of all the passages announcing Christ's return is that found in John 14:1-3, where the Lord said:

Let not your heart be troubled: believe in God, believe also in me. In my Father's house are many mansions; if it were not so, I would have told you; for I go to prepare a place for you. And if I go and prepare a place for you, I come again, and will receive you unto myself; that where I am, there ye may be also.

Surely it is heart-warming to know that our Lord has gone to prepare a place for us. This is a great encouragement to live in such a manner that we will someday be ready for the place that the Lord is now preparing for us.

As we grow older and our physical faculties fade, it is heartening to remember the words of the apostle Paul:

Wherefore we faint not; but though our outward man is decaying, yet our inward man is renewed day by day. For our light affliction, which is for the moment, worketh for us more and more exceedingly an eternal weight of glory; while we look not at the things which are seen, but at the things which are not seen: for the things which are seen are temporal; but the things which are not seen are eternal. For we know that if the earthly house of our tabernacle be dissolved, we have a building from God, a house not made with hands, eternal, in the heavens.—II Corinthians 4:16—5:1

166

A few sentences later Paul added: "For we must all be made manifest before the judgment-seat of Christ; that each one may receive the things done in the body, according to what he hath done, whether it be good or bad" (II Corinthians 5:10).

Because some of the early Christians had lost loved ones and feared that their deaths meant that they would miss the coming of the Lord and the life everlasting, the Holy Spirit guided Paul to write:

> But we would not have you ignorant, brethren, concerning them that fall asleep; that ye sorrow not, even as the rest, who have no hope. For if we believe that Jesus died and rose again, even so them also that are fallen asleep in Jesus will God bring with him. For this we say unto you by the word of the Lord, that we that are alive, that are left unto the coming of the Lord, shall in no wise precede them that are fallen asleep. For the Lord himself shall descend from heaven, with a shout, with the voice of the archangel, and with the trump of God: and the dead in Christ shall rise first; then we that are alive, that are left, shall together with them be caught up in the clouds, to meet the Lord in the air: and so shall we ever be with the Lord. Wherefore comfort one another with these words.—I Thessalonians 4:13-18

No Earthly Reign

By this beautiful and moving description of how the Lord will come we Christians are encouraged. It will certainly be a great moment when all of the saintly dead are raised and those who live on until the end of time join with them, as together they are caught up in the clouds to meet the Lord. This passage also, along with others that we have studied, indicates that when the Lord comes it will be to judge mankind and to take the righteous home with him to heaven, rather than to reign on earth for a thousand years, with Jerusalem as his headquarters city. While there are many conscientious believers in Christ who expect him to reign on earth for a millennium, their expectation is a false one based on a misunderstanding of figurative passages.

Actually, there is no scripture which indicates that Christ will ever set foot on the earth again. He will come to call forth the righteous, will meet them in the air and will take them to be with him eternally in heaven. Our Lord's kingdom is a spiritual kingdom, not a literal, physical one. If he had wished to establish a physical kingdom in Jerusalem, he could have done so when he was on earth before. There is no indication that he had such a desire then nor that he has such a desire now. We read in John 18:36 that he said to Pilate, "My kingdom is not of this world: if my kingdom were of this world, then would my servants fight, that I should not be delivered to the Jews: but now is my kingdom not from hence." The figurative, prophetic passages of the New Testament which are sometimes interpreted to mean a literal, earthly reign of a thousand years are simply indications that the gospel of Christ will bind Satan for an

167

indefinite period of time. Certainly no one literalizes the abyss and the chain of Revelation 20. Why then should he literalize the one thousand years that is part of the same verse?

Several decades had passed and the Lord had not returned. Some of the Christians began to wonder if perhaps they had misunderstood the Lord in thinking that he planned to come again. Critics mocked the Christians, saying that their hope of a returning Lord was pure imagination. It was in this situation that the Holy Spirit guided Peter to write:

> . . . in the last days mockers shall come with mockery, walking after their own lusts, and saying, Where is the promise of his coming? for, from the day that the fathers fell asleep, all things continue as they were from the beginning of the creation. For this they wilfully forget, that there were heavens from of old, and an earth compacted out of water and amidst water, by the word of God, by which means the world that then was, being overflowed with water, perished: but the heavens that now are, and the earth, by the same word have been stored up for fire, being reserved against the day of judgment and destruction of ungodly men.—II Peter 3:3-7

Just as God had destroyed the earth once by water, he has promised that he will destroy it again by fire.

DESTRUCTION OF THE EARTH

Peter then continued: "But forget not this one thing, beloved, that one day is with the Lord as a thousand years, and a thousand years as one day." This simply means that long periods of time from the human viewpoint are as nothing in God's sight. His long delay in coming is not significant, though it seems like a long period of time in man's eyes. Then, Peter gave the reason why the Lord has delayed his coming. He has delayed his return, and the judgment which will immediately follow, because he loves the souls of men and wants all men to come to repentance before the great and terrible day of judgment.

Then, the passage continues:

> But the day of the Lord will come as a thief; in the which the heavens shall pass away with a great noise, and the elements shall be dissolved with fervent heat, and the earth and the works that are therein shall be burned up. Seeing that these things are thus all to be dissolved, what manner of persons ought ye to be in all holy living and godliness, looking for and earnestly desiring the coming of the day of God, by reason of which the heavens being on fire shall be dissolved, and the elements shall melt with fervent heat? But, according to his promise, we look for new heavens and a new earth, wherein dwelleth righteousness.—II Peter 3:10-13

It is apparent from this reading that the day of the Lord will come suddenly and unexpectedly, and when it comes this earth will be destroyed by fire. Surely we do not want to be here when that terrible event takes place. It is imperative that we come to Christ and let him cleanse us from our sins and that we then follow in his footsteps as we live so that someday we may be worthy of being called forth to meet him in the air and to escape the terrible tragedy of the sinful world. A clear realization that Christ is coming and that man must face the judgment is a great encouragement toward righteous living. Faith in Christ as God's Son, made meaningful by obedience to the Lord's commands, is an imperative for each of us. There is no certainty of tomorrow, only a certainty that without becoming a Christian man is eternally lost.

Conclusion

Recently, we visited one of our dear friends, a devout Christian in her nineties, who is now bedfast. Several years ago she lost her beloved husband, a companion of more than three score years. She has no children to care for and love her in these declining years of life. With tears in her eyes she asked, "Is it wrong for me to want to die and go to heaven?" Some of her friends had chided her a bit when she had expressed such a desire, urging her to want to live on here on the earth. Our answer was, "No, it is not wrong to want to die and to go to heaven. It is Christian."

Without being dissatisfied here on earth, and without lessening our efforts for the Cause of Christ here, let us all look forward to our Lord's coming. Let us appreciate this life and use it to the full in every good and wholesome way. Let us enjoy wholesome family relationships, challenging work, and the beauties of the world about us, but let us also look forward with eagerness to a better life to come. The apostle Paul used the expression, "for it is very far better" (Philippians 1:23). Let us make every effort to be sure that we are ready when the Lord calls us home, whether he calls us in an individual way through death, or whether we live until the great day of the Lord's return. Let us learn to say, "Maranatha,"—"Our Lord, come."

Significance of Jesus
Ps. 2:7 Heb. 1:5 Lk. 1:31-35 Heb. 1:8 Heb. 5:5

John 8:32   Bethany

Lord - only head of church
Christian only name
Bible only creed
Christian character

Printed in the United States
21446LVS00006B/403-453